A CHOICE OF DRAMATIC THEMES

R. P. HEWETT

Formerly Senior English Master
Northgate Grammar School for Boys, Ipswich

HARRAP LONDON

First published in Great Britain 1973
by HARRAP LIMITED
19–23 Ludgate Hill, London EC4M 7PD

Reprinted: 1983

© *R. P Hewett. 1973*

ISBN 0 245–54052–0

Composed in Intertype Garamond.
Printed in Great Britain at
Whitstable Litho Limited
Whitstable, Kent

Harrap's
New Outlook Series

A CHOICE OF DRAMATIC THEMES

South Devon
Technical College.

(4).

Harrap's
New Outlook Series

A CHOICE OF POETS, an anthology of
poets from Wordsworth to the present day
—*by* R. P. HEWETT

7 THEMES IN MODERN VERSE—*edited
by* MAURICE WOOLLMAN

By the same author
READING AND RESPONSE
An approach to the Criticism of Literature
A FURTHER CHOICE OF POETS

Acknowledgments

The publishers would like to thank the following for their kind permission to reproduce the extracts included in this book:

Jonathan Cape Ltd, for extracts from *Chips with Everything* and from *Roots* from *The Wesker Trilogy*, by Arnold Wesker; Faber & Faber Ltd, for extracts from *A Day in the Death of Joe Egg*, by Peter Nichols; William Heinemann Ltd, for extracts from *The Long and the Short and the Tall*, by Willis Hall; Methuen & Co Ltd, for extracts from *Sergeant Musgrave's Dance*, by John Arden, *The Caucasian Chalk Circle*, by Bertholt Brecht, translated by James and Tania Stern with W. H. Auden, and *The Caretaker*, by Harold Pinter; Penguin Books Ltd, for extracts from *Live Like Pigs*, by John Arden, from *John Arden: Three Plays*; Laurence Pollinger and the Estate of the late Mrs Frieda Lawrence, for an extract from *The Widowing of Mrs Holroyd*, from *The Complete Plays of D. H. Lawrence*; David Rudkin, for an extract from *Afore Night Come*; Secker & Warburg, for extracts from *The Crucible*, by Arthur Miller, Copyright © 1952, 1953, by Arthur Miller; The Society of Authors on behalf of the Bernard Shaw Estate, for an extract from *Pygmalion*, by Bernard Shaw; Harvey Unna Ltd, for an extract from *Billy Liar*, by Keith Waterhouse.

Contents

Introduction 1

xxxxxxxxxxxxxxxxxxxxxxxxxxxxxxxxxxxxxxxxxxxxxxxxxxxxxxxxxxxxxxxxxxxxx

MAINLY FOR THE TEACHER

This is a book of extracts from plays, and I ought to start by trying to justify what is, on the face of it, a barbarous procedure. My own experience in using plays in the class-room must be common to many and perhaps most English teachers, at any rate in secondary schools; I have found a smallish selection of good one-acters, or plays of similar length for junior forms, and a real dearth of good material for pupils in early puberty, when something more substantial is needed for reading and acting. I find the Shakespeare co-medies, standard diet thirty years ago, hard going to take as a whole, because of their highly verbalized humour and 'romantic' elements, especially if one is going to try to act them. With the 'mixed ability' classes that are increasingly, and rightly, dominating English teaching, *Twelfth Night* and *As You Like It* may well be counter-productive. There are splendid and rewarding plays written mainly in England since the mid-fifties, many of them represented here; but I have often felt the need for *introducing* a wider range of material than the one full-length play a term that I seem to manage in the middle forms. I hope that the extracts offered here will give a taste of a variety of kinds of dramatic situations, and of course I hope that many of them will encourage classes and teachers to go on to the full play when it really stimulates interest.

The extracts vary from very short sequences to substantial extracts, some of which select a theme, or sub-theme, some of which stimulate further exploration, discussion or even further development dramatically, some of which may spark off on one another by juxtaposition. I have grouped them loosely under thematic headings and one or more of these, with a judicious use of the linking commentaries, might make a study lasting for several weeks, and provide material for class discussion and writing as well as acting and reading. I assume that all the extracts used in class would be given at the very least a dramatic reading (careful casting and selection of voices, some degree of production and perhaps some sound effects); actual performance at the various possible classroom levels would, of course, be better, and possibly some related or contrasted extracts might be learned, produced and presented at the same time, with or without costume and staging, to certain limited audiences—for example to other students in the same year.

When I started choosing material for this selection I was attacked by one of the occupational disorders of English teaching—a conviction that 'chronologicalizing' (a barbarous word for a barbarous assumption) would be a feature, and that somehow one would be offering a potted history of drama. I soon abandoned this as unworkable, and found that the extracts I had chosen from Ben Jonson were too difficult, from Sheridan and Goldsmith too wordy and mannered, and fell back on what I came to realize was in fact an assumption, a choice and a judgment about the actual merits of English drama, at least for this purpose—that Shakespeare and the renaissance in English drama since the mid-fifties were the only areas that could be made really interesting and perhaps even cross-fertilize each other. So the bulk of my final collection is unashamedly from Shakespeare and the moderns, including a little American drama, with one passage from Synge as the only chronological link. In fact, I have abandoned chronology, and doubt whether it exists in English drama. I have found Shaw unduly verbose, but have included a passage from *Pygmalion* which is not as burdened with stage directions as some; rather than use translations, I decided reluctantly not to include Ibsen or Chekhov, though I have made one exception to the translation rule with some short passages from Brecht.

I hope that the play extracts will make reasonable sense isolated from the plays of which they are part. The 'lead-ins' and 'run-outs' are attempts to put the extracts back into context, i.e., to say what is indispensable by way of introduction, to outline what I think necessary in summarizing the play material before the extract opens, and to drop some small hints about interpretation. The *Acting Notes* are not designed to impose any particular reading or treatment, but merely to be helpful in suggesting very broadly interpretation and therefore casting, and when appropriate to suggest some minimal equipment and small details of that kind. If the school which uses this collection is lucky enough to have an adequate drama room or mummery, the general range of experience of teachers and students may well make the acting notes redundant. They can, of course, be ignored by anyone who finds them intrusive and are included only for those who may need them. The many teachers—and classes—who have wide experience with free unscripted drama, mime and so forth, may find them a little old-fashioned; but as every educationist knows, the spectrum of development in this, as in other fields, is very wide and there are schools which still have no activity at all in drama and others where it is restricted solely to an annual school play. For these schools the acting notes may occasionally be useful or suggestive; I have put them in small type to suggest their marginal role. If, instead of always directing the performance yourself, you encourage a member of your class to do so, he or she might find the notes helpful here and there.

The run-outs, in particular, aim at encouraging further exploration, perhaps by individual students from short sets of the complete plays, perhaps by the class as a whole when their interest has been engaged and they feel in the mood to tackle the whole play.

I have not annotated the Shakespeare extracts in detail, assuming that most English stores have at least single copies with adequate notes for those who need them. Brief biographical notes on the playwrights are gathered together at the end, for reference and possibly for follow-ups.

This is not the place to hold forth on the value of classroom drama, even the most primitive. Perhaps the note on which I should prefer to end is to remind us all that the one class that nearly always seems to 'work' is the play period, and that anything lively, entertaining, exciting or moving that can be made accessible to the student starts with a great deal in its favour precisely *because* he is in a sense going to live it and become it, instead of merely contemplating it on the stage.

Introduction 2

MAINLY FOR THE STUDENT

There is a very wide difference between schools in their dramatic activities, and if you work at a school where it is a central part of English work, or a major out-of-school activity, or both, most of what I have to say here will be unnecessary. On the other hand, I know of schools which have little or no regular drama, either in the classroom or outside it, and for students in such schools the few pointers below may be of some use.

The more one thinks about acting the more mysterious an activity it is, and the more strange its relationship with other basic English school activities like writing, reading and talking. It clearly most involves the last two of these and may—if you write your own plays—involve also the first. I suppose its strangeness derives from the fulfilment one obtains from getting inside someone else's skin, and for a while becoming that character and stopping being oneself; the best actors, perhaps, are those who can do that most completely. The effort of interpreting some other person, by voice and intonation on the one hand and movement on the other, is both demanding and exciting; in the process you seem to become freer and in some way more yourself. It differs from most other classroom activities, at any rate for mid-teenagers, in using movement—a refreshing change from the static frontal class and the static facing teacher. The mysteries of acting as a craft and an art are explored in several places in this book—notably perhaps in the two extracts from Peter Nichol's *A Day in the Death of Joe Egg* (p. 16 and p. 232) which open and close the book, and in the sequence of extracts from *A Midsummer Night's Dream* (p. 21). The experience of acting belongs in part to a very primitive aspect of ourselves, as one can see from the element of acting in most, or even all, religious and tribal rituals, and from the universality of small children's acting even in the absence of any instruction or stimulus from adults.

It follows, perhaps, that everyone should have a try at acting: the most unlikely students sometimes turn out to be very good at it once they have broken through an early uneasiness or shyness or diffidence. Teachers will invite you to join in and encourage you to do so, but in the end (and this is like enjoying reading or writing a good poem or short story) the really essential thing is your own effort. Those students who join in will get enormous pleasure from it, and you will be missing this if you don't try—though you might, after a real trial, and if your teacher encourages this, try your hand at being a director rather than an actor. If later on you get involved in a full-scale play there are lots of roles that the non-actor can play, from those to do with stage design and construction, make-up, costume, prompting, lighting and sound effects, to those of props man, call-boy, front-of-the-house manager and so forth. Still, in the classroom, acting is the central thing.

In my experience younger pupils often act as it were naturally and with great pleasure and strong instinct, while at the other end of the school entry, students of sixteen to eighteen, or a fair proportion of them, don't find any difficulty in getting involved. It is the middle range—those from fourteen to sixteen—who sometimes seem reluctant to act in front of their class. This is the very group for whom this book is designed, so I hope that you will at least try it as the rewards are so great.

This book contains only bits and pieces really, though I hope each extract makes some kind of sense on its own: I've aimed at a wide variety of material, and if you are *never* amused, excited, impressed, moved or touched by any of it you must be hard to please. Even so, no one student will like all the extracts, and perhaps only a few will be on your 'wavelength'. Do nag your teachers until they get you full-length versions of the ones you like or other plays by the same dramatist, or plays parallel in theme or content. This is the way to develop; even though drama is a highly socialized activity with a lot of teamwork and so forth, each individual will be getting a different experience, and the ones that *you* value are the ones you should follow up.

Lastly, the act of acting and the experience of enjoying drama can best be supported by seeing plays at the theatre. Everyone knows how a play read privately or in class comes to life when it is performed and suddenly takes on qualities which one didn't fully recognize or understand on the page.

There are 'halfway houses' such as recordings of plays which can be very helpful, and some public libraries have these on loan if your school hasn't got them. Radio and television both produce some very good drama; but there is no entirely satisfactory substitute for seeing the live play on the stage—and this is particularly valuable if you see a full-length play after having worked on all or part of it in classroom conditions. You may not agree with the director's or actors' interpretation, and this can take you back fruitfully to the text of the play itself. Your opinions aren't really worth tuppence until you've explored, in as many dimensions or media as you can, the play itself—as print on the page, as something to read aloud, as something to act in classroom or drama room, and as something to see on the stage or on television or to hear on the radio. But then you really *are* in a position to judge, and your judgment is the decisive one. On the way to this final point you ought to enjoy yourself and use yourself fully—your voice, your body, above all your understanding and intelligence. With a full-scale school play, though your effort may be important or even decisive, you are part of a large team working jointly for a common end (and this, I think, is one of the most valuable things you can do with your time); but in the more modest achievements to which this book aims at contributing, your personal effort and your personal choice and judgment are crucial.

The poet Wordsworth once said that nothing worthwhile was ever learned except through enjoyment: this may well apply (I believe it does) to all education, but perhaps it applies most centrally of all to your work in the field of drama, which shouldn't feel like work at all. It's when you *lose yourself* in acting or working in plays that you are really getting educated.

1
By way of introduction

𝄝𝄝𝄝𝄝𝄝𝄝𝄝𝄝𝄝𝄝𝄝𝄝𝄝𝄝𝄝𝄝𝄝𝄝𝄝𝄝𝄝𝄝𝄝𝄝𝄝𝄝𝄝𝄝𝄝𝄝𝄝𝄝𝄝𝄝𝄝𝄝

I thought I should like to start with a short passage which suggests (at least to me) that teaching and drama are in some ways very much alike—the teacher is to some degree acting, and the students, though captive and not volunteers, are like a theatre audience. The passage is itself the opening of a play, and turns the theatrical situation back into the classroom one as it presents a teacher talking to his class. I hope this won't confuse; I find it interesting to think that there's an element of drama in my own job and, on the occasions when it 'works', the students—though I always hope they will participate far more than in most theatres—are in a 'drama' situation; I won't deny that it's often not much of a play.

A DAY IN THE DEATH OF JOE EGG

Lead-in
The extract that follows is the opening of Peter Nichols' remarkable play *A Day in the Death of Joe Egg*. It is available as a Faber paperback, and has recently been made into a film. As this book concludes with a longer and more central extract from the play, we are leaving discussion of the content of the play till then. All you need to know is that Bri is a schoolmaster, not very happy in his job and with a difficult class. In the theatre he opens the play by treating the audience as if they were his class, and if *you* read it in class you will be, as it were, back at the beginning, with a schoolmaster addressing his pupils. Sheila is his wife; he loves her, but is always playing confidence tricks on her.

ACTING NOTES

This is very simple to do, and will provide an opportunity for a boy or girl to try being a teacher. Bri must be aggressive, witty, contemptuous of the class—and yet perhaps fond of them; and he has very serious problems at home, of which more later; but he jokes his way through life. Sheila must be terrified at the 'toy' spider he puts on his face just before she appears; this is the only 'prop' needed—and something to serve for Sheila's teapot. The class you are in might be *his* class and respond to his orders, laugh at his jokes, especially the accidental ones, and generally be restless and 'play up'. Meanwhile, Bri should occasionally shout; more often he is coldly sarcastic. But when the scene changes to Bri and Sheila's living-room the audience stops being the class, or the class the audience: how confusing it is! I mean that you listen as you would to any other play or extract.

BRI *comes on without warning. Shouts at audience.*

BRI. That's enough! (*Pause. Almost at once, louder.*) *I said enough!* (*Pause. Stares at audience. He is thirty-three but looks younger. Hardly ever at rest, acts being maladroit but the act is skilful. Clowning may give way to ineffectual hectoring and then self-piteous gloom.*) Another word and you'll be here till five o'clock. Nothing to me, is it? I've got all the time in the world. (*Moves across without taking his eyes off them.*) I didn't even get to the end of the corridor before there was such a din all the other teachers started opening their doors as much as to say what the hell's going on there's SOMEBODY'S TALKING NOW! (*Pause, stares again, like someone facing a mad dog.*) Who was it? You? You, Mister Man? . . . I did not *accuse* you, I *asked* you. Someone in the back row? (*Stares dumbly for some seconds. Relaxes, moves a few steps. Shrugs.*) You're the losers, not me. Who's that? (*Turns on them again.*) Right—hands on heads! Come on, that includes you, put the comb away. Eyes front and sit up. All of you, sit up! (*Puts his own hands on his head for a while, watching for a move, waiting for a sound, then takes them down. Suddenly roars.*) Hands on head and eyes front! YOU I'm talking to! You'll be *tired* by the time

I've finished. Stand on your seat. And keep your hands
on your heads. Never mind what's going on outside,
that joker at the back. Keep looking out here. Eyes
front, hands on heads.

(*Moves across.*)

(*Bell rings.*)

Who said MOVE? Nobody. Said move. Hands on heads
. . . Next one to groan stands on the seat. We're going
to have one minute's perfect silence before you go.
(*Looks at his watch.*) If we have to wait till midnight.
(*Stands watching for some seconds.*) That's nice. I like
that. Now try to hold it just like that till I get to this
machine-gun over here. (*Moves upstage, turning his
back. Turns back at once.*) My fault, all right. Little
joke. No more laughing. Eyes front, hands on heads.
(*Waits for silence, looks at watch, moving across suddenly looks up, very cross again.*) Who was that? Whoever did—that—can open the window before we all get
gassed . . . Wait a minute! Three of you? What are you
—a group? One go—one nearest the window. All the
others, eyes front, hands on heads. Right. (*Looks at
watch.*) That characteristic performance from our friend
near the window means we return to Go. (*Looks
up sharply.*) Shall I make it *two* minutes? (*Looks down
again. Ten seconds pass.*) We could have had this
sooner. Then we shouldn't be wasting time sitting here
when we might be . . . well . . . let's all—think—what
we might be doing—'stead of sitting here when the rest
have all gone home—we could be . . .

(*Speaking quietly now, absently staring into space. Few
more seconds pass. When he speaks again, it is as if in
a reverie.*) Yes—eyes front . . . hands on breasts . . .
STOP the laughter! WHO wants to start another minute?
(*Looks at watch then up again.*) And whatever the great
joke is, whatever it is that has so tickled your Stone Age
sense of humour—when all my efforts have failed . . .
save it till you're outside. I'm going to get my coat from
the staff-room now. And you will be as quiet as mice—
no, fish—till I get back. All right? I don't want to hear
a sound. Not a bubble. (*Goes off.*)

(*Lights up on set behind; living room.*)

(*Pleasant and comfortable, furnished with a gallant collection of junk-shop bargains and H.P. modern. Plain
walls with two essential doors and one optional window.
Door in upstage wall leads to hall and stairs, which can
be seen when the door is opened. Door in other wall
leads to kitchen. Bird in cage, fish in tank, plants in
pots. Two paintings of cowboys are conspicuous.*)

(SHEILA, *wearing trousers and pullover, comes from
kitchen with tea on a tray. She is thirty-five, generously
built, serious and industrious. When dressed for society,
she can be captivating.*) (*Puts down tray and runs back
to kitchen door, pushing with her foot, keeping out an
animal.*)

SHEILA. Back, back, no no.

(*Shuts the door and comes back. Door slams off.* SHEILA
starts pouring tea.)

(*Shouts.*) Bri?

BRI (*off*). No.

SHEILA. (*Shouts*). Just got tea.

(*He comes on, approaches her, takes the offered kiss,
then stands close looking at her. She goes back to pouring tea and offers him a cup. He doesn't take it, so she
looks at his face. She screams, nearly spills tea.*)
What's that?

BRI. What?

SHEILA. On your face!

BRI. Where?

SHEILA. Near your eye.

BRI. What is it?

SHEILA. A black thing.

BRI. For Christ's sake—

SHEILA. A spider—

BRI. Shall I touch it?

SHEILA. A great black—get it off!

BRI. How?

SHEILA. Knock it off!

(BRI *takes it off, smiling.*)

SHEILA. Ugh!

(*He puts it on the back of his hand and shows her.*)

BRI. I confiscated it.
  (*She knocks it away angrily.*)
  From Terry Hughes.
SHEILA. Vicious sod!
BRI. He *is*. For thirteen.
SHEILA. You, I mean.
BRI. In Religious Instruction.
SHEILA. It's not funny.
BRI. What I told *him*.

Run-out

Another and longer passage from *Joe Egg* will be found at the end of this book. Here you get a first glimpse of Bri's character, and perhaps a little insight into what it might be like to be a schoolteacher; notice how he longs to go but feels obliged to stay to impose his will on the pupils. Why does he tell them to be 'as quiet as mice' and then correct himself and say 'no, fish'? What would you do in the first instance if you were left alone with this instruction, and having a war with the teacher?

2
About acting

Shakespeare was not only a great dramatist, but also an actor and possibly a stage manager. It has often been pointed out that his language and metaphors are often connected with the theatre: everyone knows the line

All the world's a stage

from *As You Like It*; and there is a sadder reflection in *Macbeth*—
> Life's but a walking shadow, a poor player
> That struts and frets his hour upon the stage,
> And then is heard no more.

In the following three extracts we have a play about a play; and ludicrous though the efforts of Bottom and Co. may be, they are involved in essentially the same process as the greatest theatrical company.

A MIDSUMMER NIGHT'S DREAM

Lead-in
A group of workmen (usually in Shakespeare's day called 'mechanicals') are having what the modern theatre calls a 'planning meeting' to prepare rehearsals for the play *Pyramus and Thisbe* which is 'intended for great Theseus' wedding day'. The first scene shows them casting the play and dealing with some of the problems involved; at the end of the scene they decide to rehearse away from the town, in a wood by moonlight, where their friends will not interfere and no one will discover their secrets ('If we meet in the city we shall be dogged with company, and our devices known').

In the second scene they meet in the forest, tackle and

solve (to *their* satisfaction!) various tricky problems involved in their production, and begin their rehearsal. What
they don't realize is that the forest is enchanted and is in
the power of the fairies. The mischievous Puck, the right-
hand man and servant of Oberon, king of the fairies, takes
the 'shallowest thickskin of that barren sort', Bottom the
weaver, and fits him up with an ass's head (a kind of poetic
justice), and when he appears thus disguised, the rest of the
company are terrified and run away, leaving Bottom alone.
Quite unknown to any of them, Oberon has had a quarrel
with his queen, Titania, and has sent Puck to find a magic
herb,

> The juice of which on sleeping eye-lids laid,
> Will make or man or woman madly dote
> Upon the next live creature that it sees.

Oberon has squeezed the juice on the sleeping Titania's eye-
lids and when Bottom sings a song to keep his courage up,
it wakes up Titania, who falls in love not only with the coarse
and ignorant Bottom but also with an ass-headed man. (If
you want to know more of this remarkable love-affair you
will have to read the play.) Oberon later decides to be re-
conciled to Titania and uses an antidote to remove the effect
of the magic herb, and Titania sees Bottom as he really is
before the ass's head is removed from him and he returns to
the town (there is a pretence on Shakespeare's part that this is
Athens, but it is quite clearly an Elizabethan town, and these
are Elizabethan workmen).

In the third and last scene we have the pleasure of watching the play itself, performed as part of the celebration of
the wedding between Duke Theseus and Hippolyta and the
wedding of two other pairs of lovers—Lysander and Hermia,
and Demetrius and Helena. *Pyramus and Thisbe* is atro-
ciously bad and extremely funny, and half the fun comes from
the fact that we not only watch the play itself and its absurdities, but also hear the reaction of the stage audience—the
courtiers and the three newly-married pairs; so that a kind
of triangular relationship is set up between the workmen acting this play, the stage audience, and the real audience out

in the auditorium. Moreover, the whole play is about love and we might easily miss the idea that *Pyramus and Thisbe*, however crudely and absurdly, also presents a story of romantic love.

The three scenes tell us an enormous amount about stage illusion, and it seemed a suitable start for a book of extracts from plays. The anxiety that the workmen feel about *this* play may well be paralleled by the anxieties of your class about your own efforts; and if you do no better than Bottom and company and make an equal number of mistakes, we can remember, in Theseus' words, that 'the *best* in this kind are but toys, and the *worst* are no worse, if imagination amend them'. This is not a bad slogan with which to begin a sequence of classroom drama.

ACTING NOTES

The first scene takes place in Quince's house and as he is a carpenter you might like to have some props to suggest a carpenter's shop. The six mechanicals must all be 'gormless' in various ways —Quince fussy and old; Bottom tremendously confident, boastful and wishing to monopolize both acting and the production; Flute perhaps tall and gawky and awkward—ideally *un*suited for the heroine's part. The other three are rather less differentiated and you can decide for yourselves how they should be played; in one stage tradition Starveling is old, bent and deaf, so deaf that he can't hear his cues; Snout is fat and thick and anxious, and Snug dim and illiterate ('I am slow of study', he says).

The second scene is in the wood and it would be great fun to do this, indeed the whole sequence, out of doors; or, if in a classroom which can be blacked out, in darkness with a lantern or two. Titania ought to be beautiful, languid and imperious and dressed if possible in something that suggests the fairy world, in contrast with the rough clothing of the workmen. The ass's head is tricky unless you can make one of *papier mâché* on a wire framework, though many dramatic stores have a donkey's head as one of the standard 'props'. Ideally it should have a movable jaw and/or ears, controlled by strings held under Bottom's jerkin. Some 'fairy' music would be nice for Titania's awakening.

The third scene in this set of extracts is in the palace; Theseus and Hippolyta might have a throne of some sort and the other pairs of lovers should sit with them. Half the stage area could be devoted to *Pyramus and Thisbe*. Quince might wear a garland as the Prologue and sometimes is shown sitting on the stage as prompter after his introduction (he must make quite sure to get his punctuation and pauses *wrong*, and Theseus and the stage audience must respond and be amused, as their comments show). Bottom might have a helmet and a wooden sword, Flute a skirt and if possible a long-haired wig. Snout will need a box structure with bricks painted on it, Snug an old rug and some sort of lion's head, and Starveling a storm-lantern, a bundle of sticks, and a dog (I once used a wooden toy dog on wheels for this, which Starveling dragged behind him). You can invent your own stage business for *Pyramus and Thisbe*, so long as you remember that the workmen themselves presumably believe in what they are doing, however absurd it may be. At the end Bottom and Flute do a rough heavy peasants' dance (a 'Bergomask') and the play (or rather our extract) ends with Theseus' beautiful short speeches, done in a kind of hush with an atmosphere of fulfilment and peace, after he has been very kind and full of compliments to the mechanicals. More music here, of a quiet sleepy kind, would be a nice way of finishing the play.

(i)   *Athens*. QUINCE'S *house*.

   Enter QUINCE, SNUG, BOTTOM, FLUTE, SNOUT *and* STARVE-
      LING.

   QUINCE. Is all our company here?

   BOTTOM. You were best to call them generally, man by man, according to the scrip.

   QUINCE. Here is the scroll of every man's name, which is thought fit, through all Athens, to play in our interlude before the duke and the duchess, on his wedding-day at night.

   BOTTOM. First, good Peter Quince, say what the play treats on, then read the names of the actors, and so grow to a point.

   QUINCE. Marry, our play is, The most lamentable comedy, and most cruel death of Pyramus and Thisby.

   BOTTOM. A very good piece of work, I assure you, and a merry. Now, good Peter Quince, call forth your actors by the scroll. Masters, spread yourselves.

QUINCE. Answer as I call you. Nick Bottom, the weaver.

BOTTOM. Ready. Name what part I am for, and proceed.

QUINCE. You, Nick Bottom, are set down for Pyramus.

BOTTOM. What is Pyramus? a lover, or a tyrant?

QUINCE. A lover, that kills himself most gallant for love.

BOTTOM. That will ask some tears in the true performing of
    it: if I do it, let the audience look to their eyes; I will
    move storms, I will condole in some measure. To the
    rest: yet my chief humour is for a tyrant: I could play
    Ercles rarely, or a part to tear a cat in, to make all split.

> The raging rocks
> And shivering shocks
> Shall break the locks
>   Of prison gates;
> And Phibbus' car
> Shall shine from far
> And make and mar
>   The foolish Fates.

This was lofty! Now name the rest of the players. This
    is Ercles' vein, a tyrant's vein; a lover is more condoling.

QUINCE. Francis Flute, the bellows-mender.

FLUTE. Here, Peter Quince.

QUINCE. Flute, you must take Thisby on you.

FLUTE. What is Thisby? a wandering knight?

QUINCE. It is the lady that Pyramus must love.

FLUTE. Nay, faith, let me not play a woman; I have a beard
    coming.

QUINCE. That's all one: you shall play it in a mask, and you
    may speak as small as you will.

BOTTOM. An I may hide my face, let me play Thisby too, I'll
    speak in a monstrous little voice, 'Thisne, Thisne'; 'Ah
    Pyramus, my lover dear! thy Thisby dear, and lady
    dear!'

QUINCE. No, no; you must play Pyramus: and, Flute, you
    Thisby.

BOTTOM. Well, proceed.

QUINCE. Robin Starveling, the tailor.

STARVELING. Here, Peter Quince.

QUINCE. Robin Starveling, you must play Thisby's mother.
    Tom Snout, the tinker.

SNOUT. Here, Peter Quince.

QUINCE. You, Pyramus' father: myself, Thisby's father. Snug, the joiner; you, the lion's part: and, I hope, here is a play fitted.

SNUG. Have you the lion's part written? pray you, if it be, give it me, for I am slow of study.

QUINCE. You may do it extempore, for it is nothing but roaring.

BOTTOM. Let me play the lion too: I will roar, that I will do any man's heart good to hear me; I will roar, that I will make the duke say 'Let him roar again, let him roar again.'

QUINCE. An you should do it too terribly, you would fright the duchess and the ladies, that they would shriek; and that were enough to hang us all.

ALL. That would hang us, every mother's son.

BOTTOM. I grant you, friends, if that you should fright the ladies out of their wits, they would have no more discretion but to hang us: but I will aggravate my voice so that I will roar you as gently as any sucking dove; I will roar you an 'twere any nightingale.

QUINCE. You can play no part but Pyramus; for Pyramus is a sweet-faced man; a proper man, as one shall see in a summer's day; a most lovely gentleman-like man: therefore you must needs play Pyramus.

BOTTOM. Well, I will undertake it. What beard were I best to play it in?

QUINCE. Why, what you will. . . . But, masters, here are your parts: and I am to entreat you, request you, and desire you, to con them by tomorrow night; and meet me in the palace wood, a mile without the town, by moonlight; there will we rehearse, for if we meet in the city, we shall be dogged with company, and our devices known. In the meantime I will draw a bill of properties, such as our play wants. I pray you, fail me not.

BOTTOM. We will meet; and there we may rehearse most obscenely and courageously. Take pains; be perfect: adieu.

QUINCE. At the duke's oak we meet.

BOTTOM. Enough; hold or cut bow-strings.
(*Exeunt.*)

i) *The wood. Titania lying asleep.*

(*Enter* QUINCE, SNUG, BOTTOM, FLUTE, SNOUT, *and*
STARVELING.)

BOTTOM. Are we all met?

QUINCE. Pat, pat; and here's a marvellous convenient place
for our rehearsal. This green plot shall be our stage,
this hawthorn-brake our tiring-house; and we will do
it in action as we will do it before the duke.

BOTTOM. Peter Quince—

QUINCE. What sayest thou, bully Bottom?

BOTTOM. There are things in this comedy of Pyramus and
Thisby that will never please. First, Pyramus must draw
a sword to kill himself; which the ladies cannot abide.
How answer you that?

SNOUT. By'r lakin, a parlous fear.

STARVELING. I believe we must leave the killing out, when
all is done.

BOTTOM. Not a whit: I have a device to make all well. Write
me a prologue; and let the prologue seem to say, we
will do no harm with our swords, and that Pyramus is
not killed indeed; and, for the more better assurance,
tell them that I Pyramus am not Pyramus, but Bottom
the weaver: this will put them out of fear.

QUINCE. Well, we will have such a prologue; and it shall be
written in eight and six.

BOTTOM. No, make it two more; let it be written in eight
and eight.

SNOUT. Will not the ladies be afeard of the lion?

STARVELING. I fear it, I promise you.

BOTTOM. Masters, you ought to consider with yourselves:
to bring in—God shield us!—a lion among ladies, is a
most dreadful thing; for there is not a more fearful wild-
fowl than your lion living; and we ought to look to 't.

SNOUT. Therefore another prologue must tell he is not a
lion.

BOTTOM. Nay, you must name his name, and half his face
must be seen through the lion's neck: and he himself

must speak through, saying thus, or to the same defect,
—'Ladies,'—or 'Fair ladies,—I would wish you,'—or
'I would request you,'—or 'I would entreat you,—,
not to fear, not to tremble: my life for yours. If you
think I come hither as a lion, it were pity of my life:
no, I am no such thing; I am a man as other men are;'
and there indeed let him name his name, and tell them
plainly he is Snug the joiner.

QUINCE. Well, it shall be so. But there is two hard things;
that is, to bring the moonlight into a chamber; for, you
know, Pyramus and Thisby meet by moonlight.

SNOUT. Doth the moon shine that night we play our play?

BOTTOM. A calendar, a calendar! look in the almanac: find
out moonshine, find out moonshine.

QUINCE. Yes, it doth shine that night.

BOTTOM. Why, then may you leave a casement of the great
chamber window, where we play, open, and the moon
may shine in at the casement.

QUINCE. Ay; or else one must come in with a bush of thorns
and a lanthorn, and say he comes to disfigure, or to
present, the person of Moonshine. Then, there is another thing: we must have a wall in the great chamber;
for Pyramus and Thisby, says the story, did talk through
the chink of a wall.

SNOUT. You can never bring in a wall. What say you, Bottom?

BOTTOM. Some man or other must present Wall: and let
him have some plaster, or some loam, or some rough-
cast about him, to signify wall; and let him hold his
fingers thus and through that cranny shall Pyramus and
Thisby whisper.

QUINCE. If that may be, then all is well. Come, sit down,
every mother's son, and rehearse your parts. Pyramus,
you begin: When you have spoken your speech, enter
into that brake: and so every one according to his cue.
(*Enter* PUCK *behind*.)

PUCK. What hempen home-spuns have we swaggering here,
So near the cradle of the fairy queen?
What, a play toward! I'll be an auditor;
An actor too, perhaps, if I see cause.

QUINCE. Speak, Pyramus. Thisby, stand forth.
BOTTOM. Thisby, the flowers of odious savours sweet,—
QUINCE. Odours, odours.
BOTTOM. —odours savours sweet:
    So hath thy breath, my dearest Thisby dear.
    But hark, a voice! stay thou but here awhile,
    And by and by I will to thee appear. (*Exit.*)
PUCK. A stranger Pyramus than e'er played here. (*Exit.*)
FLUTE. Must I speak now?
QUINCE. Ay, marry, must you; for you must understand he
    goes but to see a noise that he heard, and is to come
    again.
FLUTE. Most radiant Pyramus, most lily-white of hue,
    Of colour like the red rose on triumphant brier,
    Most brisky juvenal and eke most lovely Jew,
    As true as truest horse that yet would never tire,
    I'll meet thee, Pyramus, at Ninny's tomb.
QUINCE. 'Ninus' tomb,' man: why, you must not speak that
    yet; that you answer to Pyramus: you speak all your
    part at once, cues and all. Pyramus enter: your cue is
    past; it is 'never tire.'
FLUTE. I,—as true as truest horse, that yet would never
    tire.
    (*Re-enter* PUCK, *and* BOTTOM *with an ass's head.*)
BOTTOM. If I were fair, Thisby, I were only thine.
QUINCE. O monstrous! O strange! we are haunted. Pray,
    masters! fly, masters! Help!
  (*Exeunt* QUINCE, SNUG, FLUTE, SNOUT, *and* STARVE-
    LING.)
PUCK. I'll follow you, I'll lead you about a round,
    Through bog, through bush, through brake, through
    brier:
    Sometime a horse I'll be, sometime a hound,
    A hog, a headless bear, sometime a fire;
    And neigh, and bark, and grunt, and roar, and burn,
    Like horse, hound, hog, bear, fire, at every turn.
    (*Exit.*)
BOTTOM. Why do they run away? this is a knavery of them
    to make me afeard.
    (*Re-enter* SNOUT.)

SNOUT. O Bottom, thou art changed! what do I see on thee?

BOTTOM. What do you see? you see an ass-head of your own, do you?

(*Exit* SNOUT.)

(*Re-enter* QUINCE.)

QUINCE. Bless thee, Bottom! bless thee! thou art translated.

BOTTOM. I see their knavery: this is to make an ass of me; to fright me, if they could. But I will not stir from this place, do what they can: I will walk up and down here, and I will sing, that they shall hear I am not afraid.

(*Sings.*)   The ousel cock so black of hue,
> With orange-tawny bill,
> The throstle with his note so true,
> The wren with little quill,—

TITANIA (*Awaking*). What angel wakes me from my flowery bed?

BOTTOM (*Sings*).   The finch, the sparrow and the lark,
> The plain-song cuckoo gray,
> Whose note full many a man doth mark,
> And dares not answer nay;—

for indeed, who would set his wit to so foolish a bird? who would give a bird the lie, though he cry 'cuckoo' never so?

TITANIA. I pray thee, gentle mortal, sing again:
Mine ear is much enamour'd of thy note;
So is mine eye enthralled to thy shape;
And thy fair virtue's force perforce doth move me
On the first view to say, to swear, I love thee.

(iii) *Athens. The palace of* THESEUS.

PHILOSTRATE. So please your grace, the Prologue is address'd.

THESEUS. Let him approach.

(*Flourish of trumpets.*)

(*Enter* QUINCE *for the* Prologue.)

PROLOGUE. If we offend, it is with our good will.
That you should think, we come not to offend,
But with good will. To show our simple skill,
That is the true beginning of our end.
Consider then we come but in despite.

We do not come as minding to content you,
Our true intent is. All for your delight
We are not here. That you should here repent you,
The actors are at hand, and by their show
You shall know all that you are like to know.

THESEUS. This fellow doth not stand upon points.

LYSANDER. He hath rid his prologue like a rough colt: he knows not the stop. A good moral, my lord: it is not enough to speak, but to speak true.

HIPPOLYTA. Indeed he hath played on his prologue like a child on a recorder; a sound, but not in government.

THESEUS. His speech was like a tangled chain; nothing impaired, but all disordered. Who is next?

(*Enter* PYRAMUS *and* THISBE, WALL, MOONSHINE, *and* LION.)

PROLOGUE. Gentles, perchance you wonder at this show;
But wonder on, till truth make all things plain.
This man is Pyramus, if you would know;
This beauteous lady Thisby is certain.
This man, with lime and rough-cast, doth present
Wall, that vile Wall which did these lovers sunder;
And through Wall's chink, poor souls, they are content
To whisper. At the which let no man wonder.
This man, with lanthorn, dog, and bush of thorn,
Presenteth Moonshine; for, if you will know,
By moonshine did these lovers think no scorn
To meet at Ninus' tomb, there, there to woo.
This grisly beast, which by name Lion hight,
The trusty Thisby, coming first by night,
Did scare away, or rather did affright;
And, as she fled, her mantle she did fall,
Which Lion vile with bloody mouth did stain.
Anon comes Pyramus, sweet youth and tall,
And finds his trusty Thisby's mantle slain:
Whereat, with blade, with bloody blameful blade,
He bravely broach'd his boiling bloody breast;
And Thisby, tarrying in mulberry shade,
His dagger drew, and died. For all the rest,
Let Lion, Moonshine, Wall, and lovers twain
At large discourse, while here they do remain.

(*Exeunt* PROLOGUE, PYRAMUS, THISBE, LION, *and* MOONSHINE.)

THESEUS. I wonder if the lion be to speak.

DEMETRIUS. No wonder, my lord: one lion may, when many asses do.

WALL. In this same interlude it doth befall
That I, one Snout by name, present a wall;
And such a wall, as I would have you think,
That had in it a crannied hole or chink,
Through which the lovers, Pyramus and Thisby,
Did whisper often very secretly.
This loam, this rough-cast, and this stone doth show
That I am that same wall; the truth is so:
And this the cranny is, right and sinister,
Through which the fearful lovers are to whisper.

THESEUS. Would you desire lime and hair to speak better?

DEMETRIUS. It is the wittiest partition that ever I heard discourse, my lord.

(*Re-enter* PYRAMUS.)

THESEUS. Pyramus draws near the wall: silence!

PYRAMUS. O grim-look'd night! O night with hue so black!
O night, which ever art when day is not!
O night, O night! alack, alack, alack,
I fear my Thisby's promise is forgot!
And thou, O wall, O sweet, O lovely wall,
That stand'st between her father's ground and mine!
Thou wall, O wall, O sweet and lovely wall,
Show me thy chink, to blink through with mine eyne!
(WALL *holds up his fingers*.)
Thanks, courteous wall: Jove shield thee well for this!
But what see I? No Thisby do I see.
O wicked wall, through whom I see no bliss!
Cursed be thy stones for thus deceiving me!

THESEUS. The wall, methinks, being sensible, should curse again.

PYRAMUS. No, in truth, sir, he should not. 'Deceiving me' is Thisby's cue: she is to enter now, and I am to spy her through the wall. You shall see, it will fall pat as I told you. Yonder she comes.

(*Re-enter* THISBE.)

THISBE. O wall, full often hast thou heard my moans,
    For parting my fair Pyramus and me.
    My cherry lips have often kiss'd thy stones,
    Thy stones with lime and hair knit up in thee.
PYRAMUS. I see a voice; now will I to the chink,
    To spy an I can hear my Thisby's face.
    Thisby!
THISBE. My love thou art, my love I think.
PYRAMUS. Think what thou wilt, I am thy lover's grace;
    And like Limander, am I trusty still.
THISBE. And I like Helen, till the Fates me kill.
PYRAMUS. Not Shafalus to Procrus was so true.
THISBE. As Shafalus to Procrus, I to you.
PYRAMUS. O, kiss me through the hole of this vile wall!
THISBE. I kiss the wall's hole, not your lips at all.
PYRAMUS. Wilt thou at Ninny's tomb meet me straightway?
THISBE. 'Tide life, 'tide death, I come without delay.
    (*Exeunt* PYRAMUS *and* THISBE.)
WALL. Thus have I, Wall, my part discharged so;
    And, being done, thus Wall away doth go. (*Exit.*)
THESEUS. Now is the mural down between the two neigh-
    bours.
DEMETRIUS. No remedy, my lord, when walls are so wilful
    to hear without warning.
HIPPOLYTA. This is the silliest stuff that ever I heard.
THESEUS. The best in this kind are but shadows: and the
    worst are no worse, if imagination amend them.
HIPPOLYTA. It must be your imagination then, and not theirs.
THESEUS. If we imagine no worse of them than they of them-
    selves, they may pass for excellent men. Here come two
    noble beasts in, a man and a lion.
    (*Re-enter* LION *and* MOONSHINE.)
LION. You, ladies, you, whose gentle hearts do fear
    The smallest monstrous mouse that creeps on floor,
    May now perchance both quake and tremble here,
    When lion rough in wildest rage doth roar.
    Then know that I, one Snug the joiner, am
    A lion-fell, nor else no lion's dam;
    For, if I should as lion come in strife
    Into this place, 'twere pity on my life.

B

THESEUS. A very gentle beast, and of a good conscience.

DEMETRIUS. The very best at a beast, my lord, that e'er I saw.

LYSANDER. This lion is a very fox for his valour.

THESEUS. True: and a goose for his discretion.

DEMETRIUS. Not so, my lord; for his valour cannot carry his discretion; and the fox carries the goose.

THESEUS. His discretion, I am sure, cannot carry his valour; for the goose carries not the fox. It is well: leave it to his discretion, and let us listen to the moon.

MOON. This lanthorn doth the horned moon present;—

DEMETRIUS. He should have worn the horns on his head.

THESEUS. He is no crescent, and his horns are invisible within the circumference.

MOON. This lanthorn doth the horned moon present;
Myself the man i' the moon do seem to be.

THESEUS. This is the greatest error of all the rest: the man should be put into the lanthorn. How is it else the man i' the moon?

DEMETRIUS. He dares not come here for the candle; for, you see, it is already in snuff.

HIPPOLYTA. I am weary of this moon: would he would change!

THESEUS. It appears, by his small light of discretion, that he is in the wane; but yet, in courtesy, in all reason, we must stay the time.

LYSANDER. Proceed, Moon.

MOON. All that I have to say, is, to tell you that the lanthorn is the moon; I, the man in the moon; this thorn-bush, my thorn-bush; and this dog, my dog.

DEMETRIUS. Why, all these should be in the lanthorn; for all these are in the moon. But silence! here comes Thisbe.

(*Re-enter* THISBE.)

THISBE. This is old Ninny's tomb. Where is my love?

LION (*Roaring*). Oh— (THISBE *runs off*.)

DEMETRIUS. Well roared, Lion.

THESEUS. Well run, Thisbe.

HIPPOLYTA. Well shone, Moon. Truly, the moon shines with a good grace.

(*The* LION *shakes* THISBE's *mantle, and exit*.)

THESEUS. Well moused, Lion.

LYSANDER. And so the lion vanished.
DEMETRIUS. And then came Pyramus.
(*Re-enter* PYRAMUS.)
PYRAMUS. Sweet Moon, I thank thee for thy sunny beams;
   I thank thee, Moon, for shining now so bright;
   For, by thy gracious, golden, glittering gleams,
   I trust to take of truest Thisby sight.
          But stay, O spite!
          But mark, poor knight,
        What dreadful dole is here!
          Eyes, do you see?
          How can it be?
        O dainty duck! O dear!
          Thy mantle good,
        What, stain'd with blood!
       Approach, ye Furies fell!
          O Fates, come, come,
          Cut thread and thrum;
      Quail, crush, conclude, and quell!
THESEUS. This passion, and the death of a dear friend, would
   go near to make a man look sad.
HIPPOLYTA. Beshrew my heart, but I pity the man.
PYRAMUS. O wherefore, Nature, didst thou lions frame?
  Since lion vile hath here deflower'd my dear:
  Which is—no, no—which was the fairest dame
  That lived, that loved, that liked, that look'd with cheer.
     Come, tears, confound:
     Out, sword, and wound
    The pap of Pyramus;
     Ay, that left pap,
     Where heart doth hop: (*Stabs himself.*)
   Thus die I, thus, thus, thus.
    Now am I dead,
    Now am I fled;
  My soul is in the sky:
    Tongue, lose thy light;
    Moon, take thy flight: (*Exit Moonshine.*)
  Now die, die, die, die, die. (*Dies.*)
DEMETRIUS. No, die, but an ace, for him; for he is but one.
LYSANDER. Less than an ace, man; for he is dead; he is noth-
   ing.

THESEUS. With the help of a surgeon he might yet recover, and prove an ass.

HIPPOLYTA. How chance Moonshine is gone before Thisbe comes back and finds her lover?

THESEUS. She will find him by starlight. Here she comes; and her passion ends the play.

(*Re-enter* THISBE.)

HIPPOLYTA. Methinks she should not use a long one for such a Pyramus; I hope she will be brief.

DEMETRIUS. A mote will turn the balance, which Pyramus, which Thisbe, is the better; he for a man, God warrant us; she for a woman, God bless us.

LYSANDER. She hath spied him already with those sweet eyes.

DEMETRIUS. And thus she means, *videlicet* : —

THISBE.   Asleep, my love?
            What, dead, my dove?
          O Pyramus, arise!
            Speak, speak. Quite dumb?
            Dead, dead? A tomb
          Must cover thy sweet eyes.
            These lily lips,
            This cherry nose,
          These yellow cowslip cheeks,
            Are gone, are gone:
            Lovers, make moan:
          His eyes were green as leeks.
            O Sisters Three,
            Come, come to me,
          With hands as pale as milk;
            Lay them in gore,
            Since you have shore
          With shears his thread of silk.
            Tongue, not a word:
            Come, trusty sword;
          Come, blade, my breast imbrue:
(*Stabs herself.*)
            And farewell, friends;
            Thus Thisby ends:
          Adieu, adieu, adieu.
(*Dies.*)

THESEUS. Moonshine and Lion are left to bury the dead.

DEMETRIUS. Ay, and Wall too.

BOTTOM (*Starting up*). No, I assure you: the wall is down that parted their fathers. Will it please you to see the epilogue, or to hear a Bergomask dance between two of our company?

THESEUS. No epilogue, I pray you; for your play needs no excuse. Never excuse; for when the players are all dead, there need none to be blamed. Marry, if he that writ it had played Pyramus and hanged himself in Thisbe's garter, it would have been a fine tragedy: and so it is, truly; and very notably discharged. But, come, your Bergomask: let your epilogue alone.

(*A dance.*)

The iron tongue of midnight hath told twelve:
Lovers, to bed; 'tis almost fairy time.
I fear we shall out-sleep the coming morn
As much as we this night have overwatch'd.
This palpable-gross play hath well beguiled
The heavy gait of night. Sweet friends, to bed.
A fortnight hold we this solemnity,
In nightly revels and new jollity.

(*Exeunt.*)

Run-out

In these extracts we have only taken the scenes concerning the mechanicals—and not quite all of these. The full play is of course far richer. Much of it takes place in the fairy-haunted wood at night (as does the scene in which Titania falls in love with Bottom). Here there are complicated and amusing goings-on between the four lovers, whom we have met in the last of the printed scenes, who are 'magicked' by the herb Oberon uses against Titania; there is also the quarrel between the fairy king and queen, the character of Puck, Oberon's mischievous servant, and many other delights. The play ends with the fairies blessing the triple marriages and Puck saying farewell to the audience. I hope you will be able to read the whole play on some occasion, and that this fairly large sample will have whetted your appetite to do so. It is one of the most rewarding of Shakespeare's comedies.

3
Love

〤〤

A key subject in any life, and therefore in any drama. I have
tried to choose passages which demonstrate or explore con-
trasting aspects of this huge part of our experience. The
Shakespeare passage is bound to seem dated and formal in
comparison, say, with the extract from *Billy Liar*: yet it's
surprising how much grasp of modern ideas of love can be
extracted from it, and I suppose a good deal of this derives
from the device of the girl being dressed as a boy and therefore in a situation to mock the absurdities and exaggerations
of love while focusing and thereby intensifying them. The
short bit from *The Playboy of the Western World* seems
to me beautiful and moving. A television version did it notably well, with Pegeen's facial expression moving from
scepticism to fascination and finally to love as Christy spins
his tale; and Synge has enormous advantages in 'the fiery,
magnificent and tender' imagination of the Irish peasants he
was drawing from and the rich language through which it is
expressed. *The Caucasian Chalk Circle* extracts were, of
course, originally written in German. Their effect is, to me
at least, moving as well as dignified—and very straightforward especially in contrast to the appalling situation in which
poor Grusha finds herself in the second extract, where the
conflict element in drama, and in love, dominates: she is
married, she apparently has a child and there is a river between her and her sweetheart. The idea of a love-barrier is
an important one—the wall in Pyramus and Thisbe (see
our extract from *A Midsummer Night's Dream*, p. 21)
is a simple example—and the whole of Shakespeare's
Romeo and Juliet is a working out of the love-barrier idea.
The fourth passage, from *Billy Liar*, is much less assured in
tone—I mean that Billy doesn't really know *what* he feels,

a typically *modern* predicament—and the play ends with a question mark. All four involve the confrontation of the lovers, and incidentally they perhaps offer a sketch of historical changes in our attitudes to love as well as bringing out what is common to all.

AS YOU LIKE IT

Lead-in

To make sense of the following extract from Shakespeare's *As You Like It*, you need to know a few things about the story. Rosalind's father, Duke Senior, has had his dukedom usurped by his brother and has exiled himself to the Forest of Arden. Rosalind has been told she is a traitor and ordered to leave the court; she decides to disguise herself as a man and, taking her cousin Celia with her as a peasant girl, to seek her father in the forest. While still at the court she has fallen in love with Orlando, who has also arrived, separately, in the forest. Orlando first meets the cynical courtier Jaques, and then his love Rosalind in disguise. As is usual in Shakespearean comedy he cannot penetrate Rosalind's disguise but accepts that she is a young man called Ganymede. He confesses his love for Rosalind to this young man, and admits he has been writing verses and hanging them on trees in the forest. Rosalind undertakes to cure him of his love if he will pretend that Ganymede *is* Rosalind, and takes the opportunity of ridiculing some of the absurdities of romantic love.

ACTING NOTES

Two of the parts are quite straightforward : Celia, at least in this extract, is a mere 'feed' for Rosalind, and Orlando is a conventional lover—which, in Elizabethan terms, means that he is passionately single-minded and inclined to be sorry for himself as he cannot even see his beloved Rosalind. Jaques is proud of his melancholy, and takes a gloomy and cynical view of his fellow-man ; in strong contrast with Orlando, he despises love as lunacy. The really difficult part is that of Rosalind. He/she must be lively, energetic, witty and delighting in his/her role and expertise on love. Rosalind is a girl but in Elizabethan times her part would have been played by a boy, as women were forbidden to appear on the stage. Then she is dressed as a boy under the name of Ganymede; and then this young man undertakes to impersonate the part of Rosalind and, by his tantrums and moodiness, cure Orlando of his love for Rosalind. Thus we have a boy (young Elizabethan actor) playing a girl (Rosalind) dressed as a boy (Ganymede) pretending to be a girl. So if the actor *you* choose is a boy he's got to do all four stages, or imply them in some way; if a girl, she has to do only three stages. On the modern stage the part is usually taken by a girl (though there was an all-male production in London recently!) If you are in a co-educational class, perhaps a 'swash-buckling' girl would be best.

The forest.

ROSALIND. Good my complexion! dost thou think, though I am caparisoned like a man, I have a doublet and hose in my disposition? One inch of delay more is a South-sea of discovery; I prithee, tell me who it is quickly, and speak apace. I would thou couldst stammer, that thou mightst pour this concealed man out of thy mouth, as wine comes out of a narrow-mouthed bottle, either too much at once, or none at all. I prithee, take the cork out of thy mouth that I may drink thy tidings.

CELIA. So you may put a man in your belly.

ROSALIND. Is he of God's making? What manner of man? Is his head worth a hat, or his chin worth a beard?

CELIA. Nay, he hath but a little beard.

ROSALIND. Why, God will send more, if the man will be thankful: let me stay the growth of his beard, if thou delay me not the knowledge of his chin.

CELIA. It is young Orlando, that tripped up the wrestler's heels and your heart both in an instant.

ROSALIND. Nay, but the devil take mocking: speak sad brow and true maid.

CELIA. I' faith, coz, 'tis he.

ROSALIND. Orlando?

CELIA. Orlando.

ROSALIND. Alas the day! what shall I do with my doublet and hose? What did he when thou sawest him? What said

he? How looked he? Wherein went he? What makes
he here? Did he ask for me? Where remains he? How
parted he with thee? And when shalt thou see him
again? Answer me in one word.

CELIA. You must borrow me Gargantua's mouth first: 'tis
a word too great for any mouth of this age's size. To
say ay and no to these particulars is more than to answer
in a catechism.

ROSALIND. But doth he know that I am in this forest and in
man's apparel? Looks he as freshly as he did the day he
wrestled?

CELIA. It is as easy to count atomies as to resolve the pro-
positions of a lover; but take a taste of my finding him,
and relish it with good observance. I found him under
a tree, like a dropped acorn.

ROSALIND. It may well be called Jove's tree, when it drops
forth such fruit.

CELIA. Give me audience, good madam.

ROSALIND. Proceed.

CELIA. There lay he, stretched along, like a wounded knight.

ROSALIND. Though it be pity to see such a sight, it well becomes the ground.

CELIA. Cry 'holla' to thy tongue, I prithee; it curvets un-
seasonably. He was furnished like a hunter.

ROSALIND. O, ominous! he comes to kill my heart.

CELIA. I would sing my song without a burden: thou bring-
est me out of tune.

ROSALIND. Do you not know I am a woman? when I think,
I must speak. Sweet, say on.

CELIA. You bring me out. Soft! comes he not here?
(*Enter* ORLANDO *and* JAQUES.)

ROSALIND. 'Tis he: slink by, and note him.

JAQUES. I thank you for your company; but, good faith, I
had as lief have been myself alone.

ORLANDO. And so had I; but yet, for fashion sake, I thank
you too for your society.

JAQUES. God be wi' you: let's meet as little as we can.

ORLANDO. I do desire we may be better strangers.

JAQUES. I pray you, mar no more trees with writing love
songs in their barks.

ORLANDO. I pray you, mar no moe of my verses with reading them ill-favouredly.

JAQUES. Rosalind is your love's name?

ORLANDO. Yes, just.

JAQUES. I do not like her name.

ORLANDO. There was no thought of pleasing you when she was christened.

JAQUES. What stature is she of?

ORLANDO. Just as high as my heart.

JAQUES. You are full of pretty answers. Have you not been acquainted with goldsmiths' wives, and conned them out of rings?

ORLANDO. Not so; but I answer you right painted cloth, from whence you have studied your questions.

JAQUES. You have a nimble wit: I think 'twas made of Atalanta's heels. Will you sit down with me? and we two will rail against our mistress the world and all our misery.

ORLANDO. I will chide no breather in the world but myself, against whom I know most faults.

JAQUES. The worst fault you have is to be in love.

ORLANDO. 'Tis a fault I will not change for your best virtue. I am weary of you.

JAQUES. By my troth, I was seeking for a fool when I found you.

ORLANDO. He is drowned in the brook: look but in, and you shall see him.

JAQUES. There I shall see mine own figure.

ORLANDO. Which I take to be either a fool or a cipher.

JAQUES. I'll tarry no longer with you: farewell, good Signior Love.

ORLANDO. I am glad of your departure: adieu, good Monsieur Melancholy.

(*Exit Jaques.*)

ROSALIND (*aside to Celia*). I will speak to him like a saucy lackey and under that habit play the knave with him. Do you hear, forester?

ORLANDO. Very well: what would you?

ROSALIND. I pray you, what is't o'clock?

ORLANDO. You should ask me what time o' day: there's no clock in the forest.

ROSALIND. Then there is no true lover in the forest; else sighing every minute and groaning every hour would detect the lazy foot of Time as well as a clock.

ORLANDO. And why not the swift foot of Time? had not that been as proper?

ROSALIND. By no means, sir: Time travels in divers paces with divers persons. I'll tell you who Time ambles withal, who Time trots withal, who Time gallops withal and who he stands still withal.

ORLANDO. I prithee, who doth he trot withal?

ROSALIND. Marry, he trots hard with a young maid between the contract of her marriage and the day it is solemnized: if the interim be but a se'nnight, Time's pace is so hard that it seems the length of seven year.

ORLANDO. Who ambles Time withal?

ROSALIND. With a priest that lacks Latin and a rich man that hath not the gout, for the one sleeps easily because he cannot study and the other lives merrily because he feels no pain, the one lacking the burden of lean and wasteful learning, the other knowing no burden of heavy tedious penury; these Time ambles withal.

ORLANDO. Who doth he gallop withal?

ROSALIND. With a thief to the gallows, for though he go as softly as foot can fall, he thinks himself too soon there.

ORLANDO. Who stays it still withal?

ROSALIND. With lawyers in the vacation; for they sleep between term and term and then they perceive not how Time moves.

ORLANDO. Where dwell you, pretty youth?

ROSALIND. With this shepherdess, my sister; here in the skirts of the forest, like fringe upon a petticoat.

ORLANDO. Are you native of this place?

ROSALIND. As the cony that you see dwell where she is kindled.

ORLANDO. Your accent is something finer than you could purchase in so removed a dwelling.

ROSALIND. I have been told so of many: but indeed an old

religious uncle of mine taught me to speak, who was in his youth an inland man; one that knew courtship too well, for there he fell in love. I have heard him read many lectures against it, and I thank God I am not a woman, to be touched with so many giddy offences as he hath generally taxed their whole sex withal.

ORLANDO. Can you remember any of the principal evils that he laid to the charge of women?

ROSALIND. There was none principal; they were all like one another as half-pence are, every one fault seeming monstrous till his fellow-fault came to match it.

ORLANDO. I prithee, recount some of them.

ROSALIND. No, I will not cast away my physic but on those who are sick. There is a man haunts the forest, that abuses our young plants with carving 'Rosalind' on their barks; hangs odes upon hawthorns and elegies on brambles, all, forsooth, deifying the name of Rosalind: if I could meet that fancy-monger, I would give him some good counsel, for he seems to have the quotidian of love upon him.

ORLANDO. I am he that is so love-shaked: I pray you, tell me your remedy.

ROSALIND. There is none of my uncle's marks upon you: he taught me how to know a man in love; in which cage of rushes I am sure you are not prisoner.

ORLANDO. What were his marks?

ROSALIND. A lean cheek, which you have not, a blue eye and sunken, which you have not, an unquestionable spirit, which you have not, a beard neglected, which you have not; but I pardon you for that, for simply your having in beard is a younger brother's revenue: then your hose should be ungartered, your bonnet unbanded, your sleeve unbuttoned, your shoe untied and every thing about you demonstrating a careless desolation; but you are no such man; you are rather point-device in your accoutrements, as loving yourself, than seeming the lover of any other.

ORLANDO. Fair youth, I would I could make thee believe I love.

ROSALIND. Me believe it! you may as soon make her that

you love believe it; which, I warrant, she is apter to do
than to confess she does: that is one of the points in the
which women still give the lie to their consciences. But,
in good sooth, are you he that hangs the verses on the
trees, wherein Rosalind is so admired?

ORLANDO. I swear to thee, youth, by the white hand of Rosalind, I am that he, that unfortunate he.

ROSALIND. But are you so much in love as your rhymes speak?

ORLANDO. Neither rhyme nor reason can express how much.

ROSALIND. Love is merely a madness, and, I tell you, de-
serves as well a dark house and a whip as madmen do:
and the reason why they are not so punished and cured
is, that the lunacy is so ordinary that the whippers are
in love too. Yet I profess curing it by counsel.

ORLANDO. Did you ever cure any so?

ROSALIND. Yes, one, and in this manner. He was to imagine
me his love, his mistress; and I set him every day to woo
me: at which time would I, being but a moonish youth,
grieve, be effeminate, changeable, longing and liking,
proud, fantastical, apish, shallow, inconstant, full of
tears, full of smiles, for every passion something and
for no passion truly any thing, as boys and women are
for the most part cattle of this colour; would now like
him, now loathe him; then entertain him, then forswear
him; now weep for him, then spit at him; that I drave
my suitor from his mad humour of love to a living
humour of madness; which was, to forswear the full
stream of the world and to live in a nook merely mo-
nastic. And thus I cured him; and this way will I take
upon me to wash your liver as clean as a sound sheep's
heart, that there shall not be one spot of love in 't.

ORLANDO. I would not be cured, youth.

ROSALIND. I would cure you, if you would but call me Rosalind and come every day to my cote and woo me.

ORLANDO. Now, by the faith of my love, I will: tell me
where it is.

ROSALIND. Go with me to it and I'll show it you: and by the
way you shall tell me where in the forest you live.
Will you go?

ORLANDO. With all my heart, good youth.

ROSALIND. Nay, you must call me Rosalind. Come, sister, will you go?
(*Exeunt.*)

Run-out
There is a good deal of interest in these three short stretches of dialogue: some small bits will need explaining (e.g., 'Gargantua's mouth', 'curvets', 'right painted cloth'), but the main drift is clear enough, and it gives an amusing opportunity for Rosalind, herself desperately in love with Orlando, to ridicule the excesses and exaggerations of the kind of 'moony' love represented by Orlando, and yet establishes a strong picture of 'real' love. There is a further extract from this play on page 152.

THE PLAYBOY OF THE WESTERN WORLD

Lead-in
The following extract comes from J. M. Synge's *The Playboy of the Western World*. Christy has arrived at Pegeen's village and has become famous because he claims to have killed his father. Pegeen is reluctantly fascinated by him, and in this short sequence the main point is the power of verbal love-making that Christy shows in winning Pegeen's love.

ACTING NOTES
The rhetorical power of Christy is the vital thing here, with Pegeen starting rather coolly and becoming more and more entranced as he makes love to her by his power of speech. If Irish voices can be produced this will be a great advantage, but the lilt of Christy's imagery and Pegeen's warming response speaks for itself, so long as it is carefully, thoughtfully and richly spoken. They should not even touch until Christy puts an arm round Pegeen, but should probably be staring at one another throughout.

PEGEEN. Well, you're the lad, and you'll have great times from this out when you could win that wealth of prizes, and you sweating in the heat of noon!

CHRISTY (*looking at her with delight*). I'll have great times
if I win the crowning prize I'm seeking now, and that's
your promise that you'll wed me in a fortnight, when
our banns is called.

PEGEEN (*backing away from him*). You've right daring to
go ask me that, when all knows you'll be starting to some
girl in your own townland, when your father's rotten
in four months, or five.

CHRISTY (*indignantly*). Starting from you, is it? (*He follows her*.) I will not, then, and when the airs is warming,
in four months or five, it's then yourself and me should
be pacing Neifin in the dews of night, the times sweet
smells do be rising, and you'd see a little, shiny new
moon, maybe sinking on the hills.

PEGEEN (*looking at him playfully*). And it's that kind of a
poacher's love you'd make, Christy Mahon, on the sides
of Neifin, when the night is down?

CHRISTY. It's little you'll think if my love's a poacher's, or
an earl's itself, when you'll feel my two hands stretched
around you, and I squeezing kisses on your puckered
lips, till I'd feel a kind of pity for the Lord God is all
ages sitting lonesome in his golden chair.

PEGEEN. That'll be right fun, Christy Mahon, and any girl
would walk her heart out before she'd meet a young
man was your like for eloquence, or talk at all.

CHRISTY (*encouraged*). Let you wait, to hear me talking,
till we're astray in Erris, when Good Friday's by, drinking a sup from a well, and making mighty kisses with
our wetted mouths, or gaming in a gap of sunshine, with
yourself stretched back unto your necklace, in the flowers
of the earth.

PEGEEN (*in a low voice, moved by his tone*). I'd be nice so,
is it?

CHRISTY (*with rapture*). If the mitred bishops seen you that
time, they'd be the like of the holy prophets, I'm thinking, do be straining the bars of Paradise to lay eyes on
the Lady Helen of Troy, and she abroad, pacing back
and forward, with a nosegay in her golden shawl.

PEGEEN (*with real tenderness*). And what is it I have, Christy
Mahon, to make me fitting entertainment for the like of

you, that has such poet's talking, and such bravery of heart?

CHRISTY (*in a low voice*). Isn't there the light of seven heavens in your heart alone, the way you'll be an angel's lamp to me from this out, and I abroad in the darkness, spearing salmons in the Owen or the Carrowmore?

PEGEEN. If I was your wife, I'd be along with you those nights, Christy Mahon, the way you'd see I was a great hand at coaxing bailiffs, or coining funny nicknames for the stars of night.

CHRISTY. You, is it? Taking your death in the hailstones, or in the fogs of dawn.

PEGEEN. Yourself and me would shelter easy in a narrow bush (*with a qualm of dread*); but we're only talking, maybe, for this would be a poor, thatched place to hold a fine lad is the like of you.

CHRISTY (*putting his arm round her*). If I wasn't a good Christian, it's on my naked knees I'd be saying my prayers and paters to every jackstraw you have roofing your head, and every stony pebble is paving the lane-way to your door.

PEGEEN (*radiantly*). If that's the truth, I'll be burning candles from this out to the miracles of God have brought you from the south today, and I with my gowns bought ready, the way that I can wed you, and not wait at all.

CHRISTY. It's miracles, and that's the truth. Me there toiling a long while, and walking a long while, not knowing at all I was drawing all times nearer to this holy day.

PEGEEN. And myself, a girl, was tempted often to go sailing the seas till I'd marry a Jew-man, with ten kegs of gold, and I not knowing at all there was the like of you draw-ing nearer, like the stars of God.

CHRISTY. And to think I'm long years hearing women talk-ing that talk, to all bloody fools, and this the first time I've heard the like of your voice talking sweetly for my own delight.

PEGEEN. And to think it's me is talking sweetly, Christy Mahon, and I the fright of seven townlands for my biting tongue. Well, the heart's a wonder, and, I'm thinking, there won't be our like in Mayo, for gallant lovers, from this hour today. (*Drunken singing is heard outside.*) There's my father coming from the wake, and when he's had his sleep we'll tell him, for he's peaceful then.

Run-out

To my ears the lilt of the Irish sentences here have great beauty and one can see how important speech is as an element in love-making. Christy manages to make even poverty and humbleness attractive when transfigured by the power of love. The whole effect of the dialogue is very different from the clipped and bare speech so often used nowadays even by lovers. Synge recorded with the most loving attention the turns of speech, the metaphors and the rhythms of the peasants in the West of Ireland in the first decades of this century. The whole play is fascinating to read and watch, and if you admire the speech, you should try *Riders to the Sea* or *Deirdre of the Sorrows.*

THE CAUCASIAN CHALK CIRCLE

Lead-in

These two short extracts come from Berthold Brecht's famous play *The Caucasian Chalk Circle.* Brecht is usually considered one of the greatest German dramatists, certainly of this century. Many of his plays are radical or revolutionary in content, and he hated the Hitler régime, from which he escaped to work in the United States, finally returning to East Germany after the war and founding the famour Berliner Ensemble, a theatrical company which included his wife Helene Waigel.

The plot of *The Caucasian Chalk Circle* is complex, and only part of it concerns us here. Grusha is a servant to the Governor, Georgi Abashvili, and his wife Natella. There is a palace revolution in which the Governor is killed; his wife escapes, taking with her all her jewels and marvellous gowns, but forgetting her son Michael, who is left helpless u Grusha takes him up for pity; he is certain to be killed new régime if found. Grusha takes him on a long journey away from the city and with great difficulty and great courage cherishes him and enables him to survive. She goes through a form of marriage with a sick peasant at one stage to save the child's life.

The first extract shows a soldier, Simon Chachava, who has noticed Grusha and fallen in love with her, making an oblique but more or less formal proposal of marriage, giving her a love token and promising to return after the war to marry her.

In the second extract Simon meets Grusha for the first time since they parted and she feels obliged to explain the 'marriage'. They meet on the opposite banks of a river, and Simon soon senses that all is not well. Grusha loves him and her marriage was only a nominal one, to protect the child. The Singer explains with great power what Simon can't actually say to Grusha. He sees Michael's cap and though she immediately denies that the child is hers, she too, like Simon, can't really explain—at least, not across the river—and it is left to the Singer to tell us her real thoughts. Then, devastatingly, an Ironshirt soldier, one of those who have been searching for Michael, asks if he is her child; to protect him she must, and with great courage and selflessness does, say he is. Immediately Simon leaves and Grusha unhappily 'followed them to the city, the dangerous place'.

ACTING NOTES

These two extracts need performing very simply and directly. The first is a simple love scene with the soldier's formality and questions showing a direct, honest, and finally tender, devoted and loving attitude Grusha. The movement from prose to verse, comm comes as Grusha promises with great sincerity en he goes off to the wars. The Singer acts as commentator on the action, and is present filling in the gaps, expressing things the or themselves, and often interpreting the he Chorus in Shakespeare's *Henry V* is) This contributes towards an interesting on, so that we are always conscious that not 'a slice of life'. Brecht's plays are based on the theory of 'alienation', which means, roughly, that we in the audience are asked not to identify with the characters, but to stand sufficiently away from the action to be able to judge the moral, social and intellectual problems presented as impersonally as possible. Thus the Berliner Ensemble production of *The Caucasian Chalk Circle* used for the river (in the second extract below) a long blue cloth held horizontally by two 'extras' and shaken gently to represent the waves. A classroom production could well do the same. The Singer should be at the side of the stage area, and a guitar would be a pleasant extra, a few quiet chords being played before or after his two speeches.

(*Enter the soldier,* SIMON CHACHAVA, *searching the crowd for* GRUSHA.)

SIMON. There you are at last, Grusha! What are you going to do?

GRUSHA. Nothing. If the worst comes to the worst, I've a brother with a farm in the mountains. But what about you?

SIMON. Don't worry about me. (*Polite again.*) Grusha Vachnadze, your desire to know my plans fills me with satisfaction. I've been ordered to accompany Madam Natella Abashvili as her guard.

GRUSHA. But hasn't the Palace Guard mutinied?

SIMON (*serious*). That's a fact.

GRUSHA. But isn't it dangerous to accompany the woman?

SIMON. In Tiflis, they say: Isn't the stabbing dangerous for the knife?

GRUSHA. You're not a knife, you're a man, Simon Chachava. What has this woman to do with you?

SIMON. The woman has nothing to do with me. But I have my orders, and so I go.

GRUSHA. The soldier is a pigheaded man: he gets himself into danger for nothing—nothing at all. Now I must go into the third courtyard. I'm in a hurry.

SIMON. As there's a hurry we oughtn't to quarrel. For a good quarrel one needs time. May I ask if the young lady still has parents?

GRUSHA. No, only a brother.

SIMON. As time is short—the second question would be: Is

the young lady as healthy as a fish in water?

GRUSHA. Perhaps once in a while a pain in the right shoulder. But otherwise I'm strong enough for any work. So far no one has complained.

SIMON. Everyone knows that. Even if it's Easter Sunday and there's the question who shall fetch the goose, then it's she. The third question is this: Is the young lady impatient? Does she want cherries in winter?

GRUSHA. Impatient, no. But if a man goes to war without any reason, and no message comes, that's bad.

SIMON. A message will come. And finally the main question . . .

GRUSHA. Simon Chachava, because I've got to go to the third courtyard and I'm in a hurry, the answer is 'Yes'.

SIMON (*very embarrassed*). Hurry, they say, is the wind that blows down the scaffolding. But they also say: The rich don't know what hurry is—I come from . . .

GRUSHA. Kutsk.

SIMON. So the young lady has already made enquiries? Am healthy, have no dependents, earn ten piastres a month, as paymaster twenty, and am asking honourably for your hand.

GRUSHA. Simon Chachava, that suits me.

SIMON (*taking from his neck a thin chain from which hangs a little cross*). This cross belonged to my mother, Grusha Vachnadze. The chain is silver. Please wear it.

GRUSHA. I thank you, Simon. (*He fastens it round her neck.*)

SIMON. Now I must harness the horses. The young lady will understand that. It would be better for the young lady to go into the third courtyard. Otherwise there'll be trouble.

GRUSHA. Yes, Simon.

(*They stand together undecided.*)

SIMON. I'll just take the woman to the troops who've remained loyal. When the war's over, I'll come back. In two weeks. Or three. I hope my intended won't get tired waiting for my return.

GRUSHA. Simon Shashava, I shall wait for you.

Go calmly into battle, soldier
The bloody battle, the bitter battle

From which not everyone returns.
When you return I will be there.
I will be waiting for you under the green elm
I will be waiting for you under the bare elm
I will wait until the last soldier has returned
And even longer.
When you return from the battle
No boots will lie before the door
The pillow beside mine will be empty
And my mouth will be unkissed.
When you return, when you return
You will be able to say: all is as it was.

SIMON. I thank you, Grusha Vachnadze, and farewell! (*He bows low before her; she bows low before him. Then she runs off without looking round.*)

On turning round, GRUSHA *sees* SIMON CHACHAVA *standing on the opposite bank. He wears a shabby uniform.*)

GRUSHA. Simon!

SIMON. Is that Grusha Vachnadze?

GRUSHA. Simon.

SIMON (*politely*). A good morning, and good health to the young lady.

GRUSHA (*gets up gaily and bows deeply*). A good morning to the soldier. And thank God he has returned in good health.

SIMON. They found better fish than me, so they didn't eat me, said the haddock.

GRUSHA. Courage, said the kitchen boy. Luck, said the hero.

SIMON. How are things here? Was the winter bearable? Did the neighbour behave?

GRUSHA. The winter was a little rough, the neighbour as usual, Simon.

SIMON. May one ask if a certain person is still in the habit of putting her leg in the water when washing her linen?

GRUSHA. The answer is no. Because of the eyes in the bushes.

SIMON. The young lady is talking about soldiers. Here stands a paymaster.

GRUSHA. Is that worth twenty piastres?

SIMON. And board.

GRUSHA (*with tears in her eyes*). Behind the barracks under the date trees.

SIMON. Yes, there. I see someone has kept her eyes open.

GRUSHA. Someone has.

SIMON. And has not forgotten? (GRUSHA *shakes her head*.) And so the door is still on its hinges, as they say? (GRUSHA *looks at him in silence and shakes her head again*.) What's that mean? Is something wrong?

GRUSHA. Simon Chachava, I can never go back to Nukha. Something has happened.

SIMON. What has happened?

GRUSHA. It so happened that I knocked down an Ironshirt.

SIMON. Grusha Vachnadze will have had her reasons for that.

GRUSHA. Simon Chachava, my name is also no longer what it was.

SIMON (*after a pause*). I don't understand that.

GRUSHA. When do women change their names, Simon? Let me explain it to you: nothing stands between us. Everything between us has remained as it was. You've got to believe that.

SIMON. How can nothing stand between us and things be changed?

GRUSHA. How can I explain it to you? So fast and with the stream between us? Couldn't you cross that bridge there?

SIMON. Perhaps it's no longer necessary.

GRUSHA. It's most necessary. Come over, Simon. Quick!

SIMON. Is the young lady saying someone has come too late? (GRUSHA *looks up to him in despair, her face streaming with tears*. SIMON *stares before him. He picks up a piece of wood and starts cutting it*.)

THE SINGER. So many words are said, so many words are left unsaid.

The soldier has come. Whence he comes he doesn't say. Hear what he thought but didn't say:

The battle began at dawn, grew bloody at noon.

The first fell before me, the second behind me, the third at my side.

I trod on the first, I abandoned the second, the captain sabred the third.

My one brother died by steel, my other brother died by
smoke.

My neck was burnt by fire, my hands froze in my gloves,
my toes in my socks. For food I had aspen buds, for
drink I had maple brew, for bed I had stones in water.

SIMON. I see a cap in the grass. Is there a little one already?

GRUSHA. There is, Simon. How could I hide it? But please
don't let it worry you, it's not mine.

SIMON. They say: Once the wind begins to blow, it blows
through every crack. The woman need say no more.
(GRUSHA *lowers her head and says no more.*)

THE SINGER. There was great yearning but there was no waiting.

The oath is broken. Why was not disclosed.

Hear what she thought, but didn't say:

While you fought in the battle, soldier,

The bloody battle, the bitter battle,

I found a child who was helpless

And hadn't the heart to do away with it.

I had to care for what otherwise would have come to
harm

I had to bend down on the floor for breadcrumbs

I had to tear myself to pieces for what was not mine

But alien.

Someone must be the helper.

For the little tree needs its water

The little lamb loses its way when the herdsman is asleep

And the bleating remains unheard!

SIMON. Give me back the cross I gave you. Or better, throw
it in the stream. (*He turns to go.*)

GRUSHA (*getting up*). Simon Chachava, don't go away! It
isn't mine, it isn't mine! (*She hears the* CHILDREN *calling.*) What is it, children?

VOICES. Soldiers have come!—They are taking Michael
away.

(GRUSHA *stands aghast as* TWO IRONSHIRTS, *with*
MICHAEL *between them, come towards her.*)

IRONSHIRT. Are you Grusha? (*She nods.*) Is that your child?

GRUSHA. Yes. (SIMON *goes off.*) Simon!

IRONSHIRT. We have official orders to take this child, found in your charge, back to the city. There is suspicion that it is Michael Abashvili, son and heir of the late Governor Georgi Abashvili, and his wife, Natella Abashvili. Here is the document and the seal (*They lead the* CHILD *away*).

GRUSHA (*running after them and shouting*). Leave it here, please! It's mine!

THE SINGER. The Ironshirts took the child away, the precious child.

The unhappy girl followed them to the city, the dangerous place.

The real mother demanded the child back. The foster mother faced her trial.

Who will try the case, on whom will the child be bestowed?

Who will be the Judge? A good one, a bad one?

The city was in flames. On the Judgment Seat sat Azdak.

Run-out

Azdak, the judge mentioned at the end of the second extract, is a curious and fascinating character, a village 'scrivener' who wrote letters and documents for the illiterate—often drunk, not above taking bribes, but very far-seeing and, at least as a judge, honest; he is of course not a professional judge and has achieved the post by a series of accidents during a revolution. It is he who judges whether Natella has the right to take back Michael or whether he is now essentially Grusha's. He devises a test in which the real mother Natella and the adopted mother Grusha see who can pull the child out of a circle drawn in chalk on the stage. Natella is greedy; she wants the child not for love but because he inherits vast wealth, and is prepared to hurt the child to get him back, while Grusha can't bear to do so. Azdak perceives thus that the one to whom the child belongs is the one who has nurtured, protected and loved it—a moral which has importance quite outside this particular case. The play is very well worth reading and you would certainly find it exciting, often very funny and yet profound.

✕✕✕

BILLY LIAR

Lead-in

The following extract comes from *Billy Liar*, which appeared
as a play in 1960, based on the novel by Keith Waterhouse
and adapted for the stage by the novelist and Willis Hall
(who wrote *The Long and the Short and the Tall*; see extracts on p. 106 and p. 183). It is set in a northern industrial
town. Billy Fisher ('Billy Liar') has middle-aged parents of
working-class origin, but his father is now a garage-owner
and has aspirations to improve his class position. Billy is the
only child and now works as an undertaker's clerk, but he
claims to have been recently offered work in London 'as a
script-writer'. He is certainly a very bad clerk and his accounts and books are in a desperate muddle, and so are his
relations with his parents and his love-life. The main reason
for all of this is that Billy 'makes things up'—he is a 'patho-
logical liar', as his friend Arthur calls him—not a vicious
one, but a person who dreams his way through life and
makes up fantasies because he can't help it. He has made
promises to three girls; Barbara is his parents' favourite can-
didate; she is tidy, sensible and has her eye only on marriage
and furnishing the country cottage of her dreams. Billy has
given her a ring which he previously gave to Rita, and must
now give back. Rita is aggressive and coarse ('common and
hard' as she is described) and works in a snack-bar. Billy
tries desperately to keep each of these girls happy and ignorant of his association with the others, and they seem to represent the respectable and the slovenly. But the girl he really
likes is Liz, and she is the one his parents most despise;
Arthur has described her as scruffy-looking and says it's
time someone bought her a new skirt; his mother says 'she
looked as though a good bath wouldn't do her any harm'.
The dialogue that follows shows how Liz and Billy get on,
and how he must 'ditch' Rita and Barbara to go to London
with her; she clearly understands and accepts him in a way
neither of the others possibly can, and shares rather than

merely rejects his fantasy life.

ACTING NOTES
Liz is described as 'about the same age as Barbara and Rita' but with 'more maturity and self-possession. Although she is dressed casually and is, in fact, wearing the black skirt we have heard so much about, she is not as scruffy as we have been led to believe. . . . She is not particularly pretty but is obviously a girl of strong personality.' She is 'the only girl for whom Billy has any real feelings'. Billy is nineteen and 'slightly built'; he obviously has a real creative streak and might indeed make a good script-writer. The scene takes place in the garden with a light in the porch of the house. It requires no props—merely very good acting.

There is a slight pause as they stand and look at each other.
BILLY. . . . Hallo, Liz.
LIZ. Hallo, Billy.
BILLY. When did you get back?
LIZ. Last week.
BILLY. Why didn't you ring me up?
LIZ. I was going to.
BILLY. Thank you very much.
LIZ. No—really. I was going to. I thought I'd see you at the dance tonight. I went to the dance. I thought you'd be there.
BILLY. I couldn't go.
LIZ. No. No—I know. I heard about your grandma. I'm sorry.
BILLY. Yes. (*Changing the subject.*) I haven't seen you for months.
LIZ. Five weeks. You didn't waste much time, did you?
BILLY. Why? What do you mean?
LIZ. Getting engaged. To everybody.
BILLY. Oh—that.
LIZ. You're mad.
BILLY (*he shrugs his shoulders*). Where have you been?
LIZ. Oh—here and there.
BILLY. Why didn't you write?
LIZ. I did—once. I tore it up.
BILLY. You're always tearing it up.

LIZ (*changing the subject*). How's everything with you? How's the script-writing? How's the book coming along?

BILLY (*enthusiastically*). Oh, I've finished it. It's going to be published next Christmas. (*She gives him a long, steady look.*) I haven't started writing it yet.

LIZ. You are mad.

BILLY. I wish it was something you could tear up and start again. Life—I mean. You know—like starting a new page in an exercise book.

LIZ. Well, it's been done. Turning over a new leaf.

BILLY. I turn over a new leaf every day—but the blots show through.

LIZ. What's all this about London?

BILLY. I've been offered a job down there.

LIZ. Honestly?

BILLY. Honestly. A sort of a job.

LIZ. Good. I'm glad. Perhaps it's your new leaf.

BILLY (*proud of the phrase*). I turn over a new leaf every day—but the blots show through the page.

LIZ. Well, perhaps a new leaf isn't good enough. Perhaps you need to turn over a new volume.

BILLY. Yes.

LIZ. Are you going to take that job?

BILLY. I think so.

LIZ. You only think so?

BILLY. I don't know.

LIZ. You know, my lad, the trouble with you is that you're— what's the word?—introspective. You're like a child at the edge of a paddling pool. You want very much to go in, but you think so much about whether the water's cold, and whether you'll drown, and what your mother will say if you get your feet wet ...

BILLY (*interrupting*). All I'm doing is wondering whether to dive or swim.

LIZ. Perhaps you need a coach.

BILLY. Do you know why I'm so fascinated by London?

LIZ. No. Why?

BILLY. A man can lose himself in London. London is a big place. It has big streets—and big people.

LIZ (*giving him another look*). Mad.

BILLY. Perhaps I need to turn over a new paddling pool.
(*There is a pause as they look at each other.*)

LIZ. Who do you love?

BILLY (*adopting his thick North Country accent*). Thee, lass.

LIZ. Yes, it sounds like it, doesn't it?

BILLY. I do, lass.

LIZ. Say it properly, then.

BILLY. I do, Liz. I do.

LIZ. What about Barbara?

BILLY. Well, what about her?

LIZ. Well, *what* about her?

BILLY. All over.

LIZ. You've said that before.

BILLY. I know. This time it is all over.

LIZ. And what about the other one? Rita-whatever-her-name-is.

BILLY. That's all over, too.
(*There is a pause.* BILLY *takes out a packet of cigarettes, lights two and gives one to* LIZ.)

LIZ. I want to marry you, you know, Billy.

BILLY. I know, Liz—I know. We will—one day.

LIZ. Not one day. Now.

BILLY. Do you?

LIZ. Next week will do. Before you go to London. Or when you get there. Whichever you prefer.

BILLY. I think I get engaged a bit too often.

LIZ. I don't want to get engaged. I want to get married.

BILLY. Is that why you keep sloping off every few weeks? Because you want to get married?

LIZ. I want to get married.

BILLY. All right. All right.

LIZ. How do you mean—all right? I've just proposed to you and you say 'all right'. Aren't you supposed to say 'this is so sudden' or 'yes' or something?

BILLY. I don't know.

LIZ (*she puts her arms round him and kisses him. He responds. They break away*). Billy . . .

BILLY. Yes?

LIZ. You know what you wanted me to do? That night?

When we walked through the park? And I said 'another night'?

BILLY. I remember.

LIZ. Well, it's another night tonight, isn't it?

BILLY (*afraid but excited*). Are you sure?

LIZ. Yes.

BILLY. Where could we go?

LIZ. I've got a room. There's no one there.

BILLY. What do you think we ought to do about—you know, babies.

LIZ. Have them. Lots and lots of them.

BILLY. No, I mean tonight.

LIZ. It's all right. (*After a pause*) Billy?

BILLY. Yes?

LIZ. Ask you something?

BILLY. What?

LIZ. Do you know what *virgo intacta* means?

BILLY. Yes.

LIZ. Well, I'm not.

BILLY. No. I somehow didn't think you were.

LIZ. Want me to tell you about it?

BILLY. No. (*He kisses her.*) All right, yes. Tell me about it.

LIZ. No—not now.

BILLY. Tell me about it.

LIZ. You think that's why I'm always going away, don't you?

BILLY. I don't know.

LIZ. Ask me where I've been for the past five weeks.

BILLY. What difference does it make?

LIZ. None—I suppose. It's just that every so often I want to go away. It's not you, Billy. I want to be here with you. It's the town. It's the people we know. I don't like knowing everybody—or becoming a part of things. Do you see what I mean?

BILLY. Yes . . . yes.

LIZ. What I'd like is to be invisible. You know, to be able to move around without people knowing, and not having to worry about them. Not having to explain all the time.

BILLY. Liz . . . Liz! Listen! Listen! Liz, do you know what I do? When I want to feel invisible. I've never told

anybody. I have a sort of—well, it's an imaginary country. Where I go. It has its own people . . .

LIZ (*interrupting*). Do you do that? I knew you would.
Why are we so alike, Billy? I can read your thoughts.
A town like this. Only somewhere over by the sea.
And we used to spend the whole day on the beach. That's
what I used to think about.

BILLY. This is more than a town—it's a whole country. (*He
is getting excited.*) I'm supposed to be the Prime Minister.
You're supposed to be the Foreign Secretary—or something.

LIZ (*with mock obedience*). Yes, sir.

BILLY. I think about it for hours. Sometimes I think, if we
were married, with a house of our own, we could just
sit and imagine ourselves there.

LIZ. Yes, we could.

BILLY. I want a room, in the house, with a green baize door.
It will be a big room, and when we go into it, through
the door, that's it, that's our country. No one else would
be allowed in. No one else will have keys. They won't
know where the room is. Only we'll know. And we'll
make models of the principal cities. You know, out of
cardboard. And we could use toy soldiers. Painted. For
the people. We could draw maps. It would be a place
to go on a rainy afternoon. We could go there. No one
would find us. I thought we could have a big sloping
shelf running all the way down one wall, you know,
like a big desk. And we'd have a lot of blank paper on it
and design our own newspapers. We could even make
uniforms, if we wanted to. It would be our country . . .
(*He falters away.*)

LIZ. Let's have a model train that the kids won't be allowed
to use.

BILLY. Liz . . . ? Will you marry me?

LIZ. Yes. (*He kisses her.*) Billy?

BILLY. Yes?

LIZ. Are you really going to London or just pretending?

BILLY. I'm thinking about it.

LIZ. Only thinking?

BILLY. Well, going. Soon, anyway.

LIZ. When's soon?

BILLY. Well, soon.

LIZ. That's a bit vague. Soon. Why not now?

BILLY. It's difficult.

LIZ. No, it's easy. You just get on a train and four hours later there you are—in London.

BILLY. It's easy for you, you've had the practice.

LIZ. I'll come with you.

BILLY. That'd be marvellous—if we could.

LIZ (*she rises*). But we can, Billy. We can! What is there to stop us?

BILLY (*thinking seriously about it for the first time*). Well, there's . . . I don't know . . . you've got to make all sorts of arrangements, haven't you?

LIZ. You buy a ticket, that's all. You buy a ticket and get on a train. That's all there is to it.

BILLY. I've never thought about it like that.

LIZ. Billy, we can! We can go! We can go tonight!

BILLY. But, Liz . . .

LIZ. There's the midnight train. We can catch that. It gets in at King's Cross station. Breakfast at Lyons Corner House. Then we get a tube—we get a tube from Piccadilly Circus to Earl's Court. I've got friends there, Billy. They'll put us up. They'd give us a room.

BILLY (*almost convinced. He rises*). Tonight, Liz?

LIZ. Yes, tonight! Twelve-five from New Street Station. We'll be in London tomorrow. We can go to Hyde Park in the afternoon. We'll go to the pictures tomorrow night—the Odeon, Marble Arch. What time is it now?

BILLY (*glancing at his watch*). Just after ten.

LIZ. I'm going, Billy. Are you coming?

BILLY (*his mind made up*). Yes, Liz. I'm coming.

LIZ. Are you sure?

BILLY. I'm coming with you.

LIZ (*briskly*). Right, then, I'm going home. Now. And I'm going to pack my things. I'll meet you at the station. In that refreshment room. In an hour's time. Eleven o'clock. I'll get the tickets. Two singles to London. You won't let me down, Billy?

BILLY. I'm coming.

LIZ. What will you tell your father and mother?
BILLY. They know already—more or less.
LIZ. You won't let them talk you out of it?
BILLY. I'm coming.
> (*The lights begin to come up in the living-room.* GEOF-
> FREY *enters from the kitchen, takes up a newspaper,
> sits down and begins to read. The lights fade slightly
> in the garden.*)
LIZ (*she kisses* BILLY). Eleven o'clock.
BILLY. Eleven.
> (LIZ *goes off down the garden.* BILLY *watches her go
> and then turns and enters the house.*)

Run-out

The merits of this passage seem to lie in its honesty and
directness: Liz is much more sure than Billy, whose restricted
life perhaps accounts partly for his fantasies and indeed
lies; in comparison Liz knows her way about the world and
also her own mind. Billy is relatively scared—for example
of London and of breaking away from his family and sur-
roundings, which are safe and familiar, however dreary he
finds them. The play ends soon after this extract with some
uncertainty as to whether Billy *will* go to London with Liz.
We learn that far from being offered a job in London he
has merely been invited by an actor to 'call in for a chat the
next time you are in London'. He goes off with a packed bag
after his parents are in bed; Rita arrives with Arthur and
shouts abuse at the house and threatens the absent Billy
with punishment from 'our kid', her brother. They go off
together and the ending shows Billy returning to the house
alone, pretending to conduct some music from the radio,
and then starting to unpack his bag. Thus we in the audience
are left with a question mark; Billy *will* break away sometime, and we hope, perhaps, that it will be with Liz who understands him so well. But perhaps it won't be this time—
and his fantasies will continue until he can turn them into
reality. The language of the passage, with its directness,
simplicity and tentativeness, makes an interesting contrast
to the beautiful rhetoric of Christy and Pegeen in the extract
from *The Playboy of the Western World* (p. 46).

4
Authority

✕✕✕

The first pair of extracts shows a highly—and necessarily?—authoritarian organization, the army; first, the N.C.O. faced with a group of recruits he must 'lick into shape' and, next, the officers doing their set speeches and looking down on the same recruits 'from a great height'. The total effect, as well as being comic, is bitter and satirical and, though Corporal Hill is a good N.C.O. and in the event quite a nice person, one's sympathies are surely throughout with the underdogs, the recruits. Wesker's officers are less attractive, but at least they probably mean well. The extracts raise the question of whether authority is necessarily distorting to human relationships, whether it can avoid being a relationship of exploiters and exploited. Pip tries to find another course, but in the end joins the officers, who, in Wesker's terms, are the exploiters. It also asks us whether any organization can be run without at least a minimum of authority: an army? a hospital? a family? a school?

The two Dogberry passages from *Much Ado About Nothing* mock the absurdities of authority, gently but devastatingly. Dogberry is indeed 'cock of his own dunghill' and carries unquestioned authority with the hopeless dimwits of the watch; his pretensions are exposed in the scene with the sexton, who shows by contrast his total incompetence, so that in the end even the arrested criminals ridicule him, and he is reduced to spluttering absurdity in the last speech when he cannot believe that anyone has questioned his dignity, his utter worthiness and above all his authority. The whole idea of the 'jack in office' is exposed for ever. Shakespeare is fascinated by authority and questions it in various ways, notably in some famous lines from *Measure for Measure*:

c

> Man, proud man,
> Drest in a little brief authority,
> Most ignorant of what he's most assured,
> His glassy essence, like an angry ape,
> Plays such fantastic tricks before high heaven
> As make the angels weep.

xxxxxxxxxxxxxxxxxxxxxxxxxxxxxxxxxxxxxxxxxxxxxxxxxxxxxxxxxxxxxx

CHIPS WITH EVERYTHING

Lead-in

The first of these extracts from Wesker's play about army life, *Chips with Everything*, shows Corporal Hill, a professional soldier, drilling the National Service conscripts for the first time on the parade ground. Most of it is one long speech, or rather series of instructions, to the very raw recruits; their only part in the proceedings is to obey orders and occasionally repeat a kind of bark. This speech of Corporal Hill's reads like a parody, but in fact it's very true to life, as anyone who has ever served in the army will agree—the sarcasm, the aggressiveness, the various devices for catching out the unwary—it's a kind of standard performance to scare the new men into instant obedience and meticulous attention to details even about such apparently simple things as standing to attention. (Incidentally, Corporal Hill turns out to be quite a nice person; here he is merely doing what he has been taught to understand as his duty.)

The second extract shows the officers introducing themselves to the recruits in a lecture hall, trying to be considerate and fairly relaxed (the men are seated) compared with Corporal Hill, but revealing themselves and their pet ideas very thoroughly; notice that though they invite questions, they don't really deal with any.

ACTING NOTES

Corporal Hill has to have stamina and what the army calls 'power of command'; his long opening speech is mainly barked at the recruits. They are timid, awkward and inexperienced, and you can have fun with their mistakes. Perhaps a group of pupils (eight or so) of very different shapes and sizes might make a good 'awk-ward squad'. No rifles are needed for this scene, though Hill might perhaps have a 'swagger cane'. He must make full use of the hints in the text and demonstrate everything he describes, with grotesque precision and accuracy (you will perhaps have seen the Changing of the Guard or something similar on television to give you an idea) and he shouts the passages in capitals, especially the marvellous 'If you don't relax I'll put you on a charge!' i.e., send you for possible punishment (this one is worth thinking about). The second scene is straightforward enough : the voices of the first three officers should be 'cultured', and these are their open-ing (and often very revealing) statements to the new body of re-cruits. Smiler should be in the front row of the 'audience' and is so called because he has a continuous grin on his face; note that two of the officers pick on him, and later he gets into serious trouble and tries to run away.

Parade Ground: morning.
HILL. Out! I'll give you sixty seconds or you'll be on a charge, one, two, three, four—come on out of that hut, twenty-five, twenty-six, twenty-seven, twenty-eight. AT THE DOUBLE! Now get into a line and stop that talking, get into a line. A straight line you heaving nig-nogs, a straight line.
   This is the square. We call it a square-bashing square. I want to see you bash that square. Right, now the first thing you've got to know, you've got to know how to come to attention, how to stand at ease and easy, how to make a right turn and how to step off.
   Now to come to attention you move smartly, very smartly, to this position: heels together. STOP THAT! When I was born I was very fortunate, I was born with eyes in the back of my neck and don't be cheeky. Legs apart and wait till I give the command SHUN. When I give the command SHUN, you will move sharply, very sharply, to this position. Heels together and in a line, feet turned out to an angle of thirty degrees, knees braced, body erect and with the weight balanced evenly between the balls of the feet and the heels.
   Shoulders down and back level and square to the front.

Arms hanging straight from the shoulders.
Elbows close to the sides.
Wrists straight.
Hands closed—not clenched.
Back of the fingers close to the thighs.
Thumbs straight and to the front, close to the forefinger
and just behind the seam of the trousers. Head up, chin
in, eyes open, heels together, body erect and evenly balanced between the balls of the feet and the heels—you
didn't know you had balls on your feet did you—well
you have, use them.

Stand up straight there—keep your mouth shut and your
eyes open and to the front. Right, well, you are now
standing—somewhat vaguely—in the position of attention.

To stand at ease you keep the right foot still and carry
the left foot to the left so that the feet are about—do it
with me—so that the feet are about twelve inches apart.
At the same time force the arms behind the back, keeping
them straight, and place the back of the right hand in
the palm of the left, thumbs crossed, fingers and hands
straight and pointing towards the ground. At the same
time transfer the weight of the body slightly to the left
so as to be evenly balanced. Keep your arms straight
and don't bend at the waist. (*Inspects them.*) Right
hand inside your left, *your* left not his. Try to make
your elbows meet. When you hear me give the command SQUAD, I want you to jump to that position,
smarten up, as if you were going somewhere. We'll try
it—stand easy, relax, just relax, but keep your hands
behind your back, don't slouch, don't move your feet
and don't talk—just relax, let your head look down,
RELAX! IF YOU DON'T RELAX I'LL PUT YOU ON A
CHARGE!

Squad, squad—SHUN! As you were, I want you to do
it together. Squad—SHUN! As you were. Squad—
SHUN! STAND AT EASE!

To make a Right Turn: keeping both knees straight,
turn through ninety degrees to the right swivelling on
the heel of the right foot and the toe of the left raising

the toe of the right and the heel of the left in doing so.
Keeping the weight of the body on the right foot, on
completion of this movement the right foot is flat on the
ground, the left leg to the rear and the heel raised—both
knees braced back and the body in the position of attention. Bring the left foot into the right, good and hard,
and for the time being I want that left knee good and
high, slam your foot in good and hard and keep still.
Squad, squad—SHUN.
Turning to the right—RIGHT TURN.
All right you creepy-crawly nig-nogs, moon men that's
what you are, moon men. I want it done together. As
you were.
Squad, turning to the right—RIGHT TURN.
Now, to Step Off. When I say by the front—quick
march, I don't want your pretty left foot forward any-
ways, like this, no, it's got to be scorching smart, like a
flash of greased lightning. ONE! Like this (*Petrified
stance of a man about to step off.*) ONE! Like that, and
I want that left hand up as high as you can get it and
your right level with your breast pocket.
Now, on the word—MARCH—I want you only to take
a step forward, *not* to march. I want you only to take a
step forward, just pretend, got that? Some dimwitted
piece of merchandise is sure to carry on. Now then,
watch it. SQUAD—by the front—quick MARCH!
(*Sure enough two boys march off and collide with those
standing still, and one in the front marches off out of
sight.*)
Stop that laughing. I'll charge the next man I see smile.
(*Stands, watching the other one disappear.*)
All right, Horace, come back home. (*Airman returns,
sheepishly.*) You nit, you nit, you creepy-crawly nit.
Don't you hear, don't you listen, can't you follow
simple orders, CAN'T YOU? Shut up! Don't answer back!
A young man like you, first thing in the morning, don't
be rude, don't be rude. No one's being rude to you.
Stop that laughing. I'll charge the next man I see smile.
(*To Smiler.*) You, I said wipe off that smile. I said wipe
it off.

SMILER. I'm not smiling, Corporal, it's natural. I was born
with it.

HILL. Right then, don't ever let me see that face frown or
I'll haul you over the highest wall we've got. (*Approach-
ing one of the two marching ones.*) You. If you'd been
paying attention you might 'ave done it correctly, eh?
But you weren't, you were watching the little aeroplanes,
weren't you? You want to fly? Do you want to reach
the thundering heavens, my little lad, at an earlier age
than you imagined, with Technicolor wings? KEEP
YOUR EYES ON ME. (*To all.*) You better know from the
start, you can have it the hard way or you can have it
the easy way, I don't mind which way it is. Perhaps you
like it the hard way, suits me. Just let me know. At ease
everyone. Now, we'll try and make it easier for you.
We'll count our way along. We'll count together, and
then maybe we'll all act together. I want everything to
be done together. We're going to be the happiest family
in Christendom and we're going to move together, as
one, as one solitary man. So, when I say 'attention' you'll
slam your feet down hard and cry 'one'. Like this. And
when I say 'right turn' you'll move and bang your foot
down and cry 'one-pause-two'. Like this. Is that clear?
Is that beyond the intellectual comprehensibilities of any
of you? Good! SQUAD—wait for it—atten-SHUN!

SQUAD. ONE!

HILL. As you were, at ease. Did I say slam? Didn't I say
slam? Don't worry about the noise, it's a large square,
no one will mind. Squad—atten-SHUN.

SQUAD. ONE!

HILL. As you were. Let's hear that 'one'. Let's have some
energy from you. I want GOD to hear you crying 'ONE,
ONE, ONE—pause TWO!' Squad—atten-SHUN!

SQUAD. ONE!

HILL. Right TURN!

SQUAD. ONE—pause—TWO!

HILL. By the left—quick—MARCH!
(*The boys march off round the stage, sound of marching
and the chanting of* 'One, One, One—pause—Two!
One, One, One—pause—Two!')

1) *Sounds of marching feet. Marching stops. The lecture hall.
(Boys enter and sit down on seats. Enter the* WING COM-
MANDER, *boys rise.)*

WING COMMANDER. Sit down, please. I'm your Wing Commander. You think we are at peace. Not true. We are
never at peace. The human being is in a constant state
of war and we must be prepared, each against the other.
History has taught us this and we must learn. The reasons why and wherefore are not our concern. We are
simply the men who must be prepared. You, why do
you look at me like that?

PIP. I'm paying attention, sir.

WING COMMANDER. There's insolence in those eyes, lad—
I recognize insolence in a man; take that glint out of
your eyes, your posh tones don't fool me. We are simply
the men who must be prepared. Already the aggressors
have a force far superior to ours. Our efforts must be
intensified. We need a fighting force and it is for this
reason you are being trained here, according to the best
traditions of the R.A.F. We want you to be proud of
your part, unashamed of the uniform you wear. But you
must not grumble too much if you find that government
facilities for you, personally, are not up to standard.
We haven't the money to spare. A Meteor, fully armed,
is more important than a library. The C.O. of this camp
is called Group Captain Watson. His task is to check
any tendency in his officers to practical jokes, to dis-
countenance any disposition in his officers to gamble or
to indulge in extravagant expenditure; to endeavour,
by example and timely intervention, to promote a good
understanding and prevent disputes. Group Captain
Watson is a busy man, you will rarely see him. You,
why are you smiling?

SMILER. I'm not, sir, it's natural, I was born like it.

WING COMMANDER. Because I want this taken seriously, you
know, from all of you. Any questions?

WILFE. Sir, if the aggressors are better off than us, what are
they waiting for?

WING COMMANDER. What's your name?

WILFE. 247 Seaford, sir.

WING COMMANDER. Any other questions?

(*Exit. Enter* SQUADRON LEADER. *The boys rise.*)

SQUADRON LEADER. Sit down, please. I'm your squadron leader. My task is not only to ensure respect for authority, but also to foster the feelings of self-respect and personal honour which are essential to efficiency. It is also my task to bring to notice those who, from incapacity or apathy, are deficient in knowledge of their duties, or who do not afford an officer that support which he has a right to expect or who conduct themselves in a manner injurious to the efficiency or credit of the R.A.F. You are here to learn discipline. Discipline is necessary if we are to train you to the maximum state of efficiency, discipline and obedience. You will obey your instructors because they are well trained, you will obey them because they can train you efficiently, you will obey them because it's necessary for you to be trained efficiently. That is what you are here to learn: obedience and discipline. Any questions? Thank you.

(*Exit. Enter* PILOT OFFICER. *The boys rise.*)

PILOT OFFICER. Sit down, please. I'm your pilot officer. You'll find that I'm amenable and that I do not stick rigidly to authority. All I shall require is cleanliness. It's not that I want rigid men, I want clean men. It so happens, however, that you cannot have clean men without rigid men, and cleanliness requires smartness and ceremony. Ceremony means your webbing must be blancoed, and smartness means that your brass—all of it—must shine like silver paper, and your huts must be spick and span without a trace of dust, because dust carries germs, and germs are unclean. I want a man clean from toe nail to hair root. I want him so clean that he looks unreal. In fact I don't want real men, real men are dirty and nasty, they pick their noses—and scratch their skin. I want unreal, super-real men. Those men win wars, the others die of disease before they reach the battlefields. Any questions? You, what are you smiling at?

SMILER. I'm not, sir, it's natural. I was born like that.

PILOT OFFICER. In between the lines of that grin are formed battalions of microbes. Get rid of it.

SMILER. I can't, sir.

PILOT OFFICER. Then never let me hear of you going sick.
(*Exit. Enter* P.T. INSTRUCTOR, FLIGHT SERGEANT.)

P.T.I. As you were. I'm in charge of physical training on this camp. It's my duty to see that every minute muscle in your body is awake. Awake and ringing. Do you hear that? That's poetry! I want your body awake and ringing. I want you so light on your feet that the smoke from a cigarette could blow you away, and yet so strong that you stand firm before hurricanes. I hate thin men and detest fat ones. I want you like Greek gods. You heard of the Greeks? You ignorant troupe of anaemics, you were brought up on tinned beans and television sets, weren't you? You haven't had any exercise since you played knock-a-down-ginger, have you? Greek gods, you hear me? Till the sweat pours out of you like Niagara Falls. Did you hear that poetry? Sweat like Niagara Falls! I don't want your stupid questions!
(*Exit.*)

PIP. You have babies, you eat chips and you take orders.

CHAS. Well, look at you then, I don't see you doing different.
(*They march off. Sound of marching feet.*)

Run-out

The upper-class Pip tries to lead the recruits in a revolt against 'the system', but after several attempts he is broken into a recognition that he really belongs to the other side, and the play ends with Pip dressed as an officer and playing an officer's role. The ending is powerfully handled, though somehow not completely convincing. But there are many points of interest in this play, and Wesker, as in *Roots* (see p. 131), has a very good ear for the speech of ordinary people. Smiler is a finely-realized character, and so is Corporal Hill. The title, by the way, is explained near the beginning of the play when Pip describes his first visit to a working-class café, where every item on the menu is served with chips, and this becomes for him a symbol of the uniformity and dreariness of the life of most people.

XX

MUCH ADO ABOUT NOTHING

Lead-in

These two extracts come from Shakespeare's comedy *Much Ado About Nothing*. They offer a comic version of what is treated more seriously in *Chips with Everything*—though there is, of course, plenty of comedy there too. Dogberry is the 'Constable' of the nightwatchmen in the city of Messina. He is illiterate, long-winded, pompous and above all self-confident—a perfect picture, in fact, of what is sometimes called a 'jack in office'. Verges is a simple-minded nervy old man who makes a good foil to Dogberry; the rest of the watch are so dim that even the ignorant and conceited Dogberry stands out among them, just as Bottom does in *A Midsummer Night's Dream*.

In the first extract, he is giving the watch their instructions for the night and warning them especially of the possibility of noisy behaviour and disturbance as a result of an imminent wedding. This refers to the leading theme of the play, which needs only a brief summary here. A young lord, Claudio, is to marry Leonato's daughter Hero on the following day; the villain of the play for his own purposes has deluded Claudio that Hero has a lover and persuaded him to shame her at the church. Two of his agents, Conrade and Borachio, have been overheard, quite by chance, discussing the plot, and the second extract shows Dogberry acting as chief prosecutor, with the Sexton as scribe, and making a superb mess of it. The last speech of Dogberry in this scene is justly famous; Dogberry's glorious outburst of indignation that anyone has dared to call *him* an ass is itself a manifestation that the accusation is only too true. He fancies himself as a distinguished and dignified citizen, towards whom such insults are ludicrously misplaced, and his phrasing ('Masters, remember that I am an ass') has precisely the opposite effect of the one he intends.

Dogberry must be—in his own eyes at least—utterly reliable, self-sufficient and dignified; he is a big fish in a very small pond. His continual verbal blunders are part of his humour—he is half-educated rather than uneducated and his mistakes should be made with some relish. But this is only part of the impact he makes. Verges is a whining old man who reluctantly plays second fiddle to the more impressive Dogberry. The watch should be a motley collection of dimwits, anxious about their duties but quite unable to understand what they are; in one production in which I was involved we were fortunate to have two sixth-formers, close friends, one of whom was at least a foot shorter than the other—and armed with pikes and dressed in floppy hats, they looked superb, as you can imagine, as the first and second watchmen. In the second scene the watch bring in the two 'malefactors' as prisoners to the Sexton who should have pen, ink and a writing desk. Dogberry strides about self-importantly, fancying that he is conducting the whole proceedings, while the Sexton provides a note of sanity and orderliness.

i) *A Street.*
    (*Enter* DOGBERRY *and* VERGES *with the* Watch.)

DOGBERRY. Are you good men and true?

VERGES. Yea, or else it were pity but they should suffer salvation, body and soul.

DOGBERRY. Nay, that were a punishment too good for them, if they should have any allegiance in them, being chosen for the prince's watch.

VERGES. Well, give them their charge, neighbour Dogberry.

DOGBERRY. First, who think you the most desartless man to be constable?

FIRST WATCH. Hugh Otecake, sir, or George Seacole; for they can write and read.

DOGBERRY. Come hither, neighbour Seacole. God hath blessed you with a good name: to be a well-favoured man is the gift of fortune; but to write and read comes by nature.

SECOND WATCH. Both which, master constable,—

DOGBERRY. You have: I knew it would be your answer. Well, for your favour, sir, why, give God thanks, and make no boast of it; and for your writing and reading, let that appear when there is no need of such vanity. You are thought here to be the most senseless and fit man for the constable of the watch; therefore bear you the lantern. This is your charge: you shall comprehend all vagrom men; you are to bid any man stand, in the prince's name.

SECOND WATCH. How if a' will not stand?

DOGBERRY. Why, then, take no note of him, but let him go; and presently call the rest of the watch together and thank God you are rid of a knave.

VERGES. If he will not stand when he is bidden, he is none of the prince's subjects.

DOGBERRY. True, and they are to meddle with none but the prince's subjects. You shall also make no noise in the streets; for for the watch to babble and to talk is most tolerable and not to be endured.

WATCH. We will rather sleep than talk: we know what belongs to a watch.

DOGBERRY. Why, you speak like an ancient and most quiet watchman; for I cannot see how sleeping should offend: only, have a care that your bills be not stolen. Well, you are to call at all the ale-houses, and bid those that are drunk get them to bed.

WATCH. How if they will not?

DOGBERRY. Why, then, let them alone till they are sober: if they make you not then the better answer, you may say they are not the men you took them for.

WATCH. Well, sir.

DOGBERRY. If you meet a thief, you may suspect him, by virtue of your office, to be no true man; and, for such kind of men, the less you meddle or make with them, why, the more is for your honesty.

WATCH. If we know him to be a thief, shall we not lay hands on him?

DOGBERRY. Truly, by your office, you may; but I think they that touch pitch will be defiled: the most peaceable way for you, if you do take a thief, is to let him show himself what he is and steal out of your company.

VERGES. You have been always called a merciful man, partner.

DOGBERRY. Truly, I would not hang a dog by my will, much more a man who hath any honesty in him.

VERGES. If you hear a child cry in the night, you must call to the nurse and bid her still it.

WATCH. How if the nurse be asleep and will not hear us?

DOGBERRY. Why, then, depart in peace, and let the child wake her with crying; for the ewe that will not hear her lamb when it baes will never answer a calf when he bleats.

VERGES. 'Tis very true.

DOGBERRY. This is the end of the charge:—you, constable, are to present the prince's own person: if you meet the prince in the night, you may stay him.

VERGES. Nay, by'r lady, that I think a' cannot.

DOGBERRY. Five shillings to one on't, with any man that knows the statues, he may stay him: marry, not without the prince be willing; for, indeed, the watch ought to offend no man; and it is an offence to stay a man against his will.

VERGES. By'r lady, I think it be so.

DOGBERRY. Ha, ah, ha! Well. masters, good night: an there be any matter of weight chances, call up me: keep your fellows' counsels and your own; and good night. Come, neighbour.

WATCH. Well, masters, we hear our charge: let us go sit here upon the church-bench till two, and then all to bed.

DOGBERRY. One word more, honest neighbours. I pray you, watch about Signior Leonato's door; for the wedding being there tomorrow, there is a great coil tonight. Adieu: be vigitant, I beseech you.

(*Exeunt* DOGBERRY *and* VERGES.)

i) *A prison.*

(*Enter* DOGBERRY, VERGES, *and* SEXTON, *in gowns: and the* Watch, *with* CONRADE *and* BORACHIO.)

DOGBERRY. Is our whole dissembly appeared?

VERGES. O, a stool and a cushion for the sexton.

SEXTON. Which be the malefactors?

DOGBERRY. Marry, that am I and my partner.

VERGES. Nay, that's certain; we have the exhibition to examine.

SEXTON. But which are the offenders that are to be examined?
let them come before master constable.

DOGBERRY. Yea, marry, let them come before me. What is
your name, friend?

BORACHIO. Borachio.

DOGBERRY. Pray, write down, Borachio. Yours, sirrah?

CONRADE. I am a gentleman, sir, and my name is Conrade.

DOGBERRY. Write down, master gentleman Conrade. Masters,
do you serve God?

CONRADE
BORACHIO. } Yea, sir, we hope.

DOGBERRY. Write down, that they hope they serve God: and
write God first; for God defend but God should go
before such villains! Master, it is proved already that
you are little better than false knaves: and it will go
near to be thought so shortly. How answer you for yourselves?

CONRADE. Marry, sir, we say we are none.

DOGBERRY. A marvellous witty fellow, I assure you; but I
will go about with him. Come you hither, sirrah; a word
in your ear: sir, I say to you, it is thought you are false
knaves.

BORACHIO. Sir, I say to you, we are none.

DOGBERRY. Well, stand aside. 'Fore God, they are both in a
tale. Have you writ down, that they are none?

SEXTON. Master constable, you go not the way to examine:
you must call forth the watch that are their accusers.

DOGBERRY. Yea, marry, that's the eftest way. Let the watch
come forth. Masters, I charge you in the prince's name,
accuse these men.

FIRST WATCH. This man said, sir, that Don John, the
prince's brother, was a villain.

DOGBERRY. Write down Prince John a villain. Why, this is
flat perjury, to call a prince's brother villain.

BORACHIO. Master constable—

DOGBERRY. Pray thee, fellow, peace: I do not like thy look,
I promise thee.

SEXTON. What heard you him say else?

SECOND WATCH. Marry, that he had received a thousand

ducats of Don John for accusing the Lady Hero wrongfully.

DOGBERRY. Flat burglary as ever was committed.

VERGES. Yea, by mass, that it is.

SEXTON. What else, fellow?

FIRST WATCH. And that Count Claudio did mean, upon his
words, to disgrace Hero before the whole assembly, and
not marry her.

DOGBERRY. O villain! thou wilt be condemned into ever-
lasting redemption for this.

SEXTON. What else?

WATCH. This is all.

SEXTON. And this is more, masters, than you can deny. Prince
John is this morning secretly stolen away; Hero was
in this manner accused, in this very manner refused, and
upon the grief of this suddenly died. Master constable,
let these men be bound, and brought to Leonato's: I
will go before and show him their examination.
(*Exit.*)

DOGBERRY. Come, let them be opinioned.

VERGES. Let them be in the hands—

CONRADE. Off, coxcomb!

DOGBERRY. God's my life, where's the sexton? let him write
down the prince's officer coxcomb. Come, bind them.
Thou naughty varlet!

CONRADE. Away! You are an ass, you are an ass.

DOGBERRY. Dost thou not suspect my place? dost thou not
suspect my years? O that he were here to write me down
an ass! But, masters, remember that I am an ass; though
it be not written down, yet forget not that I am an ass.
No, thou villain, thou art full of piety, as shall be proved
upon thee by good witness. I am a wise fellow, and,
which is more, an officer, and which is more, a house-
holder, and, which is more, as pretty a piece of flesh
as any is in Messina, and one that knows the law, go to;
and a rich fellow enough, go to; and a fellow that hath
had losses, and one that hath two gowns and every thing
handsome about him. Bring him away. O that I had
been writ down an ass!
(*Exeunt.*)

Run-out

Dogberry appears in one later scene, when he produces the criminals and 'springs' the plot; this scene is very funny and well worth looking at. To analyse the twists and turns of the main plot is perhaps not necessary here, and it is enough to say that all ends happily. It is interesting to see that Dogberry and the watch are not merely comic relief but an essential part of the play; indeed, Borachio says so in so many words: 'What your wisdoms could not discover, these shallow fools (i.e. the watch) have brought to light.' As so often in Shakespeare, the comic and the serious co-exist and in the end are indistinguishable.

5
Menace

Two strongly contrasted kinds of menace are portrayed in the following extracts from *Afore Night Come* and *The Crucible*: yet they have something important in common—they both show the cruelty, or perhaps the threat of cruelty, of the majority against a minority, and they both portray the terrifying power that superstition may wield in the minds of men. Neither of these factors can be guaranteed to be absent even from the most civilized communities of the present day. The fruit-pickers in *Afore Night Comes* express their fear, especially of the unknown, by menacing (and ultimately by killing) an obnoxious, lazy, conceited but essentially harmless old man; the townsfolk of Salem in *The Crucible* are overcoming their fear, in this case of the unknown power of witchcraft, by menacing (and ultimately by executing among many others) the innocent and honest John Proctor. Both plays, on the stage and I think when read, provide a powerful illusion of actual menace (in Arthur Miller's play the girls' hysteria is a main source of this). I hope and believe that we would identify with the victim, but I am fairly sure that in the conflict we would share some of the feelings of the aggressive menacing vicious majority; a good production would bring this out and reflect in the stage conflict some degree of conflict in our feelings. The Greeks thought that our feelings would be *purged* by stage depictions of tragedy, and that we in the audience would in the end be purified by our imaginative experience of pity and terror. These two modern examples give us a chance to try out this theory. Both plays make us wonder whether we are not all capable of such absurdity and wickedness. The menace in each case is the product of a hysterical, unreasoning and violent emotion, against the feared person or group. It has been rightly said that fear begets fear, and in a world of arms races and of hijacking and urban guerrillas we cannot dismiss the menace of 'the outsider' as a matter only of history or a problem only for other people.

AFORE NIGHT COME

Lead-in

The following extract is from John Rudkin's powerful play *Afore Night Come*, which won a drama prize in 1962 and is a celebrated study of menace.

The setting is a fruit orchard in the North Midlands, near Birmingham, where a group of itinerant workers are picking pears on piece-work rates. A wandering Irishman called Roche manages to get taken on as a fruit-picker, but he does little or no work, pretends to be unwell, won't climb ladders, and generally gets himself disliked. Much more important than these failings, however, is the fact that Roche is to them an outsider; his speech is different—so different in its Irish lilt and elaborate vocabulary (he claims at one stage to be a poet, at another to have specialized medical knowledge)— that they both hate and fear him. It is a perfect example of the fear and hatred stimulated by any person from outside a group—a village, a district, a nation, a skin-colour. They call him 'Shakespeare' contemptuously. He tries to win their affection and sympathy, or at least their tolerance, but they become harder and harder towards him. A group of the men have been taken off fruit-picking by the foreman and ordered to slash old motor tyres with razor-sharp knives, for some purpose connected with the picking or packing of the pears. When this extract opens, Roche has just finished a dialogue with the foreman and is trying to find himself a job so that he doesn't go off with no wages. When they reject firmly his offers of help he takes some pears and fills his bag with them. He unwisely begins boasting again, this time about his knowledge of the Gaelic language, and claims to be an M.A. and to be writing a book. The dialogue, especially with Taffy, rapidly works up into nationalistic hatred; Taffy is convinced that the Irish are stealing English jobs, failing to support England in war and perhaps supporting her enemies, and bringing prostitution and venereal disease to England. Roche counters this by expressing his hatred of English cities and English industrial life. There is a helicopter spraying the orchard, and this becomes a powerful symbol, both in its menacing sound and in the suggestion that the chemicals it sprays on to the trees will make men infertile. Jeff, a young newcomer, suddenly whips off Roche's cloth which he wears on his head to protect it, and this too is symbolic—almost like uncrowning or even beheading someone—as well as menacing in a cruel, childish and sadistic way. Then his glasses (he is terribly shortsighted) are taken off and smashed and it becomes quite clear that this is only the beginning. Jumbo and Taffy, who might conceivably have protected him, find that they have urgent business elsewhere, and Roche is left alone to face the mindless vengeance of the men with the knives.

ACTING NOTES
Roche very much needs an Irish lilt and accent, and if possible someone in the class should be found who can manage this. Albert, George and Jeff are sitting or crouching, slashing away silently at the tyres; Jumbo and Taffy (Welsh accent if possible) are standing talking to Roche, who should be oldish, with a kind of tea-towel headdress and pebble-thick glasses or something to serve for them. In his haversack is a teapot (a prized possession) and there must be pears or some substitute for them. Jeff must be really vicious and spiteful towards Roche but also frightened of him and disgusted and horrified when he looks at him.

ROCHE. Ah. Quite so. Quite so; it would take more than the threats of a foreman the like of that one to get me gone. Wrongly dismissed I said to him. Wrongly dismissed. . . .

JEFF. Wrongfully dismissed. . . .

ROCHE. So I come back, now, to do my daily dozen on them tyres. . . . (*Pause.*) Could I be helping youse at all with them tyres? (*Pause.*) Would it be in order, at all, for me to be assisting you?
(ROCHE *kneels, touches* ALBERT'S *tyres.*)

ALBERT. Out on it.

ROCHE. I'll just be ...

JUMBO (*uneasy, warning*). Shakespeare ...

> (*Disturbed pause.* ROCHE *looks to* JUMBO *and* TAFFY; *finds only embarrassment, grim hardness on their faces. Moves towards* GINGER.)

ROCHE. Just assist youse in the small way I have ...

GINGER. Heard us, didn't you?

> (ROCHE, *rudely shocked, retreats.*)

ROCHE. To take the bare look off me ... Standing here, and youse working; and me with my two arms the one length ... I have two arms!

> (JEFF *sniggers.*)

> The same as any one of you!

JEFF. Want to do something for us, Shakespeare? Do us a favour? (*Pause.*) Turn into a scab, and drop off.

> (*On a decision,* ROCHE *takes bag, lifts out teapot, begins to pack away as many pears as he can.*)

JUMBO. Going home?

ROCHE. The moment I draw my wage, I'll be away from this. Into the town.

JIM. Going to Brummagem, Shakespeare?

ROCHE. I'll not stay here, now that youse none of youse need me any more. ...

> (*Struggles to fit last pear in.*)

JUMBO. You seen them working in them factories all day? All pale?

TAFFY. Yeah, they're all bent over, Paddy. The people in Birmingham are all bent over, from going up and down steep hills all bloody day.

> (ROCHE *fits in last pear; struggles to pack teapot.*)

> Short of teachers, though.

ROCHE. Ay. They are.

JUMBO. What could you teach, Shakespeare? Ballet dancing?

ROCHE. I taught in my time. Many things. For instance the Gaelic. The language of the kings. ...

JEFF. Yeah. I speak that fluent.

ROCHE. You see? Youse didn't know that. I taught the Gaelic at the Ring. The Ring, in the county Waterford; where they have a Gaelic summer school. Every verb in the

Gaelic tongue has the dual system of stems. One for the asseverative moods, and a separate stem for the oblique. You see, I have the photographic memory.

JEFF. Get a pair of socks, first—

TAFFY. Short of teachers, I said; not short of tramps.

(*Pause.* ROCHE *halted.* JUMBO *is laughing to himself, shaking his head, muttering 'Shakespeare' over and over to himself. Laughter grows, spreading.*)

ROCHE. Is the city too good for me, then? Is it? I tell you! It's writing a book I am. A book will explode in the face of all the earth! I am a Master of Arts.

(*More laughter.*)

I'll be a bricklayer, if need be! Ay. There must be thousands of houses building in Birmingham there; after the great war they had.

JUMBO. They?

(ROCHE *crams teapot on top of pears, leaves bag unclosed.*)

ROCHE. The moment the foreman comes, I'll be away.

JUMBO (*shaking* ROCHE *roughly by the shoulder*). Plenty of Brummies out of jobs. Without looking for no Irish bastards to cater for. Shoved yourselves off, didn't you? Out to bloody sea? Got your new Jerusalem? Crawl bloody home, then, to your own little emerald bog, and work there. Coming over here with your bloody tuberculosis and venereal disease.

TAFFY. Yeah. You know something, Paddy? One prostitute in ten on the streets of this country comes from Southern Ireland. One in ten.

ROCHE. It was the English brought prostitution to Ireland in the first place.

TAFFY. And when you go over there, what do you see? Bloody newspapers, with articles and speeches by parish priests and cardinals, addressed to young Irish virginals, giving them advice on how to keep themselves pure and spotless when they come over here, to the land of sin and crime.

ROCHE. Ah, the English are a terrible high-sexed race. The lubricity of them, it's positively gi-normous.

TAFFY. Over here! What happens you? What's rotten in

your young ones that's what I want to know; turn into vermin no sooner than leave the holy island of saints and scholars. What's rotten in you?

ROCHE. I'd be taking no jobs from none of you. Seeing youse are so entitled, I'd not deprive you. I'll be away from this. Some other place. Your great, rotten, putrefying city. I seen you; crawling into your city in the morning time; like the maggots and grubs squirming and squeezing in and out of a side of rotten meat in a bin of garbage and the bin burning! A city of sin, thon! A city of terrible perversion and evil and sin. I need no telling; I need only be looking at the filth in their eyes. Ay! And the country around its edge is rightly named. The Black. The sphincter of the earth! (ROCHE *shakes with fury.*)

JEFF. Don't half look funny when you'm cross, Shakespeare. (ROCHE *turns towards him.*)

Got no eyes . . . No eyes, Shakespeare . . . (JEFF *clutches knife, worried.*) Look stupid . . . Look how horrible his face is, Ginge. Look how his flesh am all rotten. All diseased. Got leprosy, Shakespeare?

(ROCHE *stands before him, angry, powerless. Now, for the first time, steady drone of helicopter, swooping, zooming; but not seeming to approach.*
Suddenly JEFF *whips off head-cloth.*)

ROCHE. Give me!

(JEFF *teases him as* ROCHE *impotently chases him.*)
My cloth! My head-cloth! The damp will destroy my head! I'll have my headache pains all over again . . .
(JEFF *skites it off stage.*)

JEFF. Wind took it, Shakespeare.
(*Whips off* ROCHE'*s glasses.*)

ROCHE (*in panic*). My eyeglasses . . . give me!
(JEFF *treads on them; they are destroyed.*)

JEFF. Busted.
(ROCHE *looks round at workers; they are expressionless, slashing as before. Fear crosses his heart. He turns to* JUMBO *and* TAFFY.)

JUMBO. Let's wander, Taff.
TAFFY. Yeah. Let's go.

JUMBO. Got a job, Taff. Haven't we?

TAFFY. Yeah. Got to hurry.

(ROCHE *clutches his bag.*)

Lots of work to do, Pat. Sorry.

ROCHE. Jumbo . . .

JUMBO. Painting beams, Taff.

TAFFY. Yeah. Fast falls the eventide.

(TAFFY *and* JUMBO *make to go.* ROCHE *gapes at them, stupefied.*)

Don't cross them, Paddy. That's all I say. You'll be all right. Don't you worry.

JUMBO (*motioning*). Taff . . .

TAFFY. Only don't cross them, that's all I say. . . .

ROCHE. Jumbo. Stay with me.

(*They are gone.*)

Welshman. . . . (*Pause.* ROCHE *turns to workers with sudden alarm, first touch of propitiation*) I'll be away from this, the moment I've drawn my wage and my insurance card. Youse are not bad men. Only a wee bit rough.

Run-out

Roche is indeed murdered—a ritual murder with hints of primitive sacrifice, as the helicopter screams above. He is the scapegoat, and these ignorant simple casual workers believe in a confused way that they can expiate their misery, poverty and misfortune, even their own sins, by executing him. The play is very strong meat, but some of you might like to read it. Roche has no proper records and will not be missed as he is only a tramp, and Rudkin insinuates the idea that such ritual murders are not unknown even in modern England. The main idea, however, is certainly the horror and fear that the figure of the Other and the Outsider presents to many of us, and its moral is that none of us, even the most educated and tolerant, are immune from this fear. The relevance of the play to many aspects of recent and indeed contemporary history, is obvious enough; one has only to think of South Africa, Northern Ireland, and immigration in Britain. We all have to learn to control the dark fear and hatred in our own souls, and to realize that Roche, the menacing, alien and sneering Outsider, is really only a harmless, pathetic, half-demented old man who couldn't and wouldn't harm a fly; he is a bogy-man, and only those who are emotionally and mentally immature could feel for him anything but pity.

❧❧

THE CRUCIBLE

Lead-in

This passage from the third Act of Arthur Miller's famous play *The Crucible* is exciting to act (especially with a mixed class), but needs a fair amount of explanation. The play is set in Salem, a large village or small town in the American county of Massachusetts in 1692, and is historically accurate in broad outline. It covers a period of superstitious fear and terror of witchcraft which swept the newly founded American colonies at this time and resulted in many deaths. The plot must be briefly recounted so that this episode is intelligible. The Reverend Parris is the local parson—mean, crabbed and self-centred. At the outset of the play his daughter Betty is sick and it is believed that she is bewitched. A group of girls have been dancing, possibly naked, in the forest and going through certain rituals, perhaps led by a Negro slave called Tituba, and the witch hunt, already established in neighbouring villages, rapidly infects this village too. One of the girls, a precocious and beautiful eighteen-year-old called Abigail Williams, has had a secret love affair with the honest and noble farmer John Proctor; she tries to retain his love but he rejects her because he really loves his wife Elizabeth, so in vengeance she accuses his wife, and later him, of witchcraft. One witness at the outset against the Proctors is their servant, an innocent girl called Mary Warren, and Proctor has persuaded her to tell the truth—that there was in fact no witchcraft. But this presents a difficulty in a hysterical and terrified community, because the other girls have confessed and she will be tried either for witchcraft or for false witness. At the outset of this extract she is being cross-questioned by the Deputy-Governor, Danforth, a noted 'witch-finder', who has sent for the other girls to check her story. The other characters can be fairly speedily dealt with: Ezekiel Cheever is clerk to the court, Hathorne is the local judge; the Reverend Hale is a visiting priest of great learning, especially about witchcraft, but honest within his lights; Giles Corey is an old farmer, whose wife is hanged and who is himself killed later. Elizabeth is already in prison, accused of witchcraft and of possessing a 'poppet' (a doll which witches were said to use for sympathetic magic by sticking pins in them and so hurting the people on whom they were modelled); she knows of her husband's adultery, but wishes to keep it hidden for his sake.

The extract opens with the arrival of the girls, led by Abigail, to confront Mary Warren's challenge. Abby denies her story, as she must. Mary, backed by Proctor, sticks to the actual truth, that she 'saw no spirits', but she is among enemies and is viciously cross-questioned; she hasn't the vocabulary to say that she was in a semi-hysterical state. Suddenly Abigail pretends to go into a trance and to be bewitched; Mary knows that she is pretending but is terrified and fears her powers. Proctor challenges her as 'a whore' and in desperation confesses that he has been her lover, and accuses her of 'a whore's vengeance', implying that Abby, formerly his servant, was sent away by his wife Elizabeth because 'she knew a whore when she saw one'. Danforth brings Elizabeth from prison into court, but she tries to conceal her husband's love affair. Abby, frightened that she will be exposed in spite of this, pretends that Mary is bewitching her in the form of a yellow bird which they 'see' up on the rafters. Mary declares that she is only pretending, but the girls work themselves up to a state of hysteria, culminating in a scream. Suddenly Mary is 'infected', rejects Proctor and declares that he is an agent of the devil. Proctor, in despair, is aware that he is trapped and cannot escape, as Abby and Mary embrace. The Reverend Hale denounces the proceedings and the scene ends in disaster.

ACTING NOTES

Some of the needs of performance are described in the detailed description above. Danforth is 'a grave man in his sixties', a lawyer of standing and dignity, completely convinced of his cause as a witch-finder. Proctor is a farmer in the middle thirties, strong and confident. His wife is younger. Parris is in his forties, a widower with a strong sense of being persecuted. The girls are young—sixteen to eighteen, and only the two opponents, Abigail and Mary, are really conspicuous. The main acting point is the hysteria of the girls, which rises to a crescendo as they imitate and repeat Mary's words, and at the climax stamp and scream; they must actually get involved in the hysteria they begin by pretending, and this also, mysteriously, happens on the stage to some extent.

A mixed class would of course be ideal for this extract; I think that girls alone could do all the parts, but I'm not sure whether boys could produce convincingly the hysterical shrieks that are essential if the scene is to 'work'.

> . . . *Enter* SUSANNA WALCOTT, MERCY LEWIS, BETTY PARRIS, *and finally* ABIGAIL. CHEEVERS *comes to* DANFORTH.

CHEEVER. Ruth Putnam's not in court, sir, nor the other children.

DANFORTH. These will be sufficient. Sit you down, children. (*Silently they sit.*) Your friend, Mary Warren, has given us a deposition, in which she swears that she never saw familiar spirits, apparitions, nor any manifest of the Devil. She claims as well that none of you have seen these things either. (*Slight pause.*) Now, children, this is a court of law. The law, based upon the Bible, and the Bible, writ by Almighty God, forbid the practice of witchcraft, and describe death as the penalty thereof. But likewise, children, the law and Bible damn all bearers of false witness. (*Slight pause.*) Now then. It does not escape me that this deposition may be devised to blind us; it may well be that Mary Warren has been conquered by Satan, who sends her here to distract our sacred purpose. If so, her neck will break for it. But if she speak true, I bid you now drop your guile and confess your pretence, for a quick confession will go easier with you. (*Pause.*) Abigail Williams, rise.

(ABIGAIL *slowly rises.*)

Is there any truth in this?

ABIGAIL. No, sir.

DANFORTH (*thinks, glances at* MARY, *then back to* ABIGAIL.) Children, a very augur bit will now be turned into your souls until your honesty is proved. Will either of you change your positions now, or do you force me to hard questioning?

ABIGAIL. I have naught to change, sir. She lies.

DANFORTH (*to* MARY). You would still go on with this?

MARY WARREN (*faintly*). Aye, sir.

DANFORTH (*turning to* ABIGAIL). A poppet were discovered in Mr Proctor's house, stabbed by a needle. Mary Warren claims that you sat beside her in the court when she made it, and that you saw her make it and witnessed how she herself stuck her needle into it for safe-keeping. What say you to that?

ABIGAIL (*with a slight note of indignation*). It is a lie, sir.

DANFORTH (*after a slight pause*). While you worked for Mr Proctor, did you see poppets in that house?

ABIGAIL. Goody Proctor always kept poppets.

PROCTOR. Your honour, my wife never kept no poppets. Mary Warren confesses it was her poppet.

CHEEVER. Your Excellency.

DANFORTH. Mr Cheever.

CHEEVER. When I spoke with Goody Proctor in that house, she said she never kept no poppets. But she said she did keep poppets when she were a girl.

PROCTOR. She has not been a girl these fifteen years, Your Honour.

HATHORNE. But a poppet will keep fifteen years, will it not?

PROCTOR. It will keep if it is kept, but Mary Warren swears she never saw no poppets in my house, nor anyone else.

PARRIS. Why could there not have been poppets hid where no one ever saw them?

PROCTOR (*furious*). There might also be a dragon with five legs in my house, but no one has ever seen it.

PARRIS. We are here, Your Honour, precisely to discover what no one has ever seen.

PROCTOR. Mr Danforth, what profit this girl to turn herself about? What may Mary Warren gain but hard questioning and worse?

DANFORTH. You are charging Abigail Williams with a marvellous cool plot to murder, do you understand that?

PROCTOR. I do, sir. I believe she means to murder.

DANFORTH (*pointing at* ABIGAIL, *incredulously*). This child would murder your wife?

PROCTOR. It is not a child. Now hear me, sir. In the sight of the congregation she were twice this year put out of this meetin' house for laughter during prayer.

DANFORTH (*shocked, turning to* ABIGAIL). What's this? Laughter during—!

PARRIS. Excellency, she were under Tituba's power at that time, but she is solemn now.

GILES. Aye, now she is solemn and goes to hang people!

DANFORTH. Quiet, man.

HATHORNE. Surely it have no bearing on the question, sir. He charges contemplation of murder.

DANFORTH. Aye. (*He studies* ABIGAIL *for a moment, then*) Continue, Mr Proctor.

PROCTOR. Mary. Now tell the Governor how you danced in the woods.

PARRIS (*instantly*). Excellency, since I come to Salem this man is blackening my name. He—

DANFORTH. In a moment, sir. (*To* MARY WARREN, *sternly, and surprised*). What is this dancing?

MARY WARREN. I— (*She glances at* ABIGAIL, *who is staring down at her remorselessly. Then, appealing to* PROCTOR) Mr Proctor—

PROCTOR (*taking it right up*). Abigail leads the girls to the woods, Your Honour, and they have danced there naked—

PARRIS. Your Honour, this—

PROCTOR (*at once*). Mr Parris discovered them himself in the dead of night! There's the 'child' she is!

DANFORTH (*it is growing into a nightmare, and he turns, astonished, to* PARRIS). Mr Parris—

PARRIS. I can only say, sir, that I never found any of them naked, and this man is—

DANFORTH. But you discovered them dancing in the woods? (*Eyes on* PARRIS, *he points at* ABIGAIL). Abigail?

HALE. Excellency, when I first arrived from Beverly, Mr Parris told me that.

DANFORTH. Do you deny it, Mr Parris?

PARRIS. I do not, sir, but I never saw any of them naked.

DANFORTH. But she have *danced*?

PARRIS (*unwillingly*). Aye, sir.

   (DANFORTH, *as though with new eyes, looks at* ABIGAIL.)

HATHORNE. Excellency, will you permit me? (*He points at* MARY WARREN.)

DANFORTH (*with great worry*). Pray, proceed.

HATHORNE. You say you never saw no spirits, Mary, were never threatened or afflicted by any manifest of the Devil or the Devil's agents.

MARY WARREN (*very faintly*). No, sir.

HATHORNE (*with a gleam of victory*). And yet, when people accused of witchery confronted you in court, you would faint, saying their spirits came out of their bodies and choked you—

MARY WARREN. That were pretence, sir.

DANFORTH. I cannot hear you.

MARY WARREN. Pretence, sir.

PARRIS. But you did turn cold, did you not? I myself picked you up many times, and your skin were icy. Mr Danforth, you—

DANFORTH. I saw that many times.

PROCTOR. She only pretended to faint, Your Excellency. They're all marvellous pretenders.

HATHORNE. Then can she pretend to faint now?

PROCTOR. Now?

PARRIS. Why not? Now there are no spirits attacking her, for none in this room is accused of witchcraft. So let her turn herself cold now, let her pretend she is attacked now, let her faint. (*He turns to* MARY WARREN.) Faint!

MARY WARREN. Faint?

PARRIS. Aye, faint. Prove to us how you pretended in the court so many times.

MARY WARREN (*looking to* PROCTOR). I cannot faint now, sir.

PROCTOR (*alarmed, quietly*). Can you not pretend it?

MARY WARREN. I— (*She looks about as though searching for*

the passion to faint.) I—have no *sense* of it now, I—

DANFORTH. Why? What is lacking now?

MARY WARREN. I—cannot tell, sir, I—

DANFORTH. Might it be that here we have no afflicting spirit loose, but in the court there were some?

MARY WARREN. I never saw no spirits.

PARRIS. Then see no spirits now, and prove to us that you can faint by your own will, as you claim.

MARY WARREN (*stares, searching for the emotion of it, and then shakes her head*). I—cannot do it.

PARRIS. Then you will confess, will you not? It were attacking spirits made you faint!

MARY WARREN. No, sir, I—

PARRIS. Your Excellency, this is a trick to blind the court!

MARY WARREN. It's not a trick! (*She stands.*) I—I used to faint because I—I thought I saw spirits.

DANFORTH. *Thought* you saw them!

MARY WARREN. But I did not, Your Honour.

HATHORNE. How could you think you saw them unless you saw them?

MARY WARREN. I—I cannot tell how, but I did. I—I heard the other girls screaming, and you, Your Honour, you seemed to believe them, and I— It were only sport in the beginning, sir, but then the whole world cried spirits, spirits, and I—I promise you, Mr Danforth, I only thought I saw them but I did not.

(DANFORTH *peers at her.*)

PARRIS (*smiling, but nervous because* DANFORTH *seems to be struck by* MARY WARREN'S *story*). Surely Your Excellency is not taken by this simple lie.

DANFORTH (*turning worriedly to* ABIGAIL). Abigail. I bid you now search your head and tell me this—and beware of it, child, to God every soul is precious and His vengeance is terrible on them that take life without cause. Is it possible, child, that the spirits you have seen are illusion only, some deception that may cross your mind when—

ABIGAIL. Why, this—this—is a base question, sir.

DANFORTH. Child, I would have you consider it—

ABIGAIL. I have been hurt, Mr Danforth; I have seen my

blood runnin' out! I have been near to murdered every
day because I done my duty pointing out the Devil's
people—and this is my reward? To be mistrusted, denied, questioned like a—

DANFORTH (*weakening*). Child, I do not mistrust you—

ABIGAIL (*in an open threat*). Let *you* beware, Mr Danforth.
Think you to be so mighty that the power of Hell may
not turn *your* wits? Beware of it! There is—
(*Suddenly, from an accusatory attitude, her face turns,
looking into the air above—it is truly frightened.*)

DANFORTH (*apprehensively*). What is it, child?

ABIGAIL (*looking about in the air, clasping her arms about
as though cold*). I—I know not. A wind, a cold wind,
has come. (*Her eyes fall on* MARY WARREN.)

MARY WARREN (*terrified, pleading*). Abby!

MERCY LEWIS (*shivering*). Your Honour, I freeze!

PROCTOR. They're pretending!

HATHORNE (*touching* ABIGAIL'S *hand*). She is cold, Your
Honour, touch her!

MERCY LEWIS (*through chattering teeth*). Mary, do you send
this shadow on me?

MARY WARREN. Lord, save me!

SUSANNA WALCOTT. I freeze, I freeze!

ABIGAIL (*shivering visibly*). It is a wind, a wind!

MARY WARREN. Abby, don't do that!

DANFORTH (*himself engaged and entered by* ABIGAIL). Mary
Warren, do you witch her? I say to you, do you send
your spirit out?
(*With a hysterical cry* MARY WARREN *starts to run.* PROC-
TOR *catches her.*)

MARY WARREN (*almost collapsing*). Let me go, Mr Proctor.
I cannot, I cannot—

ABIGAIL (*crying to Heaven*). Oh, Heavenly Father, take
away this shadow!
(*Without warning or hesitation,* PROCTOR *leaps at* ABI-
GAIL *and, grabbing her by the hair, pulls her to her feet.
She screams in pain.* DANFORTH, *astonished, cries, 'What
are you about?' and* HATHORNE *and* PARRIS *call, 'Take
your hands off her!' and out of it all comes* PROCTOR'S
roaring voice.)

PROCTOR. How do you call Heaven! Whore! Whore!
(HERRICK *breaks* PROCTOR *from her*.)

HERRICK. John!

DANFORTH. Man! Man, what do you—

PROCTOR (*breathless and in agony*). It is a whore!

DANFORTH (*dumbfounded*). You charge—?

ABIGAIL. Mr Danforth, he is lying!

PROCTOR. Mark her! Now she'll suck a scream to stab me
with but—

DANFORTH. You will prove this! This will not pass!

PROCTOR (*trembling, his life collapsing about him*). I have
known her, sir. I have known her.

DANFORTH. You—you are a lecher?

FRANCIS (*horrified*). John, you cannot say such a—

PROCTOR. Oh, Francis, I wish you had some evil in you that
you might know me! (*To* DANFORTH) A man will not
cast away his good name. You surely know that.

DANFORTH (*dumbfounded*). In—in what time? In what
place?

PROCTOR (*his voice about to break, and his shame great*).
In the proper place—where my beasts are bedded. On
the last night of my joy, some eight months past. She
used to serve me in my house, sir. (*He has to clamp his
jaw to keep from weeping*.) A man may think God
sleeps, but God sees everything, I know it now. I beg
you, sir, I beg you—see her what she is. My wife, my
dear good wife, took this girl soon after, sir, and put
her out on the highroad. And being what she is, a lump
of vanity, sir— (*He is being overcome*.) Excellency,
forgive me, forgive me. (*Angrily against himself, he
turns away from the Governor for a moment. Then, as
though to cry out is his only means of speech left*.)
She thinks to dance with me on my wife's grave! And
well she might, for I thought of her softly. God help
me, I lusted, and there *is* a promise in such sweat. But
it is a whore's vengeance, and you must see it; I set myself entirely in your hands. I know you must see it
now.

DANFORTH (*blanched, in horror, turning to* ABIGAIL). You
deny every scrap and tittle of this?

ABIGAIL. If I must answer that, I will leave and I will not come back again!

(DANFORTH *seems unsteady*.)

PROCTOR. I have made a bell of my honour. I have rung the doom of my good name—you will believe me, Mr Danforth! My wife is innocent, except she knew a whore when she saw one!

ABIGAIL (*stepping up to* DANFORTH). What look do you give me?

(DANFORTH *cannot speak*.)

I'll not have such looks! (*She turns and starts for the door*.)

DANFORTH. You will remain where you are! (HERRICK *steps into her path. She comes up short, fire in her eyes*.) Mr Parris, go into the court and bring Goodwife Proctor out.

PARRIS (*objecting*). Your Honour, this is all a—

DANFORTH (*sharply to* PARRIS). Bring her out! And tell her not one word of what's been spoken here. And let you knock before you enter. (PARRIS *goes out*.) Now we shall touch the bottom of this swamp. (*To* PROCTOR) Your wife, you say, is an honest woman.

PROCTOR. In her life, sir, she have never lied. There are them that cannot sing, and them that cannot weep— my wife cannot lie. I have paid much to learn it, sir.

DANFORTH. And when she put this girl out of your house, she put her out for a harlot?

PROCTOR. Aye, sir.

DANFORTH. And knew her for a harlot?

PROCTOR. Aye, sir, she knew her for a harlot.

DANFORTH. Good, then. (*To* ABIGAIL) And if she tell me, child, it were for harlotry, may God spread His mercy on you! (*There is a knock. He calls to the door*.) Hold! (*To* ABIGAIL) Turn your back. Turn your back. (*To* PROCTOR) Do likewise.

(*Both turn their backs*—ABIGAIL *with indignant slowness*.)

Now let neither of you turn to face Goody Proctor. No one in this room is to speak one word, or raise a

D

gesture aye or nay. (*He turns toward the door, calls*)
Enter!

(*The door opens.* ELIZABETH *enters with* PARRIS. PAR-
RIS *leaves her. She stands alone, her eyes looking for*
PROCTOR.)

Mr Cheever, report this testimony in all exactness. Are
you ready?

CHEEVER. Ready, sir.

DANFORTH. Come here, woman. (ELIZABETH *comes to
him, glancing at* PROCTOR'S *back.*) Look at me only,
not at your husband. In my eyes only.

ELIZABETH (*faintly*). Good, sir.

DANFORTH. We are given to understand that at one time you
dismissed your servant, Abigail Williams.

ELIZABETH. That is true, sir.

DANFORTH. For what cause did you dismiss her?

(*Slight pause. Then* ELIZABETH *tries to glance at* PROC-
TOR.)

You will look in my eyes only and not at your husband.
The answer is in your memory and you need no help
to give it to me. Why did you dismiss Abigail Williams?

ELIZABETH (*not knowing what to say, sensing a situation,
wetting her lips to stall for time*). She—dissatisfied me.
(*Pause.*) And my husband.

DANFORTH. In what way dissatisfied you?

ELIZABETH. She were— (*She glances at* PROCTOR *for a
cue.*)

DANFORTH. Woman, look at me! (ELIZABETH *does.*) Were
she slovenly? Lazy? What disturbance did she cause?

ELIZABETH. Your Honour, I—in that time I were sick. And
I— My husband is a good and righteous man. He is
never drunk as some are, nor wastin' his time at the
shovelboard, but always at his work. But in my sickness—you see, sir, I were a long time sick after my
last baby, and I thought I saw my husband somewhat
turning from me. And this girl—

(*She turns to* ABIGAIL.)

DANFORTH. Look at me.

ELIZABETH. Aye, sir. Abigail Williams— (*She breaks off.*)

DANFORTH. What of Abigail Williams?

ELIZABETH. I came to think he fancied her. And so one night I lost my wits, I think, and put her out on the high-road.

DANFORTH. Your husband—did he indeed turn from you?

ELIZABETH (*in agony*). My husband—is a goodly man, sir.

DANFORTH. Then he did not turn from you.

ELIZABETH (*starting to glance at* PROCTOR). He—

DANFORTH (*reaches out and holds her face, then*): Look at me! To your own knowledge, has John Proctor ever committed the crime of lechery? (*In a crisis of inde-cision she cannot speak.*) Answer my question! Is your husband a lecher!

ELIZABETH (*faintly*). No, sir.

DANFORTH. Remove her, Marshal.

PROCTOR. Elizabeth, tell the truth!

DANFORTH. She has spoken. Remove her!

PROCTOR (*crying out*). Elizabeth, I have confessed it!

ELIZABETH. Oh, God!

(*The door closes behind her.*)

PROCTOR. She only thought to save my name!

HALE. Excellency, it is a natural lie to tell; I beg you, stop now before another is condemned! I may shut my con-science to it no more—private vengeance is working through this testimony! From the beginning this man has struck me true. By my oath to Heaven, I believe him now, and I pray you call back his wife before we—

DANFORTH. She spoke nothing of lechery, and this man has lied!

HALE. I believe him! (*Pointing at* ABIGAIL) This girl has always struck me false! She has—

(ABIGAIL, *with a weird, wild, chilling cry, screams up to the ceiling.*)

ABIGAIL. You will not! Begone! Begone, I say!

DANFORTH. What is it, child?

(*But* ABIGAIL, *pointing with fear, is now raising up her frightened eyes, her awed face, toward the ceiling —the girls are doing the same—and now* HATHORNE, HALE, PUTNAM, CHEEVER, HERRICK, *and* DANFORTH *do the same.*)

What's there? (*He lowers his eyes from the ceiling, and*

now he is frightened; there is real tension in his voice.)
Child!
(*She is transfixed—with all the girls she is whimpering open-mouthed, agape at the ceiling.*)
Girls! Why do you—?

MERCY LEWIS (*pointing*). It's on the beam! Behind the rafter!

DANFORTH (*looking up*). Where!

ABIGAIL. Why—? (*She gulps.*) Why do you come, yellow bird?

PROCTOR. Where's a bird? I see no bird!

ABIGAIL (*to the ceiling*). My face? My face?

PROCTOR. Mr Hale—

DANFORTH. Be quiet!

PROCTOR (*to* HALE). Do you see a bird?

DANFORTH. Be quiet!

ABIGAIL (*to the ceiling, in a genuine conversation with the 'bird', as though trying to talk it out of attacking her*). But God made my face; you cannot want to tear my face. Envy is a deadly sin, Mary.

MARY WARREN (*on her feet with a spring, and horrified, pleading*). Abby!

ABIGAIL (*unperturbed, continuing to the 'bird'*). Oh, Mary, this is a black art to change your shape. No, I cannot, I cannot stop my mouth; it's God's work I do.

MARY WARREN. Abby, I'm *here*!

PROCTOR (*frantically*). They're pretending, Mr Danforth!

ABIGAIL—(*now she takes a backward step, as though in fear the bird will swoop down momentarily*). Oh, please, Mary! Don't come down.

SUSANNA WALCOTT. Her claws, she's stretching her claws!

PROCTOR. Lies, lies.

ABIGAIL (*backing farther, eyes still fixed above*). Mary, please don't hurt me!

MARY WARREN (*to* DANFORTH). I'm not hurting her!

DANFORTH (*to* MARY WARREN). Why does she see this vision?

MARY WARREN. She sees nothin'!

ABIGAIL (*now staring full front as though hypnotized, and mimicking the exact tone of* MARY WARREN'S *cry*). She sees nothin'!

MARY WARREN (*pleading*). Abby, you mustn't!

ABIGAIL AND ALL THE GIRLS (*all transfixed*). Abby, you mustn't!

MARY WARREN (*to all the girls*). I'm here, I'm here!

GIRLS. I'm here, I'm here!

DANFORTH (*horrified*). Mary Warren! Draw back your spirit out of them!

MARY WARREN. Mr Danforth!

GIRLS (*cutting her off*). Mr Danforth!

DANFORTH. Have you compacted with the Devil? Have you?

MARY WARREN. Never, never!

GIRLS. Never, never!

DANFORTH (*growing hysterical*). Why can they only repeat you?

PROCTOR. Give me a whip—I'll stop it!

MARY WARREN. They're sporting. They—!

GIRLS. They're sporting!

MARY WARREN (*turning on them all hysterically and stamping her feet*). Abby, stop it!

GIRLS (*stamping their feet*). Abby, stop it!

MARY WARREN. Stop it!

GIRLS. Stop it!

MARY WARREN (*screaming it out at the top of her lungs, and raising her fists*). Stop it!!

GIRLS (*raising their fists*). Stop it!!

(MARY WARREN, *utterly confounded, and becoming overwhelmed by* ABIGAIL'S—*and the girls'—utter conviction, starts to whimper, hands half raised, powerless, and all the girls begin whimpering exactly as she does.*)

DANFORTH. A little while ago you were afflicted. Now it seems you afflict others; where did you find this power?

MARY WARREN (*staring at* ABIGAIL). I—have no power.

GIRLS. I have no power.

PROCTOR. They're gulling you, Mister!

DANFORTH. Why did you turn about this past two weeks? You have seen the Devil, have you not?

HALE (*indicating* ABIGAIL *and the* GIRLS). You cannot believe them!

MARY WARREN. I—

PROCTOR (*sensing her weakening*). Mary, God damns all liars!

DANFORTH (*pounding it into her*). You have seen the Devil, you have made compact with Lucifer, have you not?

PROCTOR. God damns liars, Mary!

(MARY *utters something unintelligible, staring at* ABIGAIL, *who keeps watching the 'bird' above.*)

DANFORTH. I cannot hear you. What do you say?

(MARY *utters again unintelligibly.*)

You will confess yourself or you will hang! (*He turns her roughly to face him.*) Do you know who I am? I say you will hang if you do not open with me!

PROCTOR. Mary, remember the angel Raphael—do that which is good and—

ABIGAIL (*pointing upward*). The wings! Her wings are spreading! Mary, please, don't, don't—!

HALE. I see nothing, Your Honour!

DANFORTH. Do you confess this power! (*He is an inch from her face.*) Speak!

ABIGAIL. She's going to come down! She's walking the beam!

DANFORTH. Will you speak!

MARY WARREN (*staring in horror*). I cannot!

GIRLS. I cannot!

PARRIS. Cast the Devil out! Look him in the face! Trample him! We'll save you, Mary, only stand fast against him and—

ABIGAIL (*looking up*). Look out! She's coming down!

(*She and all the girls run to one wall, shielding their eyes. And now, as though cornered, they let out a gigantic scream, and* MARY, *as though infected, opens her mouth and screams with them. Gradually* ABIGAIL *and the girls leave off, until only* MARY *is left there, staring up at the 'bird', screaming madly. All watch her, horrified by this evident fit.* PROCTOR *strides to her.*)

PROCTOR. Mary, tell the Governor what they— (*He has hardly got a word out when, seeing him coming for her, she rushes out of his reach, screaming in horror.*)

MARY WARREN. Don't touch me—don't touch me!

(*At which the girls halt at the door.*)

PROCTOR (*astonished*). Mary!

MARY WARREN (*pointing at* PROCTOR). You're the Devil's man!

(*He is stopped in his tracks.*)

PARRIS. Praise God!

GIRLS. Praise God!

PROCTOR (*numbed*). Mary, how—?

MARY WARREN. I'll not hang with you! I love God, I love God.

DANFORTH (*to* MARY). He bid you do the Devil's work?

MARY WARREN (*hysterically, indicating* PROCTOR). He come at me by night and every day to sign, to sign, to—

DANFORTH. Sign what?

PARRIS. The Devil's book? He come with a book?

MARY WARREN (*hysterically, pointing at* PROCTOR, *fearful of him*). My name, he want my name. 'I'll murder you', he says, 'if my wife hangs! We must go and overthrow the court,' he says!

(DANFORTH'S *head jerks toward* PROCTOR, *shock and horror in his face.*)

PROCTOR (*turning, appealing to* HALE). Mr Hale!

MARY WARREN (*her sobs beginning*). He wake me every night, his eyes were like coals and his fingers claw my neck, and I sign, I sign . . .

HALE. Excellency, this child's gone wild!

PROCTOR (*as* DANFORTH'S *wide eyes pour on him*). Mary, Mary!

MARY WARREN (*screaming at him*). No, I love God; I go your way no more. I love God, I bless God. (*Sobbing, she rushes to* ABIGAIL.) Abby, Abby, I'll never hurt you more!

(*They all watch, as* ABIGAIL, *out of her infinite charity, reaches out and draws the sobbing* MARY *to her, and then looks up to* DANFORTH.)

DANFORTH (*to* PROCTOR). What are you? (PROCTOR *is beyond speech in his anger.*) You are combined with anti-Christ, are you not? I have seen your power; you will not deny it! What say you, Mister?

HALE. Excellency—

DANFORTH. I will have nothing from you, Mr Hale! (*To

PROCTOR) Will you confess yourself befouled with Hell, or do you keep that black allegiance yet? What say you?

PROCTOR (*his mind wild, breathless*). I say—I say—God is dead!

PARRIS. Hear it, hear it!

PROCTOR (*laughs insanely, then*): A fire, a fire is burning! I hear the boot of Lucifer, I see his filthy face! And it is my face, and yours, Danforth! For them that quail to bring men out of ignorance, as I have quailed, and as you quail now when you know in all your black hearts that this be fraud—God damns our kind especially, and we will burn, we will burn together!

DANFORTH. Marshal! Take him and Corey with him to the jail!

HALE (*starting across to the door*). I denounce these proceedings!

PROCTOR. You are pulling Heaven down and raising up a whore!

HALE. I denounce these proceedings, I quit this court! (*He slams the door to the outside behind him.*)

DANFORTH (*calling to him in a fury*). Mr Hale! Mr Hale!

Run-out

As there is a further extract from this play later in the book, I propose to leave general comments on it till then. The effect of this extract if well done can be electrifying, as I know from two performances—one at a grammar school, which I saw some years ago, the other a production I helped to produce quite recently.

6
Communication

ⵧⵧⵧⵧⵧⵧⵧⵧⵧⵧⵧⵧⵧⵧⵧⵧⵧⵧⵧⵧⵧⵧⵧⵧⵧⵧⵧⵧⵧⵧⵧ

Communication is understood now to be a key factor in teaching and learning, and indeed a key factor in all human relations, including those between nations. The passages chosen all feature communication as a central issue, though of course they differ widely in their treatment of it. The first, from *The Long and the Short and the Tall*, shows the development of a basic and primitive kind of communication between the Cockney Bamforth and the captured Japanese soldier, who cannot speak a word of English, and in fact does not speak throughout the play; yet through non-verbal communication—imitation of actions, exchange of photographs and small possessions—a relationship is established that the previously cynical and heartless Bamforth is prepared to risk his life for. *Live Like Pigs* shows how the language used by the officials is totally incomprehensible to the gypsies, with whom, in spite of a fair amount of goodwill, they make absolutely no contact. *Roots* is I think in essence a play *about* communication, and Beatie after her love affair with Ronnie spends most of her time with her parents and relatives desperately trying to set up a situation in which she can 'talk, really *talk*' to them and they to her; the irony is that she fails, her love affair breaks up because Ronnie feels he has never been able to communicate with her, and the splendid ending leaves Beatie at last able to talk without merely echoing Ronnie —but the family isn't listening or attending—she has no audience; or rather, she is communicating only with the audience in the theatre. The short passage from *As You Like It* illustrates (as do those from *Roots* and *Live Like Pigs* to some extent) the *class* barriers of communication, and Touchstone's awareness of how he can confuse the peasant William merely by using the courtly language he pretends is his own.

Finally the famous opening of *Pygmalion* shows this class aspect as Shaw sees it in the early part of this century: Liza has only to learn 'to speak posh' and she can be passed off as a duchess; this still has some uncomfortable truth about it.

Real communication, as all these extracts remind us in their different ways, is a two-way process. This is the main reason why, among so many other things, all teaching should have a discussion component, why all plays need an audience, and why an increasing number of plays invite audience participation of some kind—not merely applause, but some sort of actual involvement. In schools we are at last less interested in producing speakers of standard English (see Shaw) and more interested in finding ways of communicating between teacher and student. (For this purpose a circle is better than serried ranks with the teacher in front, and it is often a good way, too, of producing a play—in the *middle* of the room—theatre-in-the-round.)

THE LONG AND THE SHORT AND THE TALL

Lead-in

The situation is fairly easy to explain. During the Second World War, a small British patrol has been sent out from the front line in Malaya to try to discover the position held by the Japanese enemy. They have recently captured a solitary Japanese soldier, who speaks no English. The patrol is led by Sergeant Mitchem, with Corporal Johnstone as his second-in-command. The others are Macleish, recently appointed acting lance-corporal; Smith, an amiable north-countryman; Evans, a Welshman; Whitaker, a timid private who works the radio; and Bamforth, a cynical, intelligent but rather vicious cockney. This section, which concludes Act I, speaks for itself in its treatment of the theme of communication.

ACTING NOTES

The hut in which the patrol is 'holed up' feels very claustrophobic, with the menacing probability of Japanese forces surrounding it at any time; try to invent some way of getting this feeling in your own classroom. You may be able to improvize belts and arms for the soldiers; certainly you will need something to serve for a bren gun and a bayonet. Bamforth, who is truculent, aggressive and full of Cockney wit, has been, up to this point in the play, mostly unpleasant, ridiculing his equals and trying to trip up not only the unpleasant Corporal Johnstone but also the honest and reliable Sergeant Mitchem. The extract which follows shows the development of a real relationship with the Japanese, to whom he can't speak except in a kind of international sign language; steadily he develops a surprising but entirely convincing affection for his 'enemy', and the significance of this is not hard to see. He comes to recognize that he shares a common humanity with the Japanese, and within a few minutes is defending him against his own comrades. His curious and illiterate idea of Japanese speech, which is almost a comic-paper version with l's substituting for r's, ironically *does* communicate, and a relationship is established. The Japanese is a *comic* figure, earlier described as absurd but pathetic. Everybody is jumpy, especially at the end of the scene, when they hear the menacing radio voice of some possibly huge Japanese force—the illiterate English of which exactly corresponds with Bamforth's illiterate Japanese.

MITCHEM. Bamforth!

BAMFORTH. Sarge?

MITCHEM (*offering his Sten to* BAMFORTH). Here. Cop on for this. You're looking after Tojo here. I think he fancies you. If he tries to come it on he gets it through the head. No messing. He's on your charge. Look after him.

BAMFORTH (*shakes his head, refusing the Sten*). Like he was my only chick. (BAMFORTH *picks up the* PRISONER'*s bayonet from the table*.) I'll settle for this. (*He crosses towards the* PRISONER.) Down, Shorthouse. (*He motions the* PRISONER *to sit on the form*.) Put your hands up on your head. (*The* PRISONER *looks at* BAMFORTH *in bewilderment*.) I said, get your hands up on your head! Like this! See! Flingers on the blonce! Alllight? (BAMFORTH *demonstrates and the* PRISONER *complies*. BAMFORTH *is delighted*.) Hey, Taff! See that, did you? He did it like I said! Flingers up on blonce. I only talk the lingo natural!

EVANS (*turning at window*). I always knew you were an

Oriental creep at heart, man!

BAMFORTH. You've not seen nothing yet—get this. (*To the* PRISONER.) Allee-lightee. Flingers up to touch the loof. Come on, come on! Touch the loof, you asiatic glet! (BAMFORTH *raises the bayonet and the* PRISONER *cringes away.*) He's a rotten ignoramus.

MITCHEM. All right, that'll do. Pack it in. Now listen, all of you. We're taking this boy back to camp with us. I want to get him there in one piece.

JOHNSTONE. It's a bit dodgy, isn't it, Mitch?

MITCHEM. Happen.

JOHNSTONE. It's going to be a dodgy number as it is. You don't know how many more of them there are out there.

MITCHEM. Not yet.

JOHNSTONE. They could be coming down in strength.

MITCHEM. They might.

JOHNSTONE. And if they are we're up the creek all right. We've got enough on getting this lot back. They've no experience. We'll have to belt it like the clappers out of hell. We can't afford to hang about.

MITCHEM. We'll shift.

JOHNSTONE. But if we're going to cart a prisoner along as well . . .

MITCHEM. He'll go the pace. I'll see to that.

JOHNSTONE. You're in charge.

MITCHEM. That's right. Corporal Macleish! Smith!

MACLEISH. Sergeant?

SMITH. Sarge?

MITCHEM. I've got a job for you two. Outside. (MACLEISH *and* SMITH *exchange glances.*) I want the pair of you to nip down as far as the main track. Look for any signs of any more of them. O.K.?

MACLEISH. You want us to go down now, Sarge?

MITCHEM. Straight away. If the coast's clear we want to belt off back. Smartish.

MACLEISH. Right.

MITCHEM. Take it steady—careful—but don't make a meal out of it. The sooner we can make a start from here the better.

(MACLEISH *and* SMITH *strap on their ammunition pouches.*)

MACLEISH. Supposing we should . . . make contact?

MITCHEM. Don't. Not if you can help it. If you see anything that moves—turn back. Mac, you'd better take a Sten. Take mine. (MACLEISH *crosses and takes Sten and a couple of slips of ammunition from* MITCHEM. SMITH *unsheaths his bayonet and clips it on his rifle.*) Come on. (MITCHEM, MACLEISH *and* SMITH *cross to the door.*) What's it like out, Evans?

EVANS. Quiet. Quiet as a grave.

WHITAKER. Nothing this side, Sarge.

MITCHEM. Cover them as far as you can down the track. (EVANS *and* WHITAKER *nod.* MITCHEM *opens door slowly and ushers* SMITH *and* MACLEISH *on to the veranda.*) Off you go.

EVANS. So long, Smudger, Jock.

MITCHEM (*closes door and crosses to where* BAMFORTH *is guarding the* PRISONER). How's he behaving himself?

BAMFORTH (*fingering the bayonet*). All right. He hasn't got much choice.

MITCHEM (*to the* PRISONER). You listen to me. Understand? You come with us. We take you back. We take you back with us. Oh, blimey . . . Look . . . Bamforth.

BAMFORTH. Yeh?

MITCHEM. Tell him he can drop his hands. He isn't going to run away.

BAMFORTH. Hey, Tojo! Flingers off blonce. Flingers off blonce! (*The* PRISONER *raises his hands in the air.*) Not that, you nit! Here, that's not bad though, is it? He's coming on. He knows his flingers already. Good old Tojo! (*The* PRISONER *smiles.*) Now let them dlop. Dlop, see! Down! (BAMFORTH *demonstrates and the* PRISONER *slowly drops his hands.*) He picks up quick. He's a glutton for knowledge.

MITCHEM (*speaks slowly and carefully*). You—come—with —us! Back! We—take—you—back! (*The* PRISONER *is mystified.*) Back to camp! (MITCHEM *turns away.*) What's the use . . . (MITCHEM *crosses to table.*)

BAMFORTH. I'll work on him. I'll chat him up a bit.

JOHNSTONE. We should have done him first time off.

MITCHEM. I'm giving the orders!

BAMFORTH. Flingers on blonce. (*The* PRISONER *complies happily.*) Dlop flingers. (*Again the* PRISONER *obeys.*) Get that! He dlops them like a two-year-old!

JOHNSTONE. Just keep him quiet, Bamforth, that's all. We don't want any of the funny patter!

BAMFORTH. I'm teaching him to talk!

JOHNSTONE. Well don't! Mitch, we've got fifteen miles to slog it back. We've got no set. We know the Japs are coming through—so someone's waiting for a report—and quick. We can't drag him along—suppose he tries to come it on? One shout from him with any of his boys around and we're in the cart. The lot of us.

MITCHEM. So what do you suggest?

JOHNSTONE. Get rid of him. Right now. You going soft?

MITCHEM. And if we do? You want to make out the report when we get back?

JOHNSTONE. Report! You want to make out a report! Because we do a Jap? We whip him out and knock him off, that' all. We can't take prisoners. We're out to do a job.

MITCHEM. Reports on him don't bother me. And if I've got to do for him—I will. I'll knock him off myself. You think I'm stuffing my nut worrying about a Jap? One Jap? I've got six men. They're my responsibility. But more than that, and like you say, I've got a job to do. So all right. So I'll do it. Now you tell me what's going on out there? (MITCHEM *indicates the window.*) Just tell me how many Nips have broken through and where they are right now. You want to wait and count them for yourself?

JOHNSTONE. I want to slog it back!

MITCHEM. All right. That's what we're going to do. With him. (*Points to the* PRISONER.) With Tojo there. Because if anybody knows the strength of Nips behind our lines it's him. So far on this outing out it's been the biggest muck-up in the history of the British army, and that's saying a lot. We've wandered round, the set's packed in, we've no idea what's going on and if there

ever was an organized shambles—my God, this is it.
Now things have changed. We've copped on to a lad
who's going to make this detail worth its while. If I
can get him back to camp what they'll get out of him
could do more good than you if you should serve a score
and one. So he's important for what he knows. And
I'll leave any man on this patrol behind—including you
—before I'll say good-bye to him. Going soft? Do you
think I give a twopenny damn about his life? It's what
he knows.

JOHNSTONE. Suppose he comes the ab-dabs on the way?

MITCHEM. He won't.

JOHNSTONE. But if he does? He only needs to start playing
it up at the wrong time. He only wants to start coming
it on when we're close to his muckers.

MITCHEM. I've said he won't.

JOHNSTONE. What if he does?

(MITCHEM *and* JOHNSTONE *glance across at the* PRI-
SONER.)

MITCHEM. I'll put the bayonet in his guts myself. (*Pause.*)
You'd better check these Jap grenades. Might come in
handy.

(MITCHEM *and* JOHNSTONE *turn to table to check the
grenades. The* PRISONER'S *hand goes up to his breast
pocket.* BAMFORTH *raises the bayonet threateningly.*)

BAMFORTH. Watch it, Tojo boy! Just watch your step! I'll
have it in as soon as look at you!

MITCHEM (*glancing round*). What's up with him?

BAMFORTH. Going for his pocket.

(*The* PRISONER *gestures towards his pocket.*)

MITCHEM. All right. See what he wants.

BAMFORTH (*still threatening with the bayonet, he opens the
PRISONER'S breast pocket and takes out a cheap leather
wallet*). It's his wallet.

JOHNSTONE. Sling it out the window.

MITCHEM. Let him have it. Check it first.

(BAMFORTH *briefly inspects the interior of the wallet.*)

JOHNSTONE. You're going to let him have it!

MITCHEM. It costs us nothing. No point in getting him
niggly before we start.

BAMFORTH. Looks all right, Sarge.

MITCHEM. Give it him.

> (BAMFORTH *hands the wallet to the* PRISONER, *who opens it, extracts a couple of photographs and hands one to* BAMFORTH.)

BAMFORTH. It's a photo! It's a picture of a Nippo bint! (*The* PRISONER *points proudly to himself.*) Who's this, then, eh? You got wife? Your missis? (*The* PRISONER *points again to himself.*) It's his old woman! Very good. Plenty of humpy. Japanese girl very good, eh? Good old Tojo! She's a bit short in the pins, that's all. But very nice. I wouldn't mind a crack at her myself. (*The* PRISONER *passes another photograph to* BAMFORTH.) Here! Get this! Nippo snappers, Sarge. Two Jap kids. Couple of chicos. You got two chicos, eh? (*The* PRISONER *does not understand.* BAMFORTH *points to photograph and holds up two fingers.*) Two! See? You got two kids. (*The* PRISONER *shakes his head and holds up three fingers.*) Three? No, you stupid raving imbecile! Two! (BAMFORTH *points again to the photograph.*) One and one's two! Dinky-doo-number two! (*The* PRISONER *holds up his hands to indicate a baby.*) What, another? Another one as well! Well, you crafty old devil! You're a bit fond of it, aren't you? You're a rotten old sex maniac, you are. You're as bad as Smudge. (BAMFORTH *returns the photographs to the* PRISONER, *who replaces them carefully in his wallet and returns it to his pocket.*) Let's see if you still know your lessons. Flingers up on blonce! (*The* PRISONER *complies.*) Dlop flingers! (*Again the* PRISONER *is happy to obey.*) Stroll on! See that! He got it right both times! He's almost human this one is!

MITCHEM. All right, Bamforth, jack it in!

JOHNSTONE. We should have done him when he first turned up.

MITCHEM (*crossing to* EVANS). Where have them two got to?

EVANS. No sign yet, Sarge.

> (MITCHEM *peers out of window.* BAMFORTH *takes out a packet of cigarettes and puts one in his mouth. He*

replaces the packet in his pocket and feels for a box of
matches as his glance falls on the PRISONER, *who is*
looking up at him. BAMFORTH *hesitates, then transfers*
the cigarette from his own mouth to the PRISONER'S.
He takes out another cigarette for himself. JOHNSTONE
rises and crosses to BAMFORTH. BAMFORTH *is still look-*
ing for a match as JOHNSTONE *takes out a box, strikes*
one and offers BAMFORTH *a light.*)

BAMFORTH. Ta. (JOHNSTONE *holds out the match for the*
PRISONER. *As the* PRISONER *leans across to get a light,*
JOHNSTONE *knocks the cigarette from his mouth with*
the back of his hand.) What's that in aid of!

JOHNSTONE. He gets permission first!

BAMFORTH. I gave him it!

JOHNSTONE. Since when have you been calling out the time!

BAMFORTH. I don't ask you before I give a bloke a fag!

JOHNSTONE. This one you do!

BAMFORTH. Who says!

JOHNSTONE. I do, lad! (*Making a sudden grab for the* PRI-
SONER *and attempting to tear open his breast pocket.*)
I'll fix his photos for the Herb as well!

MITCHEM (*turns*). Corporal Johnstone!

BAMFORTH (*drops the bayonet and clutches* JOHNSTONE *by*
his jacket lapels. He brings his knee up in JOHNSTONE'S
groin and, as JOHNSTONE *doubles foward,* BAMFORTH
cracks his forehead across the bridge of JOHNSTONE'S
nose). Have that!

MITCHEM (*crossing towards the fight*). Bamforth!
(BAMFORTH, *unheeding, strikes* JOHNSTONE *in the sto-*
mach and pushes him to the floor.)

JOHNSTONE (*pulling himself to his feet*). All right. You've
done it this time, Bamforth! You've shot your load.
As sure as God you'll get three years for that.

BAMFORTH (*picks up bayonet*). You try and make it stick.

MITCHEM. You're on a charge, Bamforth. You're under open
arrest.

BAMFORTH. He started it!

MITCHEM. Tell that to the C.O.

EVANS (*raising his rifle*). Sarge! There's someone coming
up the track!

MITCHEM (*crosses to window*). Whereabouts?

EVANS. Just coming through the trees.

> (JOHNSTONE *picks up his Sten and crosses to join* WHITAKER.)

MITCHEM. It's all right. It's Macleish and Smith. Cover them up the track.

JOHNSTONE (*aiming the Sten*). I've got them.

EVANS. Looks as if they're in a hurry over something.

> (*A pause before we hear* MACLEISH *and* SMITH *clatter up on to the veranda.* MITCHEM *opens the door and they enter the room. They lean against the wall exhausted.*)

MITCHEM. Anybody after you? (MACLEISH *shakes his head.*) What's up then?

EVANS. What's the hurry, Smudger boy? You look as if you've had the whole of the Japanese army on your tail.

SMITH (*out of breath*). We have . . . Near enough.

MITCHEM. Sit down a tick. (SMITH *and* MACLEISH *cross to the table and sit down.* MITCHEM *crosses to join them.*) Now, come on—give. Let's be having it.

MACLEISH (*regaining his breath*). They've broken through. In strength. There's hundreds of them moving down the main trail back.

MITCHEM. Go on.

SMITH. They must have come through our defence lines like a dose of salts. They're pouring down. Happy as a lot of sand boys. Not a mark on any one of them. Up front the whole damn shoot's collapsed.

MITCHEM. You weren't spotted?

MACLEISH (*shakes his head*). They're not even looking for anybody. They seem to know they've got this area to themselves. Smudge and myself got down in the long grass. They've got no scouts out. Nothing. Just strolling down the trail as if they owned the jungle . . .

MITCHEM. Do you think they'll find this place?

MACLEISH. Not yet a while. We watched about a company march past. There was a break then in the file. We managed to cover up the entrance of the trail up here.

SMITH. We stuffed it up with bits of branch and stuff.

MITCHEM. Good.

MACLEISH. The next batch came along as we were finishing. We patched up what we could and scooted back.

JOHNSTONE. So what happens now?

MITCHEM. It's put the kybosh on the journey back. We can't move out of here just yet, and that's a certainty.

MACLEISH. You never saw so many Japs. There must be, at least, a thousand of them now between ourselves and base. We're right behind their forward lines.

MITCHEM (*crosses downstage and turns*). Let's say, for now, they march without a stop. That brings them close up on the camp before tomorrow night. If they've got stuff up in the air to back them up—and if they don't know back at base they've broken through—the base mob gets wiped up.

MACLEISH. But they'll know by now the Japs are through.

MITCHEM. We can't count on that.

JOHNSTONE. If the main road's free, they'll have heavy transport loads of Nips chugging down before to-morrow.

MITCHEM. Let's hope the Engineers have sewn that up. They'll have it mined at least. No, this is the back way in. Cross country—and it's hard graft cutting trail—they'll have to do the lot on foot.

JOHNSTONE. So?

MITCHEM. So that means we can put the blocks on them. We get there first.

JOHNSTONE. You think the Japs are going to open ranks and let us pass?

MITCHEM. What's the time now? (*He glances at his watch.*) It'll be dark in just over an hour. We might make it then.

JOHNSTONE. And so you think we stand a chance at creeping through a regiment of ruddy Nips!

MITCHEM. What's your suggestion?

JOHNSTONE. We haven't got a chance.

MITCHEM. We've got no choice. We might make it in the dark and in that shrub. They'll be blundering about themselves. At least we know the way—we've done it coming up. It's all new ground to them. We might creep through.

JOHNSTONE (*indicating the* PRISONER). What? With him in tow?

MITCHEM (*glancing across at the* PRISONER). No . . . We're ditching him. Whitaker!

WHITAKER (*turning at window*). Sarge?

MITCHEM (*indicating set*). Come on. You'd better give it one more try.

WHITAKER. I don't think it'll do any good, Sarge. The battery's nigh on stone dead.

MITCHEM. Try it, lad! Don't argue. Relieve him, Smith.

(SMITH *crosses to take* WHITAKER'*s place at the window as* WHITAKER *crosses to table and sits at set. He switches on to 'transmit' and pauses.*)

MITCHEM. Come on, lad! Get on with it! We haven't time to mess about.

WHITAKER (*turning in his chair to speak to* MITCHEM). If there are any Japs near here switched to receive they'll get a fix on us.

MITCHEM. That can't be helped. Come on, come on!

WHITAKER (*putting on headphones and tuning in*). Blue Patrol to Red Leader . . . Blue Patrol to Red Leader . . . Are you receiving me . . . Are you receiving me . . . Come in Red Leader . . . Come in Red Leader . . . Over . . . (WHITAKER *switches to 'receive' and tunes in. We hear the crackle of interference.*) Nothing yet . . .

MITCHEM. Come in, Sammy son, come on . . .

WHITAKER (*adjusting tuning dial*). There's something here . . . (*The interference dies away and we hear the voice of the Japanese* RADIO OPERATOR.) It's the Jap transmitting. Same as before.

MITCHEM. Get off the ruddy line, you Nip!

(*The voice continues in Japanese for a few seconds and then stops. It continues in taunting broken English.*)

OPERATOR. Johnee! . . . Johnee! . . . British Johnee! We—you—come—to—get . . . We—you—come—to—get.

(WHITAKER *starts up in fear and* MITCHEM *pushes him back into his chair. The patrol turn and look at the* PRISONER. *The* PRISONER, *noting that all attention is*

*centred on himself, and feeling that he is expected to
entertain the patrol, raises his hands in the air and slowly
places them on his head. He smiles round blandly in
search of approbation.*)

Curtain

Run-out

We don't propose to tell you 'what happens next', as we
have a long extract from the play later on in this book (p. 183),
where the tragic outcome is revealed.

✕✕

LIVE LIKE PIGS

Lead-in

Three short scenes or extracts follow from *Live Like Pigs*,
John Arden's play about gipsies whom the authorities try
to settle into a council house.

The first shows the 'Housing Official' talking to (or trying
to talk to) two of the women, Rachel and Rosie, and Rosie's
child, Sally. The official finds the gipsies totally incomprehensible: they seem quite uninterested in the house they are
to live in, and clearly preferred the 'broken tramcar' they
used to live in before it was condemned. Trying to be kind,
but being in fact very clumsy, he says 'I wouldn't put pigs'
(in such a place), and this later on becomes a ground for a
quarrel with Rachel's man, Sailor, who has certainly heard
this phrase before. Meanwhile Sally, the child, has crept upstairs to play with the bathroom taps, which to her are a great
novelty—but has left the plug in the basin and flooded the
floor. Rachel is very suspicious of the Official but also genu-
inely seeks information—'When *can* we run water?'—and
can't understand, if the bathroom is theirs, why he has ticked
off Sally. The Official is relieved at the prospect of getting
away, but is interrupted by the arrival of Sailor and Col with
the household furniture on a barrow. A further row immediately develops and Sailor turns the Official out.

The second passage shows an attempt by a neighbour, Mrs
Jackson, to make friends with the newcomers, but the in-
comprehension is again total. Rachel has never heard such

talk as hers, and her attitude is immediately one of rejection and aggression.

The third passage shows the Sawneys' attitude of deep suspicion towards anything official, in this case two letters; they can scarcely read, and believe that the official respectable world will always do them down, so their instinct is always to burn any official communication. The Official has been sent to warn them that there have been complaints about the state of the house: no curtains, the garden untended and an increasing number of casual lodgers, including a menacing young man called Blackmouth and an old woman known as the Old Croaker with her dreadful daughter Daffodil. The police arrive looking for someone who stabbed a policeman the previous night. Daffodil accidentally or through stupidity gives Blackmouth away. The police and the Official go off together having warned Sawney to clear up the place and get rid of the lodgers.

Two general points may be made about these extracts. The first is that what they illustrate above all is a total lack of communication between the 'respectable' world, represented by the Official, Mrs Jackson, the Town Hall letters and the police on the one side, and the anarchic but fiercely loyal Sawneys on the other: the language used by each reflects their own set of attitudes, and they cannot meet at any point. The second general point is that Arden is exploring the formidable difficulty, if not impossibility, of embodying minority groups such as gipsies into any settled community. He keeps cool about the rights and wrongs: it is clear, for example, that Blackmouth is a psychotic criminal and Old Croaker more or less mad—yet one feels that his basic sympathy is with the Sawneys, who in their own way are free, as against the suffocating forces of conformism which are trying to remodel them in a standard image. What do *you* think?

ACTING NOTES

Sailor and Rachel are very tough and speak roughly, perhaps in a dialect; Rosie is a younger version. Sally is, from a standard point of view, a spoiled child with a high-pitched whine. Mrs Jackson is a typical amiable housewife, house-proud and smug. The Official should have an 'official' kind of voice—he's used to buttering people up and trying to be reasonable, but is quite out of his depth with the Sawneys. The little verses at the beginning of the scenes could be spoken, but are intended to be sung in a folk-song style, perhaps with a guitar or other accompaniment. The barrow can probably be mimed. Watery noises off stage would be amusing when Sally turns on the taps, and a box of some kind could serve as a gramophone, probably stolen. The Sawneys must be really vicious and menacing to the Official, and Daffodil is sarcastic at the expense of the police sergeant, who tries hard to keep his dignity.

SONG

O England was a free country
So free beyond a doubt
That if you had no food to eat
You were free to go without.

But if you want your freedom kept
You need to fight and strive
Or else they'll come and catch you, Jack,
And bind you up alive.

So rob their houses, tumble their girls,
Break their windows and all,
And scrawl your dirty words across
The whitewashed prison wall.

Interior. Evening.
The OFFICIAL *is discovered halfway up the stairs, discoursing on the house.* ROSIE *sits in the living room with her baby in a shawl and* RACHEL *stands in the hall. Both women have brought in several untidy bundles.*
OFFICIAL. And up the stairs we're into the bedrooms. There's the two bedrooms, one big, one small; and there's your bathroom off the landing. You didn't have a bathroom down on the caravan site, did you? Mrs Sawney! I say Mrs Sawney; aren't you coming up to look at your bathroom? (*He comes back down into the hall.*) Oh come on, missus, I've not got all day.

Blimey, you'd think I was showing you round a condemned cell or summat.

ROSIE. Did you say it was a bathroom?

OFFICIAL. God help us. Of course, love, I said it was a bathroom. (SALLY *has entered through the open front door*.)

SALLY. Bathroom? Is there water? Is there taps of water,
mister?

RACHEL (*slapping her*). You shut your noise, Sally.

ROSIE (*angry*). Don't you go knocking her, she's not yourn,
she's not yourn to go knocking her like that.
(SALLY *howls*.)

ROSIE. Shut your noise when you're told.
(ROSIE *slaps her*. SALLY *shuts up and then begins
stealthily climbing the stairs*.)

OFFICIAL. Now look here, missus, do you want to see upstairs or don't you?

RACHEL. Why? We've no choice, have we? You've put us to
live here. Why can't we take our own bloody time looking at the place? So what if we *don't* like it? We've got
no bloody choice.

OFFICIAL (*exasperated*). Eh God, I'm a reasonable man . . .
(*The baby cries and* ROSIE *rocks it and croons*.)

OFFICIAL. But where did you get all this fat nonsense from,
hey? 'No choice', 'put you to live here'—*who* put you
to live here?

RACHEL. You put us. Coppers put us—all the lot of narks.

OFFICIAL. Now, wait, wait. I'm not the police, I mean look
at me, Mrs Sawney, did you ever see a policeman my
shape of figure? All that's happened is: Your old place
down by the caravans has had to be condemned, well
I mean: rightly—I mean a broken tramcar with no
wheels no windows, I wouldn't put pigs—all the rain
coming in on you and all, why . . .

RACHEL. Our place, mister.

OFFICIAL. But *this* is your place. *This is* your place. You've
to pay rent, of course, it's not much, though. You'll
easy afford it; if not, you can go on the Assistance, you
see . . . Why it's a *good* house. It's only five years old
at most: I mean look at it . . .
(*There is the sound of running water from the bath-*

room into which SALLY *has slipped. The* OFFICIAL
turns angrily and hurries up the stairs.)

OFFICIAL. What's that? Sounds like running water. . . .
Where's that kid gone—God help us, in the bathroom.
Hey lovey, hey, little girly, hey hey, what do you think
you're playing at with them taps, water all over the
bloody floor.

(*He goes into the bathroom and* SALLY *comes running
out, down the stairs, and off through the front door.
The* OFFICIAL *turns the taps off and comes slowly down
himself.*)

OFFICIAL. I don't know. I don't know. A lovely house, I'd
call it. I've not got a house like this, you know. *I* have
to live in furnished lodgings, and like it.

(*There is a pause.*)

RACHEL. It's time Col was here with Sailor and the barrow.
Why don't he come?

ROSIE (*nervously to* OFFICIAL). Can we: can we—is
that . . . ?

OFFICIAL. What is it, missus?

ROSIE. Upstairs, you chased the kid off, she was only running water. Who's to tell us when we *can* run water?

OFFICIAL. What are you talking about? Nobody's to tell
you. It's your bathroom. You can use it when you
like.

ROSIE. Then what for do you chase the kid off? She was
only running water.

OFFICIAL. She's left the plug in the basin, it was all over
the floor.

ROSIE. She's not your kid to chase. She was just having her
play, that's all.

RACHEL. They ought to be here with the barrow. Wait all the
bloody evening.

OFFICIAL (*embarrassed*). Well, I'll have to be off to the
Town Hall. I've given you the keys, I've done my job,
and precious thanks I've got for it. (*He moves to the
door.*) Just a while, and you'll get settled all right, Mrs
Sawney. You know, you'll like living here. Honest, you
will.

(SALLY *runs in again.*)

SALLY (*very excited*). He's coming, Col's coming, Col's coming, Col, Col, Col's coming.
(*She dances up and down.* SAILOR *and* COL *come in through the front door pushing a home-made barrow consisting of a packing case mounted on pram wheels. It is loaded with a great pile of household junk, topped by a chamber pot and an old-fashioned horn gramophone. They also both carry bundles. We hear their voices before they appear, grumbling angrily.*)

SAILOR. Two men to pull the barrow, one man pulls the barrow, one man walks beside it, that's *his* way.

COL. Ah, hold your old gob, will you, I'm leading as much of the weight as you—

SAILOR. One man to pull it, one man to walk beside—it's the strong lad, he walks beside; the old man, he has to pull; that's *his* way. (*He sees the* OFFICIAL.) Who's this?

COL (*to the women*). All the road up from the back bottom of the hill, he's carrying-on. Why don't I smash his face for him? (*He sees the* OFFICIAL.) Who's this?

OFFICIAL. Mr Sawney? I'm from the Corporation, I've just been opening the house up for your good ladies and like showing them around. I think everything's in right order for you—if there's anything you want to know about—

SAWNEY. Want to know, is it? Do *you* know where we've been living, mister, until today, d'ye know *that*?

OFFICIAL. Yes, I know. Down the far side of the railway yard, on what they call the caravan site. No drains, no fresh water, no nothing.

SAILOR (*satirically*). Ye wouldn't keep pigs in it, hey?

RACHEL. That's what he said to *us*.

SAILOR. Oh hoho, he's the grand man to talk. And look at the grand palace he gives us. (*He goes up the stairs.*) Look at it. Lovely. Lovely . . . Mister!

OFFICIAL. Er, yes?

SAILOR (*calling sharply from the big bedroom*). Whose is this house?

OFFICIAL. Well, er—

SAILOR. Whose is it?

OFFICIAL. Well, you might say it's yours, now, Mr Sawney.

RACHEL. That's what he said to *us*.

SAILOR. Then that being so, mister, then that being so—I'll give ye one half minute to get off this ground.

COL (*violently*). Go on, you heard him, go on. Jump your bloody feet to t'other side o' that door.

OFFICIAL. Now just a moment, you can't do this sort of thing here—

COL. Are you going?

OFFICIAL. This is very silly of you, you know, this is very silly indeed . . .

(*He hurries out of the house as* COL *advances threateningly.*)

RACHEL (*shouting after him*). Calling us pigs, would you! How'd you like a real screaming sow to raven your paunch for you, hey?

COL. I'll show him pigs.

SAILOR. Has he gone?

COL. Aye, he's gone. Ought to have put the boot through him. I'll show him pigs.

SAILOR. Bring the dunnage into the house, Col. Here we are and here we've got to live. But we're keeping *them* out from us, every bloody one of them. (*He stands astride and terrible.*) They call me Sailor Sawney and no man slaps his natter at *me*. Rachel, Rosie, help Col carry the dunnage.

(COL *and the women bring in more possessions from outside, including a very battered pram into which* ROSIE *puts her baby and leaves it in the living room.*)

SALLY. Col told him, Col told him right proper. You told him proper, didn't you, Col?

COL. Get out the road, kid. Run away to Sailor.

(SALLY *creeps timidly upstairs and peeps at* SAILOR *in the bedroom.*)

SAILOR. Come away in, Sally, come away in, to Sailor.

SALLY. It's water in there. Taps of water. He chased me cos I run it. He did.

SAILOR. Never you mind for him, little daisy, little sparrow. You run it when you're minded. Our house, our taps of water.

(*He sings*)
> Oh when I was a strong young man
> I wandered on the sea
> And many were the ladies
> That called unto me:
> With golden hair and scaly tails
> And eyes of bright green
> So many were the mermaid girls
> That swam all in the stream.

(ii) MRS JACKSON (*very friendly*). Excuse me: it's Mrs Sawney, isn't it? The rent collector gave me your name, he said you were coming to live here, so I thought, well, I'd just pop round the door and have a word—like, it's your first day here, and why not be neighbourly, I thought, and give 'em a call? Eh, isn't it a lovely day?

RACHEL. Who are you?

MRS JACKSON. I live next door, you see, so I thought why not be neighbourly; like, it's such a lovely day. Jackson's the name. My husband, my husband he works for the Co-op you know; like, he's their agent, drives around the villages all day in his van to the local branches; just in the grocery he used to be, but he got made agent last year. By, he wor pleased, I can tell you. He's got his van, you see: he's like his own master now. . . . What do you think to the Housing Scheme?

RACHEL (*dourly*). Housing Scheme, is it?

MRS JACKSON. Well of course, I mean, we think it's lovely. We've been here nigh on two year. I'll tell you where we used to live—you know when you went past the Town Hall, down by the Catholic Church—all them little mucky streets—eh it wor terrible. But they moved us out, moved us all out and pulled the lot down. That's where they're building new Corporation Offices, you know, now. Isn't it lovely here, though? Wide streets, bits of garden, and all. Of course, it's a long way from the shops and there's only the one public. But my husband, he reckons that's a good thing. He says—

RACHEL. Oh go to hell, you and your fizzing husband.

MRS JACKSON (*stopped gasping in midstream*). I beg your pardon! . . .
  (SALLY *runs out of the Sawney House and stares at* MRS JACKSON.)

RACHEL. I says go to hell. You're not wanted here. Keep to your own garden, you like it so much.

SALLY. Mam, Mam, she's as fat as a pig, ent she?

SAILOR (*from indoors*). Rachel! Rachel!

RACHEL (*shouts back*). Oh so you're out of your bed at last! What d'you want then?

SAILOR (*appearing at an upper window*). Chase that bloody cow out o' here, and get me a sup o' tea. Well, move to it! (*He shuts the window.*)

RACHEL (*to* MRS JACKSON). Go on, get out of it.

MRS JACKSON. Well . . . Of all the—
  (RACHEL *goes into the house.*)

ROSIE (*wearily*). Why don't you folk leave us alone? We didn't come cos we wanted; but now we *are* here you ought to leave us be. (*To the baby*) It's time you had your dinner, Geordie. In we go, in we go, in we go to dinner.
  (ROSIE *goes in too.*)

SALLY. Pig, pig, pig pig, fat fat pig.

MRS JACKSON. Why, you little— (*She offers a blow to* SALLY, *but* SAILOR *indoors shouts again:*'RACHEL!' *and* MRS JACKSON *nervously lets her arm drop.*) I'll tell my husband of this. I never heard the like. (*She goes into her house.*)

SONG

It's whether you come or whether you go
Or whether you bide at home:
They're always right behind you, Jack,
And never leave you alone.

In your footsteps they will plant their feet
For every step you tread,
They trample on your shadow, Jack
They trample on your head.

Interior. Afternoon.

*The stage is empty. Two letters fall through the letterbox
    in the front door, and there is a pair of raps on the
    knocker.*

RACHEL (*from the kitchen*). What d'ye want then!
    (*She comes out of the kitchen, eating. She picks up the
    letters and looks at them dubiously.*)
SAILOR (*from the kitchen*). Who is it? What's he after?
RACHEL. It's more of them letters.
SAILOR. Oh?
    (*He appears in the kitchen doorway.* SALLY *runs out
    into the hall underneath his arm.*)
SALLY. Is it letters, is it? Who's sending us letters, eh? Eh?
    Eh?
RACHEL. Get out of it.
    (SAILOR *takes the letters and looks at them.* ROSIE
    comes out of the kitchen.)
ROSIE. Sally, come here.
SALLY. Who sends us letters, Mam?
ROSIE. I don't know, lovey. It's not so good, whoever it is.
    Now you bide quiet and don't make Sailor mad while
    he's thinking on what to do.
SAILOR. It's second lot this week.
RACHEL. Maybe we ought to open *these*, y'know.
SAILOR. Why?
RACHEL. I don't like to burn things always. Jocky Faa once
    tell'd me he burned a whole quid in a letter one time.
SAILOR. Aye, aye. But what a daft bloody trick that, put a
    quid in a letter. Am I opening these, or not?
RACHEL (*uneasily*). It'd be better, so.
SAILOR. All right then. Let's have a look. (*He opens the
    letters and looks at them uncomprehending.*) There's
    one is printed and there's this other is type-wrote. I don't
    like it. Read 'em. (*He hands the letters to* RACHEL.)
    What do they say?
RACHEL. This printed one. It's a form. For filling-in, see.
SAILOR. Then burn it. We've never had it.
RACHEL. Ach, I dunno. It's the National Insurance.
SAILOR. What about it? Those bastards'd chase ye from New-
    castle to Cornwall. They're worse nor the bloody
    Peelers.

RACHEL. There might be an Entitlement, though. Like, you and your bad leg.

SAILOR. Na na. I said burn it . . . What's the typewriting all about?

RACHEL. I can't make it clear yet. It's from the Corporation.

SAILOR (*in alarm*). Oh . . . It is, eh? That's not so good, neither. Go on, read it.

RACHEL. He says, 'Complaints relating to condition of—of aforesaid residence. And gardens appertaining.' Ach, all that it is—words.

ROSIE. They send these words at us under the door all the time. It's not right. What can *we* do when we get them? They put us, it's like a dog in a box, you can stick spikes through every corner at him and he's no place to turn at all.

(*There is a knock on the door. They look at one another. There is another knock.* RACHEL *opens the door. The* OFFICIAL *from the Housing Department comes in.*)

OFFICIAL. Good afternoon, Mrs Sawney . . . Mr Sawney . . . er, Mrs er . . . Hello love . . . I dare say, you remember me, eh? aye, well . . . You had a letter last week from the Department, didn't you? And you should have had another today. Aye there it is, you've got it, I can see. Have you read it yet?

RACHEL. We've opened it. So what?

OFFICIAL (*embarrassed*). It's a bit awkward for me, is this, missus : you see, after all, I'm only the bottle-washer in the department—I mean.

SAILOR. What have you come for, mister?

OFFICIAL. The fact is, Mr Sawney, you've hardly been in this house two month, have you? And it's in a shocking state. I mean, look at it . . . Eh dear. There's been complaints, that's all. And what are we going to do about it, eh?

SAILOR. Aye. What *are* we going to do about it?

OFFICIAL. Well. My instructions, Mr Sawney, are to tell you that unless something *is* done, steps will be taken, Mr Sawney, by the Department, to put you out; and that's that. I'm sorry. There it is.

SAILOR. And where will we go? The institution, isn't it?

Cos you've burnt the tram-car we used to live in. We can't go on the road, we've two little kids with us. We've not got money for a wagon. So what do we do?

OFFICIAL. If you take my advice, you'll clean the house. Hang some curtains up. Tidy the garden. And get rid of your lodgers.

RACHEL. We ain't got no lodgers.

OFFICIAL. No?

RACHEL. No.

(*She has moved round behind him till she is standing between him and the closed front door. The others close in on him a little. He looks round nervously. A car is heard driving up outside.*)

OFFICIAL. It's no use you trying to intimidate me. I told you before, *I'm* not responsible. If you lot get evicted, you've only yourselves to thank—

(*There is a sharp double knock on the door. They look at one another.*)

OFFICIAL. Aren't you going to see who it is?

(*The knock is repeated, very loudly, and a voice shouts:* 'Police!' *The* POLICE SERGEANT *opens the door and comes in abruptly.*)

SERGEANT. You're very ready to answer, aren't you? Sawney's house?

SAILOR. It is.

SERGEANT. Are you Sawney?

(SAILOR *shrugs.*)

SERGEANT. Proper mucky hole you've got here, and all . . . (*He sees the* OFFICIAL.) Who are you?

OFFICIAL. Oh I'm from the Town Hall, Officer. Housing Department.

SERGEANT. Ah . . . Sawneys, eh? You were down on the old caravan site, weren't you, before they sorted you out?

SAILOR. We were.

SERGEANT. They were none too soon in shifting you, neither. (*He is wandering about the ground floor of the house, looking at everything, and throwing his comments over his shoulder at them.*) There was a Police Constable wounded last night. At approximately twelve forty-five a.m. Near the junction of Market Hill and

Princess Adelaide Street. Know anything about it? Nasty dark place, that, middle of the night. So, you see, he couldn't see who stabbed him. Could he?

SAILOR. It wasn't none of us, now.

SERGEANT. Not? You see, our lad couldn't see who stabbed him, but he could hear. It was a man, probably drunk, shouting out the name Sawney. Shouting out your name. There aren't many Sawneys, are there, in this town; specially ones as go stabbing policemen. Come on, then. Who was it?

SAILOR. It wasn't none of us.

ROSIE. We was all in the house, middle of the night. *You* can't prove no different. No.

SERGEANT. You know who did it. I been fifteen year at this game. You can't play it clever with *me*, so don't think you can. Very well. We'll try it another way. (*He picks up the gramophone from the living room floor.*) Where did you get this?

RACHEL. That's mine. I bought it fair. *You* can't prove no different.

SERGEANT. Not? You've got a receipt for it, have you?

RACHEL (*taken aback*). A what?

SERGEANT. A receipt. I'll bet you haven't. Now an instrument like this seems to me an unlikely item for folk in your sort of circumstances to possess. Don't it? So I am now going to Take you In—suspected In Possession of Stolen Property. Come on. And you—Sawney—you can come too. You live with her, don't you? Aiding and Abetting. Come on.

SAILOR. Wait a minute; you can't go taking us like this—

SERGEANT. Not? Who are you to tell me what I can do? (*He puts his whistle to his mouth.*)

(DAFFODIL *comes in through the kitchen. When she sees the* SERGEANT *she recoils in terror.*)

SERGEANT (*springing at her*). And who are *you*, young lady? ... Well? Another Sawney? Are you?

RACHEL. She's with us. So?

SERGEANT (*pinning* DAFFODIL *in a corner*). What's your name? ... Eh? What? Can't hear you!

DAFFODIL. What—what—

E

SERGEANT. Now then. *You* tell me. Who knifed the Constable last night down Adelaide Street, shouting the
name of Sawney?

DAFFODIL. Why Blackmouth did. Least, I suppose, he did—

SERGEANT. Who's Blackmouth?

DAFFODIL (*now recovering herself*). Oh don't you know who
Blackmouth is? Ooh, you want to go for *him*, Captain.
He'll give you promotion, he will!

SERGEANT. Blackmouth? . . . *I* know. Wait a moment . . .
(*He takes a notebook out and thumbs through the
pages*.) Blackmouth . . . Aha! What about this: William
Lewis, otherwise known as Blackmouth. Escaped from
Strangeways Gaol, thirteenth of last month, after severe
assault upon Prison Officer. Age twenty-eight, five foot
ten tall, black hair, swarthy features, general gipsy-like
appearance. That the lad, is it?

(DAFFODIL *nods and smiles*.)

SERGEANT. Where is he?

DAFFODIL. Sheffield.

SERGEANT. How do you know?

DAFFODIL. He said he wor going. He went, see. Last night.
You catch him, Captain. Ah.

SERGEANT. All right, I will. (*He goes to the door*.) Now
you behave yourselves. I'm warning.

OFFICIAL. Er—Officer. I wonder could you give me a lift to
the Town Hall, if you're going that way.

SERGEANT. Oh, I don't mind, sir. I'll take you as far as the
Station, anyroad . . . I'm warning. (*He goes out*.)

OFFICIAL. And bear in mind what *I* said, too. And *don't*
let's be finding you've got lodgers here. I know. (*He
goes out with a meaning look at* DAFFODIL.)

Run-out

These three extracts show us a confrontation between different worlds, and, as we have said, there is no communication
or comprehension between them; this can be brought out in
their speech and movement. The play raises, bitterly and
perhaps unanswerably, the question of what attitude those
of us—the majority—who live in a settled society and within
a structure of law and tradition, can take to the unknown,

wild, untameable world of gipsies, tramps, wanderers, and in more recent times, the people we call 'drop-outs'. Arden explores this difficult question with great power.

✖✖✖

ROOTS

Lead-in
Wesker's famous play *Roots* is part of a trilogy—a group of three plays which follows the fortunes of the Kahn family, East-End Jews who have immigrated to England from Poland. The first play, *Chicken Soup with Barley*, is set in the East End of London, and is largely about the reactions of the family to the growing fascist movement in the late nineteen-thirties which endangered all Jews there and many others: it is well worth reading, though perhaps not so successful on the whole as *Roots*. In this play the only member of the Kahn family involved is a son of the family called Ronnie, and he never actually appears. A young girl called Beatie Bryant has met him while they were both working in the kitchens of a hotel in Norwich and she has fallen in love with him and gone to London to live with him. Now she is on a visit to her parents in a Norfolk village, and Ronnie, whom she expects to marry, is to visit her and her family, as you will see in the second extract.

The first extract tells the story of the first day of Beatie's visit to her parents (she has previously been visiting her sister a short distance away). Her parents, Mr and Mrs Bryant, have quarrelled, and her mother is refusing to speak to her father. Beatie is going to have a bath and as the cottage has neither bathroom nor hot running water, the copper has been lit to heat the water.

The main point of this passage is that Beatie is trying desperately to communicate with her mother, whose conversation tends to be restricted to village gossip and tales which Beatie has already heard many times. Mrs Bryant, it appears, does little thinking, and has been shown in the previous scene as listening all day long only to the shoddiest pop music very loud on the radio. Here Beatie tries very hard to introduce her to the joys of listening to serious, or at least more serious, music; she has picked up this sort of interest from her association with Ronnie—indeed, she is continually quoting him, directly or obliquely. From Ronnie she has learned something about intellectual and cultural interests, though these don't yet go very deep—and above all she has learned the joys of talking on a variety of subjects. This is what she wants to 'teach' her mother, above all. The first extract which follows shows her succeeding in finding a moment of unity with her mother as she dances after her bath to the music and her mother shares her happiness.

In the second extract the whole of the Bryant family is assembled to greet Beatie's fiancé on his first visit to her village. Beatie is excited at the prospect of Ronnie's arrival and the extract opens with her challenge to her mother for passing 'snap judgements' without discussing and considering them properly. Mr Bryant has had his wages reduced, but the older Bryants regard such a matter as private, and refuse to discuss the problem with the rest of the family. The other people present need only be briefly mentioned; they are Jenny, Beatie's sister and her husband Jimmy, a motor mechanic, and Frankie, her brother, a farm worker, with his wife Pearl. Beatie tries to get them really talking by setting them a 'moral problem'. As she shows rising excitement and quotes Ronnie at length the postman brings a letter which announces that Ronnie has funked the visit and 'ditched' Beatie, convinced that he has made no real impression in Beatie's life or beliefs and that their marriage could never be successful. He refers to her in his letter as stubborn, and Mrs Bryant suddenly realizes that the attacks her daughter has been making on *her* are just as applicable to Beatie herself. There is a violent quarrel when Mrs Bryant shows that she can't help Beatie and says triumphantly that she is in fact exactly like her mother, with all her limitations—'the apple don't fall far from the tree'—or, as we might say, 'like mother, like daughter'. But the play ends with a triumph in spite of this and the non-arrival of Ronnie; because Beatie finds that she *can* talk, on her own, without merely quoting Ronnie and this is what he has given her, even if the relationship has ended. The irony is that she is talking to herself—

or rather to us in the audience—while the rest of the family, who will never change, tuck into the feast prepared in Ronnie's honour. Beatie is 'articulate at last'. It is a splendid ending to the play, and well worth a lot of discussion.

ACTING NOTES

The key character in both extracts is obviously Beatie. She must be lively, energetic and positive—she is twenty-two and, basically, still a country girl. Mrs Bryant is in her fifties and her husband is a bent old man who says little. Frank is friendly and good-tempered, Jimmy a pleasant but stubborn man in his thirties; Jenny is described as plump and cheerful. A main problem for people who don't live in East Anglia is the speech, which reflects very exactly, in its rhythms and structure as well as vowel-sounds and word-choice, the dialect of Norfolk; my own pupils do this splendidly as they live in Suffolk—and though there are differences between Suffolk and Norfolk they are not very audible to people from outside the area. But Wesker writes it in a helpful way and if you read it aloud carefully and fairly slowly you will certainly get some of the right effect. The pauses, when no one says anything and they just think, are important in the play and common in real life, perhaps especially in East Anglia.

Properties are simple and clothing hardly matters, though the Bryants would be in their best clothing for the party in the second extract. A gramophone or tape-recorder will be needed in the first half, and Beatie's 'bath' can take place behind a curtain or a cupboard door. For the second extract a table and chairs with something to represent food ('a large spread') will be needed, and a parcel and letter for the postman to bring.

Lunch has been eaten, MR BRYANT *is sitting at the table rolling himself a cigarette.* MRS BRYANT *is collecting the dishes and taking them to a sink to wash up.* BEATIE *is taking things off the table and putting them into the larder—jars of sauce, plates of sliced bread and cakes, butter, sugar, condiments, and bowl of tinned fruit.*

MRS BRYANT (*to* BEATIE). Ask him what he want for his tea.

MR BRYANT. She don't ever ask me before, what she wanna ask me now for?

MRS BRYANT. Tell him it's his stomach I'm thinking about—

I don't want him complaining to me about the food I
cook.

MR BRYANT. Tell her it's no matters to me—I ent got no pain
now besides.

BEATIE. Mother, is that water ready for my bath?

MRS BRYANT. Where you hevin' it?

BEATIE. In the kitchen of course.

MRS BRYANT. Blust gal, you can't bath in this kitchen during
the day, what if someone call at the door?

BEATIE. Put up the curtain then, I shan't be no more'n ten
minutes.

MR BRYANT. 'Sides, who want to se her in her dickey suit.

BEATIE. I know men as 'ould pay to see me in my dickey suit.
(*Posing her plump outline.*) Don't you think I got a
nice dickey suit?
(MR BRYANT *makes a dive and pinches her bottom.*)
Ow! Stoppit Bryants, stoppit!
(*He persists.*)
Daddy, stop it now!

MRS BRYANT. Tell him he can go as soon as he like, I want
your bath over and done with.

BEATIE. Oh Mother, stop this nonsense do. If you want to
tell him something tell him—not me.

MRS BRYANT. *I* don't want to speak to him, hell if I do.

BEATIE. Father, get the bath in for me please. Mother,
where's them curtains.
(MR BRYANT *goes off to fetch a long tin bath—wide at
one end, narrow at the other—while* MRS BRYANT *leaves
washing up to fish out some curtains which she hangs
from one wall to another concealing thus a corner of the
kitchen. Anything that is in the way is removed.* BEATTIE
*meanwhile brings out a change of underwear, her
dressing-gown, the new frock, some soap, powder, and
towel. These she lays within easy reach of the curtain.*)

BEATIE. I'm gonna wear my new dress and go across the
fields to see Frankie and Pearl.

MRS BRYANT. Frankie won't be there, what you on about?
He'll be gettin' the harvest in.

BEATIE. You makin' anything for the harvest festival?

MR BRYANT (*entering with bath, places it behind curtain*).

Your mother don't ever do anything for the harvest festival—don't you know that by now.

BEATIE. Get you to work father Bryant. I'm gonna plunge
in water and I'll make a splash.

MRS BRYANT. Tell him we've got kippers for tea and if he
don' want none let him say so now.

BEATIE. She says it's kippers for tea.

MR BRYANT. Tell her I'll eat kippers. (*Goes off, collecting
bike on the way.*)

BEATIE. He says he'll eat kippers. Right now, Mother, you
get cold water an' I'll pour the hot.
(*Each now picks up a bucket.* MRS BRYANT *goes off out
to collect the cold water and* BEATIE *plunges bucket
into boiler to retrieve hot water. The bath is prepared
with much childlike glee.* BEATIE *loves her creature
comforts and does with unabashed, almost animal, enthusiasm that which she enjoys. When the bath is prepared,* BEATIE *slips behind the curtain to undress and
enter.*)

MRS BRYANT. You hear about Jimmy Skelton? They say
he've bin arrested for accosting some man in the
village.

BEATIE. Jimmy Skelton what own the pub?

MRS BRYANT. That's him. I know all about Jimmy Skelton
though. He were a young boy when I were a young girl.
I always partner him at whist drives. He's been to law
before you know. Yes! An' he won the day too! Won
the day he did. I don't take notice though, him and me
gets on all right. What do Ronnie's mother do with her
time?

BEATIE. She've got a sick husband to look after.

MRS BRYANT. She an educated woman?

BEATIE. Educated? No. She's a foreigner. Nor ent Ronnie
educated neither. He's an intellectual, failed all his
exams. They read and things.

MRS BRYANT. Oh, they don't do nothing then?

BEATIE. Do nothing? I'll tell you what Ronnie do, he work
till all hours in a hot ole kitchen. An' he teach kids in a
club to act and jive and such. And he don't stop at
week-ends either 'cos then there's political meetings and

such and I get breathless trying to keep up wi' him. OOOhh, Mother it's hot. . . .

MRS BRYANT. I'll get you some cold then.

BEATIE. No—ooh—it's lovely. The water's so soft Mother.

MRS BRYANT. Yerp.

BEATIE. It's so soft and smooth. I'm in.

MRS BRYANT. Don't you stay in too long gal. There go the twenty-minutes-past-one bus.

BEATIE. Oh Mother, me bath cubes. I forgot me bath cubes. In the little case by me pick-up.

(MRS BRYANT *goes to find bath cubes and hands them to* BEATIE.)

MRS BRYANT (*continuing her work*). I shall never forget when I furse heard on it. I was in the village and I was talking to Reggie Fowler. I say to him, there've bin a lot o' talk about Jimmy ent there? Disgustin', I say. Still, there's somebody wanna make some easy money, you'd expect that in a village wouldn't you? Yes, I say to him, a lot of talk. An' he stood there, an' he were a-lookin' at me an' a-lookin' as I were a-talkin' and then he say, Mrs, he say, I were one o' the victims! Well, you could've hit me over the head wi' a hammer. I was one o' the victims, he say.

BEATIE. Mother, these bath cubes smell beautiful. I could stay here all day.

MRS BRYANT. Still, Jimmy's a good fellow with it all—do anything for you. I partner him at whist drives; he bin had up scores o' times though.

BEATIE. Mother, what we gonna make Ronnie when he come?

MRS BRYANT. Well, what do he like?

BEATIE. He like trifle and he like steak and kidney pie.

MRS BRYANT. We'll make that then. So long as he don't complain o' the guts ache. Frankie hev it too sometimes and Jenny's husband James.

BEATIE. Know why? You all eat too much. The Londoners think we live a healthy life but they don't know we stuff ourselves silly till our guts ache. Look at that lunch we had. Lamb chops, spuds, runner beans and three Yorkshire puddings.

MRS BRYANT. But you know what's wrong wi' Jimmy Beales? It's indigestion. He eat too fast.

BEATIE. What the hell's indigestion doin' a'tween his shoulder blades?

MRS BRYANT. 'Cos some people get it so bad it go right through their stomach to the back.

BEATIE. You don't get indigestion in the back Mother, what you on about?

MRS BRYANT. Don't you tell me gal, I hed it!

BEATIE. Owee! The soap's in me eyes—Mother, towel, the towel, quickly the towel!

(MRS BRYANT *hands in towel to* BEATIE. *The washing up is probably done by now, so* MRS BRYANT *sits in a chair, legs apart and arms folded, thinking what else to say.*)

MRS BRYANT. You heard that Ma Buckley hev been taken to Mental Hospital in Norwich? Poor ole dear. If there's one thing I can' abide that's mental cases. They frighten me—they do. Can't face 'em. I'd sooner follow a man to a churchyard than the mental hospital. That's a terrible thing to see a person lose their reason—that 'tis. Well, I tell you what, down where I used to live, down the other side of the Hall, years ago we moved in next to an old woman. I only had Jenny and Frank then—an' this woman she were the sweetest of people. We used to talk and do errands for each other—Oh she was a sweet ole dear. And then one afternoon I was going out to get my washin' in and I saw her. She was standin' in a tub o' water up to her neck. She was! Up to her neck. An' her eyes had that glazed, wonderin' look and she stared straight at me she did. Straight at me. Well, do you know what? I was struck *dumb*. I was *struck* dumb wi' shock. What wi' her bein' so nice all this while, the sudden comin' on her like that in the tub fair upset me. It did! And people tell me afterwards that she's bin goin' in an' out o' hospital for years. Blust, that scare me. That scare me so much she nearly took me round the bend wi' her.

(BEATIE *appears from behind the curtain in her dress-ing-gown, a towel round her head.*)

BEATIE. There! I'm gonna hev a bath every day when I'm
married.
(BEATIE *starts rubbing her hair with towel and fiddles
with radio. She finds a programme playing Mendels-
sohn's Fourth Symphony, the slow movement, and
stands before the mirror, listening and rubbing.*)

BEATIE (*looking at her reflection*). Isn't your nose a funny
thing, and your ears. And your arms and legs, aren't they
funny things—sticking out of a lump.

MRS BRYANT (*switching off radio*). Turn that squit off!

BEATIE (*turning on her mother violently*). *Mother!* I could
kill you when you do that. No wonder I don't know
anything about anything. You give me nothing that was
worthwhile, nothing. I never knowed anything about
the news because you always switched off after the head-
lines. I never read any good books 'cos there was never
any in the house. I never heard nothing but dance music
because you always turned off the classics. I can't even
speak English proper because you never talked about
anything important.

MRS BRYANT. What's gotten into you now gal?

BEATIE. God in heaven Mother, you live in the country but
you got no—no—no majesty. You spend your time
among green fields, you grow flowers and you breathe
fresh air and you got no majesty. Your mind's cluttered
up with nothing and you shut out the world. What kind
of a life did you give me?

MRS BRYANT. Blust gal, I weren't no teacher.

BEATIE. But you hindered. You didn't open one door for
me. Even *his* mother cared more for me than what you
did. Beatie, she say, Beatie, why don't you take up evening classes and learn something other than waitressing.
Yes, she say, you won't ever regret learnin' things. But
did you care what job I took up or whether I learned
things? You didn't even think it was necessary.

MRS BRYANT. I fed you. I clothed you. I took you out to the
sea. What more d'you want. We're only country folk
you know. We ent got no big things here you know.

BEATIE. Squit! Squit! It makes no difference country or
town. *All* the town girls I ever worked with were just

like me. It makes no difference country or town—that's
squit. Do you know when I used to work at the holiday
camp and I sat down with the other girls to write a letter
we used to sit and discuss what we wrote about. An'
we all agreed, all on us, that we started: 'Just a few
lines to let you know', and then we get on to the weather
and then we get stuck so we write about each other and
after a page an' half of big scrawl end up: 'Hoping
this finds you as well as it leaves me.' There! We
couldn't say any more. Thousands of things happening
at this holiday camp and we couldn't find words for
them. All of us the same. Hundreds of girls and one
day we're gonna be mothers, and you *still* talk to me of
Jimmy Skelton and the ole woman in the tub. Do you
know I've heard that story a dozen times. A dozen
times. Can't you hear yourself Mother? Jesus, how can
I bring Ronnie to this house.

MRS BRYANT. Blust gal, if Ronnie don't like us then he—

BEATIE. Oh, he'll like you all right. He like most people.
He'd've liked ole Stan Mann. Ole Stan Mann would've
understood everything Ronnie talk about. Blust! That
man liked livin'. Besides, Ronnie says it's too late for
the old 'uns to learn. But he says it's up to us young
'uns. And them of us that know hev got to take them of
us as don't know and bloody well teach them.

MRS BRYANT. I bet he hev a hard time changing you gal!

BEATIE. He's *not* trying to change me Mother. You can't
change people, he say, you can only give them some love
and hope they'll take it. And that's what he's tryin' to
do with me and I'm tryin' to understand—do you see
that Mother?

MRS BRYANT. I don't see what that's got to do with music
though.

BEATIE. Oh my God! (*Suddenly*) I'll show you. (*Goes off
to front room to collect pick-up and a record.*) Now
sit you down gal and I'll show you. Don't start iron-
ing or reading or nothing, just sit there and be prepared
to learn something. (*Appears with pick-up and switches
on.*) You aren't too old, just you sit and listen. That's
the trouble you see, we ent ever prepared to learn any-

thing, we close our minds the minute anything unfamiliar appear. *I* could never listen to music. I used to like some on it but then I'd lose patience, I'd go to bed in the middle of a symphony, or my mind would wander 'cos the music didn't mean anything to me so I'd go to bed or start talking. 'Sit back woman', he'd say, 'listen to it. Let it happen to you and you'll grow as big as the music itself'.

MRS BRYANT. Blust he talk like a book.

BEATIE. An' sometimes he talk as though you didn't know where the moon or the stars was. (BEATIE *puts on record of Bizet's L'Arlésienne Suite.*) Now listen. This is a simple piece of music, it's not highbrow but it's full of living. You want to dance to it. And that's what he say socialism is. 'Christ', he say. 'Socialism isn't talking all the time, it's living, it's singing, it's dancing, it's being interested in what go on around you, it's being concerned about people and the world'. Listen Mother. (*She becomes breathless and excited.*) Listen to it. It's simple isn't it? Can you call that squit?

MRS BRYANT. I don't say it's all squit.

BEATIE. You don't have to frown because it's alive.

MRS BRYANT. No, not all on it's squit.

BEATIE. See the way the other tune comes in? Hear it? Two simple tunes, one after the other.

MRS BRYANT. I aren't saying it's all squit.

BEATIE. And now listen, listen, it goes together, the two tunes together, they knit, they're perfect. Don't it make you want to dance? (*She begins to dance a mixture of a cossack dance and a sailor's hornpipe.*) (*The music becomes fast and her spirits are young and high.*) Listen to that Mother. Is it difficult? Is it squit? It's light. It make me feel light and confident and happy. God, Mother, we could all be so much more happy and alive. Wheeeee. . . .

(BEATIE *claps her hands and dances on and her* MOTHER *smiles and claps her hands and*—)

The Curtain Falls

(ii) FRANK (*reading the paper*). I see that boy what assaulted the ole woman in London got six years.

MRS BRYANT. Blust! He need to! I'd've given him six years and a bit more. Bloody ole hooligans. Do you give me a chance to pass sentence and I'd soon clear the streets of crime, that I would! Yes, that I would.

BEATIE (*springing into activity*). All right Mother—we'll give you a chance. (*Grabs Jimmy's hat and umbrella. Places hat on* MOTHER'S *head and umbrella in her arms.*) There you are, you're a judge. Now sum up and pass judgement.

MRS BRYANT. I'd put him in prison for life.

FRANK. You gotta sum up though. Blust, you just can't stick a man in prison and say nothing.

MRS BRYANT. Good-bye, I'd say.

BEATIE. Come on Mother, speak up. You sit there and you say you'd clear the streets o' crime an' I hear you pass judgement all the time, now you do it in the proper way. Anybody can say 'go to prison', but *you* want to be a judge. Well, you show a judge's understanding. Talk! Come on Mother, talk!

(*Everyone leans forward eagerly to hear* MOTHER *talk. She looks startled and speechless.*)

MRS BRYANT. Well I—I—yes I—well I— Oh, don't be so soft.

FRANK. The mighty head is silent.

BEATIE. Well yes, she would be wouldn't she.

MRS BRYANT. What do you mean, I would be? You don't expect me to *know* what they say in courts do you? I aren't no judge.

BEATIE. Then why do you sit and pass judgement on people? If someone do something wrong you don't stop and think why. No discussin', no questions, just (*snap of fingers*)—off with his head. I mean look at Father getting less money. I don't see the family sittin' together and discussin' it. It's a problem! But which of you said it concerns you?

MRS BRYANT. Nor don't it concern them. I aren't hevin' people mix in my matters.

BEATIE. But they aren't just people—they're your family for hell's sake!

MRS BRYANT. No matters, I aren't hevin' it!

BEATIE. But Mother I—

MRS BRYANT. Now shut you up Beatie Bryant and leave it alone. I shall talk when I hev to and I never shall do, so there!

BEATIE. You're so stubborn.

MRS BRYANT. So you keep saying.

(MR BRYANT *enters, he is clean and dressed in blue pin-striped suit.*)

MR BRYANT. You brewed up yit?

MRS BRYANT (*jumping up and going to kitchen*). Oh hell, yes—I forgot the tea look.

MR BRYANT. Well, now we're all waitin' on him.

JENNY. Don't look as if Susie's comin'.

BEATIE. Stubborn cow!

(*Silence.*)

JENNY. Hev you seen Susie's television set yet?

BEATIE. I seen it.

FRANK. Did you know also that when they first had it they took it up to bed wi' them and lay in bed wi' a dish of chocolate biscuits?

PEARL. But now they don't bother—they say they've had it a year now and all the old programmes they saw in the beginning they're seein' again.

MRS BRYANT (*entering with tea*). Brew's up!

BEATIE. Oh, for Christ's sake let's stop gossiping.

PEARL. I aren't gossiping. I'm making an intelligent observation about the state of television, now then.

MR BRYANT. What's up wi' you now?

BEATIE. You weren't doin' nothin' o' the sort—you was gossiping.

PEARL. Well, that's a heap sight better'n quotin' all the time.

BEATIE. I don't quote all the time, I just tell you what Ronnie say.

FRANK. Take it easy gal—he's comin' soon—don't need to go all jumpin' an' frantic.

BEATIE. Listen! Let me set you a problem.

JIMMY. Here we go.

BEATIE. While we're waitin' for him I'll set you a moral problem. You know what a moral problem is? It's a problem about right and wrong. I'll get you buggers thinking if it's the last thing I do. Now listen. There are four huts—

FRANK. What?

BEATIE. Huts. You know—them little things you live in. Now there are two huts on one side of a stream and two huts on the other side. On one side live a girl in one hut and a wise man in the other. On the other side live Tom in one hut and Archie in the other. Also there's a ferryman what run a boat across the river. Now —listen, concentrate—the girl loves Archie but Archie don't love the girl. And Tom loves the girl but the girl don't go much on Tom.

JIMMY. Poor bugger.

BEATIE. One day the girl hears that Archie—who don't love her, remember—is going to America, so she decides to try once more to persuade him to take her with him. So listen what she do. She go to the ferryman and ask him to take her across. The ferryman say, I will, but you must take off all your clothes.

MRS BRYANT. Well, whatever do he wanna ask that for?

BEATIE. It don't matter why—he do! Now the girl doesn't know what to do so she ask the wise man for advice, and he say, you must do what you think best.

FRANK. Well that weren't much advice was it!

BEATIE. No matters—he give it. So the girl thinks about it and being so in love she decides to strip.

PEARL. Oh I say!

MR BRYANT. Well, this is a rum ole story ent it?

BEATIE. Shut up Father and listen. Now, er—where was I?

MR BRYANT. She was strippin'.

BEATIE. Oh yes! So, the girl strips and the ferryman takes her over—he don't touch her or nothing—just takes her over and she rushes to Archie's hut to implore him to take her with him and to declare her love again. Now Archie promises to take her with him and so she sleeps with him the night. But when she wake up in the morning he've gone. She's left alone. So she go across to Tom and explain her plight and ask for help. But soon ever he knowed what she've done, he chuck her out see? So there she is. Poor little gal. Left alone with no clothes

and no friends and no hope of staying alive. Now—
this is the question, think about it, don't answer quick
—who is the person most responsible for her plight?

JIMMY. Well, can't she get back?

BEATIE. No, she can't do anything. She's finished. She've
hed it! Now, who's to blame?
(*There is a general air of thought for the moment and*
BEATIE *looks triumphant and pleased with herself.*)

MRS BRYANT. Be you a'drinkin' on your tea look. Don't you
worry about no naked gals. The gal won't get cold but
the tea will.

PEARL. Well I say the girl's most responsible.

BEATIE. Why?

PEARL. Well, she made the choice didn't she?

FRANK. Yes, but the old ferryman made her take off her
clothes.

PEARL. But she didn't hev to.

FRANK. Blust woman, she were in love!

BEATIE. Good ole Frank.

JENNY. Hell if I know.

BEATIE. Jimmy?

JIMMY. Don't as me gal—I follow decisions, I aren't
makin' none.

BEATIE. Father?

MR BRYANT. I don't know what you're on about.

BEATIE. Mother?

MRS BRYANT. Drink you your tea gal—never you mind what
I think.
(*This is what they're waiting for.*)

PEARL. Well—what do Ronnie say?

BEATIE. He say the gal is responsible only for makin' the
decision to strip off and go across and that she do that
because she's in love. After that she's the victim of two
phoney men—one who don't love her but take advantage of her and one who say he love her but don't love
her enough to help her, and that the man who say he
love her but don't do nothin' to help her is most responsible because he were the last one she could turn to.

JENNY. He've got it all worked out then!

BEATIE (*jumping on a chair she thrusts her fists into the air like* RONNIE *and glories in what is the beginning of an hysterical outburst of his quotes*). 'No one do that bad that you can't forgive them.'

PEARL. He's sure of himself then?

BEATIE. 'We can't be sure of everything but certain basic things we must be sure about or we'll die.'

FRANK. He think everyone is gonna listen then?

BEATIE. 'People *must* listen. It's no good talking to the converted. *Everyone* must argue and think or they will stagnate and rot and the rot will spread.'

JENNY. Hark at that then.

BEATIE (*her strange excitement grows; she has a quote for everything*). 'If wanting the best things in life means being a snob then glory hallelujah I'm a snob. But I'm not a snob Beatie, I just believe in human dignity and tolerance and co-operation and equality and—'

JIMMY (*jumping up in terror*). He's a communist!

BEATIE. 'I'm a socialist!'

(*There is a knock on the front door.*)

BEATIE (*jumping down joyously as though her excited quotes have been leading to this one moment*). He's here, he's here! (*But at the door it is the* POSTMAN, *from whom she takes a letter and a parcel*). Oh, the silly fool, the fool. Trust him to write a letter on the day he's coming. Parcel for you Mother.

PEARL. Oh that'll be your dress from the club.

MRS BRYANT. What dress is this then? I didn't ask for no dress from the club.

PEARL. Yes you did, you did ask me, didn't she ask me Frank? Why, we were looking through the book together Mother.

MRS BRYANT. No matters what we was doin' together I aren't hevin' it.

PEARL. But Mother you distinctly—

MRS BRYANT. I aren't hevin' it so there now!

(BEATIE *has read the letter—the contents stun her. She cannot move. She stares round speechlessly at everyone.*)

MRS BRYANT. Well, what's the matter wi' you gal? Let's have a read. (*Takes letter and reads contents in a dead flat but loud voice—as though it were a proclamation*) 'My dear Beatie. It wouldn't really work would it? My ideas about handing on a new kind of life to people are quite useless and romantic if I'm really honest. If I were a healthy human being it might have been all right but most of us intellectuals are pretty sick and neurotic—as you have often observed—and we couldn't build a world even if we were given the reins of government—not yet any-rate. I don't blame you for being stubborn. I don't blame you for ignoring every suggestion I ever made— I only blame myself for encouraging you to believe we could make a go of it. We've had precious moments together. But now two weeks of your not being here has given me the cowardly chance to think about it and decide and I—'

BEATIE (*snatching letter*). SHUT UP!

MRS BRYANT. Oh—so we know now do we?

MR BRYANT. What's this then—ent he comin'?

MRS BRYANT. Yes, we know now.

MR BRYANT. Ent he comin' I ask?

BEATIE. NO HE ENT COMIN'.

(*An awful silence ensues. Everyone looks uncomfortable.*)

JENNY (*softly*). Well blust gal, didn't you know this was going to happen?

(BEATIE *shakes her head.*)

MRS BRYANT. So *we're* stubborn are we?

JENNY. Shut you up Mother, the girl's upset.

MRS BRYANT. Well I can see that. I can see that, he ent coming, I can see that, and we're here like bloody fools, I can see that.

PEARL. Well did you quarrel all that much Beatie?

BEATIE (*as if discovering this for the first time*). He always wanted me to help him but I never could. Once he tried to teach me to type but soon ever I made a mistake I'd give up. I'd give up every time! I couldn't bear making mistakes. I don't know why, but I couldn't bear making mistakes.

MRS BRYANT. Oh—so we're hearin' the other side o' the story now are we?

BEATIE. He used to suggest I start to copy real objects on to my paintings instead of only abstracts and I never took heed.

MRS BRYANT. Oh, so you never took heed.

JENNY. Shut you up I say.

BEATIE. He gimme a book sometimes and I never bothered to read it.

FRANK (*not maliciously*). What about all this discussion we heard of?

BEATIE. I *never* discussed things. He used to beg me to discuss things but I never saw the point on it.

PEARL. And he got riled because of that?

BEATIE (*trying to understand*). I didn't have any patience.

MRS BRYANT. Now it's coming out.

BEATIE. I couldn't help him—I never knew patience. Once he looked at me with terrified eyes and said, 'We've been together for three years but you don't know who I am or what I'm trying to say—and you don't care do you?'

MRS BRYANT. And there she was tellin' me.

BEATIE. I never knew what he wanted—I didn't think it mattered.

MR BRYANT. And there she was gettin' us to solve the moral problem and now we know she didn't even do it herself. That's a rum 'un, ent it?

MRS BRYANT. The apple don't fall far from the tree—that it don't.

BEATIE (*wearily*). So you're proud on it? You sit there smug and you're proud that a daughter of yours wasn't able to help her boy friend? Look at you. All of you. You can't say anything. You can't even help your own flesh and blood. Your daughter's bin ditched. It's your problem as well isn't it? I'm part of your family aren't I? Well, help me then! Give me words of comfort! Talk to me—for God's sake, someone talk to me. (*She cries at last.*)

MR BRYANT. Well, what do we do now?

MRS BRYANT. We sit down and we eat that's what we do now.

JENNY. Don't be soft Mother, we can't leave the girl crying like that.

MRS BRYANT. Well, blust, 'tent my fault she's cryin'. I did

what I could—I prepared the food, I'd've treated him
as my own son if he'd come but he hevn't! We got a
whole family gathering specially to greet him, all on us
look, but he hevn't come. So what am I supposed to do?

BEATIE. My God, Mother, I hate you—the only thing I ever
wanted and I weren't able to keep him, I didn't know
how. I hate you, I hate . . .

(MRS BRYANT *slaps* BEATIE'S *face. Everyone is a little
shocked at this harsh treatment.*)

MRS BRYANT. There! I hed enough!

MR BRYANT. Well what d'you wanna do that for?

MRS BRYANT. I hed enough. All this time she've bin home
she've bin tellin' me I didn't do this and I didn't do
that and I hevn't understood half what she've said and
I've hed enough. She talk about bein' part o' the family
but she've never lived at home since she've left school
look. Then she go away from here and fill her head wi'
high-class squit and then it turn out she don't understand any on it herself. It turn out she do just the same
things she say I do. (*Into* BEATIE'S *face*) Well, am I
right gal? I'm right ent I? When you tell me I was
stubborn, what you mean was that *he* told you *you* was
stubborn—eh? When you tell me I don't understand
you mean *you* don't understand isn't it? When you tell
me I don't make no effort you mean *you* don't make
no effort. Well, what you blaming me for? Blaming
me all the time! I haven't bin responsible for you since
you left home—you bin on your own. She think I like
it, she do! Thinks I like it being cooped up in this
house all day. Well I am telling you my gal—I don't!
There! And if I had a chance to be away working somewhere the whole lot on yous could go to hell—the lot
on yous. All right so I am a bloody fool—all right!
So I know it! A whole two weeks I've bin told it. Well,
so then I can't help you my gal, no that I can't, and
you get used to that once and for all.

BEATIE. No you can't Mother, I know you can't.

MRS BRYANT. I suppose doin' all those things for him weren't
enough. I suppose he weren't satisfied wi' goodness
only.

BEATIE. Oh, what's the use.

MRS BRYANT. Well, don't you sit there an' sigh gal like you was Lady Nevershit. I ask you something. Answer me. You do the talking then. Go on—you say you know something we don't so *you* do the talking. Talk—go on, talk gal.

BEATII (*despairingly*). I can't Mother, you're right—the apple don't fall far from the tree do it? You're right, I'm like you. Stubborn, empty, wi' no tools for livin'. I got no roots in nothing. I come from a family o' farm labourers yet I ent got no roots—just like town people —just a mass o' nothin'.

FRANK. Roots, gal? What do you mean, roots?

BEATIE (*impatiently*). Roots, roots, roots! Christ, Frankie, you're in the fields all day, you should know about growing things. Roots! The things you come from, the things that feed you. The things that make you proud of yourself—roots!

MR BRYANT. You got a family ent you?

BEATIE. I am not talking about family roots—I mean—the —I mean— Look! Ever since it begun the world's bin growin' hasn't it? Things hev happened, things have bin discovered, people have bin thinking and improving and inventing but what do we know about it all?

JIMMY. What is she on about?

BEATIE (*various interjections*). What do you mean, what am I on about? I'm talking! Listen to me! I'm tellin' you that the world's bin growing for two thousand years and we hevn't noticed it. I'm telling you that we don't know what we are or where we come from. I'm telling you something's cut us off from the beginning. I'm telling you we've got no roots. Blimey Joe! We've all got large allotments, we all grow things around us so we should know about roots. You know how to keep your flowers alive don't you Mother? Jimmy—you know how to keep the roots of your veges strong and healthy. It's not only the corn that need strong roots, you know, it's us too. But what've we got? Go on, tell me, what've we got? We don't know where we push up from and we don't bother neither.

PEARL. Well, I aren't grumbling.

BEATIE. You say you aren't—oh yes, you say so, but look at you. What've you done since you come in? Hev you said anythin'? I mean really said or done anything to show you're alive? Alive! Blust, what do it mean? Do you know what it mean? Any of you? Shall I tell you what Susie said when I went and saw her? She say she don't care if that ole atom bomb drop and she die— that's what she say. And you know why she say it? I'll tell you why, because if she had to care she'd have to do something about it and she find *that* too much effort. Yes she do. She can't be bothered—she's too bored with it all. That's what we all are—we're all too bored.

MRS BRYANT. Blust woman—bored you say, bored? You say Susie's bored, with a radio and television an' that? I go t'hell if she's bored.

BEATIE. Oh yes, we turn on a radio or a TV set maybe, or we go to the pictures—if them's love stories or gangsters —but isn't that the easiest way out? Anything so long as we don't have to make an effort. Well, am I right? You know I'm right. Education ent only books and music—it's asking questions, all the time. There are millions of us, all over the country, and no one, not one of us, is asking questions, we're all taking the easiest way out. Everyone I ever worked with took the easiest way out. We don't fight for anything, we're so mentally lazy we might as well be dead. Blust, we are dead! And you know what Ronnie say sometimes? He say it serves us right! That's what he say—it's our own bloody fault.

JIMMY. So that's us summed up then—so we know where *we* are then!

MRS BRYANT. Well if he don't reckon we count nor nothin', then it's as well he didn't come. There! It's as well he didn't come.

BEATIE. Oh, *he* thinks we count all right—living in mystic communion with nature. Living in mystic bloody communion with nature (indeed). But us count? Count Mother? I wonder. Do we? Do you think we really count? You don' wanna take any notice of what them ole papers say about the workers bein' all-important these days—that's all squit! 'Cos we aren't. Do you think when the really talented people in the country get to work they get to work for us? Hell if they do! Do you think they don't know we 'ont make the effort? The writers don't write thinkin' we can understand, nor the painters don't paint expecting us to be interested—that they don't, nor don't the composers give out music thinking we can appreciate it. 'Blust', they say, 'the masses is too stupid for us to come down to them. Blust,' they say, 'if they don't make no effort why should we bother?' So you know who come along? The slop singers and the pop writers and the film makers and women's maga-zines and the Sunday papers and the picture strip love stories—that's who come along, and you don't have to make no effort for them, it come easy. 'We know where the money lie,' they say, 'hell we do! The workers've got it so let's give them what they want. If they want slop songs and film idols we'll give 'em that then. If they want words of one syllable, we'll give 'em that then. If they want the third-rate, BLUST! We'll give 'em THAT then. Anything's good enough for them 'cos they don't ask for no more!' The whole stinkin' commercial world insults us and we won't care a damn. Well, Ron-nie's right—it's our own bloody fault. We want the third-rate—we got it! We got it! We . . .

(*Suddenly* BEATIE *stops as if listening to herself. She pauses, turns with an ecstatic smile on her face—*)

D'you hear that? D'you hear it? Did you listen to me? I'm talking, Jenny, Frankie, Mother—I'm not quoting no more.

MRS BRYANT (*getting up to sit at table*). Oh hell, I hed enough of her—let her talk a while she'll soon get fed up.

(*The others join her at the table and proceed to eat and murmur.*)

BEATIE (*as though a vision were revealed to her*). God in heaven, RONNIE! It does work, it's happening to me, I can feel it's happened, I'm beginning, on my own two feet—I'm beginning . . .

(*The murmur of the family sitting down to eat grows*

> *as* BEATIE'S *last cry is heard. Whatever she will do they will continue to live as before. As* BEATIE *stands alone, articulate at last—*)
> ### Curtain

Run-out

The power of speech is one of our main marks of distinction from animals; but many of us use speech only for simple practical purposes or gossip, Wesker implies. Communication is clearly the main theme here—the communication of thought and feeling. Perhaps Ronnie's relationship with Beatie wasn't a failure at all after all, as she learned from him how to express herself—a gift which she will never lose; this priceless gift validates the relationship, and Beatie will go on, one feels, to find herself, though she will probably not be able to communicate fully with her family, who are too set in their ways. The whole play is well worth reading; it's often funny, sometimes touching, and of great interest in its study of the contrasts between village and town life, between the generations, and between the 'accepters' and the 'challengers'.

The third play in the trilogy *I'm Talking About Jerusalem* concerns the attempt and failure of another part of the Kahn family to set up as makers of hand-made furniture in a village: it is perhaps less interesting than the other two, but has some splendid scenes. Elsewhere in this book you will find some extracts from Wesker's later play about army life, *Chips with Everything* (p. 66).

XXXXXXXXXXXXXXXXXXXXXXXXXXXXXXXXXXXXXXXXXXXXXXXXXXXXXXXXXXXXXXXXXXX

AS YOU LIKE IT

Lead-in

From the earlier extract from *As You Like It* (see p. 39) you will have learned something of the plot. Touchstone is a jester—a professional court clown—who for reasons we needn't go into in detail finds himself exiled with the Duke, his master, and the court in the forest of Arden. To pass the time he flatters and attracts a country girl, Audrey, and even goes through a form of marriage with her conducted by a false 'priest', a so-called 'hedge-priest', Sir Oliver Martext. Now he meets Audrey's previous lover, a simpleton called William, and with his sophisticated language makes rings round him. At one point he even translates what he pretends to be his natural, rather learned, language into simpler speech for William's benefit; he is, of course, putting on airs, and is probably no more than a jumped-up peasant himself. It is an attractive small study in the educational and class barriers of language.

ACTING NOTES
Touchstone is a smart-alec—confident, calculating, full of wit, above all patronizing. He really cares nothing for Audrey (elsewhere he describes her to another courtier in the immortal words 'An ill-favoured thing, sir, but mine own'). Audrey is simple, a bit sluttish ('Hold thyself more seemly' he rebukes her at one point) but fascinated by the relatively elegant creature Touchstone with his apparent confidence and superiority. William is completely gormless, and understands very little of what is said to him : this is typified by his marvellous remark after Touchstone's long speech of abuse and threat—'God rest you merry, sir.' Given the right actors and some contrast of accents (Touchstone very superior, the other two rustic) it can be very funny.

The Forest.
(*Enter* TOUCHSTONE *and* AUDREY.)
TOUCHSTONE. We shall find a time, Audrey : patience, gentle Audrey.
AUDREY. Faith, the priest was good enough, for all the old gentleman's saying.
TOUCHSTONE. A most wicked Sir Oliver, Audrey; a most vile Martext. But, Audrey, there is a youth here in the forest lays claim to you.
AUDREY. Ay, I know who 't is : he hath no interest in me in the world : here comes the man you mean.
(*Enter* WILLIAM.)
TOUCHSTONE. It is meat and drink to me to see a clown : by my troth, we that have good wits have much to answer for; we shall be flouting; we cannot hold.
WILLIAM. Good even, Audrey.

AUDREY. God ye good even, William.

WILLIAM. And good even to you, sir.

TOUCHSTONE. Good even, gentle friend. Cover thy head, cover thy head; nay, prithee, be covered. How old are you, friend?

WILLIAM. Five-and-twenty, sir.

TOUCHSTONE. A ripe age. Is thy name William?

WILLIAM. William, sir.

TOUCHSTONE. A fair name. Wast born i' the forest here?

WILLIAM. Ay, sir, I thank God.

TOUCHSTONE. 'Thank God'; a good answer. Art rich?

WILLIAM. Faith, sir, so so.

TOUCHSTONE. 'So so', is good, very good, very excellent good; and yet it is not; it is but so so. Art thou wise?

WILLIAM. Ay, sir, I have a pretty wit.

TOUCHSTONE. Why, thou sayest well. I do now remember a saying, 'The fool doth think he is wise, but the wise man knows himself to be a fool.' The heathen philosopher, when he had a desire to eat a grape, would open his lips when he put it into his mouth; meaning thereby that grapes were made to eat and lips to open. You do love this maid?

WILLIAM. I do, sir.

TOUCHSTONE. Give me your hand. Art thou learned?

WILLIAM. No, sir.

TOUCHSTONE. Then learn this of me: to have, is to have; for it is a figure in rhetoric that drink, being poured out of a cup into a glass, by filling the one doth empty the other; for all your writers do consent that *ipse* is he: now, you are not *ipse*, for I am he.

WILLIAM. Which he, sir?

TOUCHSTONE. He, sir, that must marry this woman. Therefore, you clown, abandon—which is in the vulgar leave, —the society,—which in the boorish is, company,— of this female,—which in the common is, woman; which together is, abandon the society of this female, or, clown, thou perishest; or, to thy better understanding, diest; or, to wit, I kill thee, make thee away, translate thy life into death, thy liberty into bondage: I will deal in poison with thee, or in bastinado, or in steel; I will bandy with thee in faction; I will o'er-run thee with policy; I will kill thee a hundred and fifty ways: therefore tremble, and depart.

AUDREY. Do, good William.

WILLIAM. God rest you merry, sir. (*Exit.*)

(*Enter* CORIN.)

CORIN. Our master and mistress seeks you: come, away, away!

TOUCHSTONE. Trip, Audrey! trip, Audrey! I attend, I attend. (*Exeunt.*)

Run-out

Audrey and Touchstone are married in the end. Jaques, the bitter commentator of *As You Like It*, congratulating the three pairs of lovers who are to marry at the end of the play, says of this fourth pair 'And you to wrangling; for thy loving voyage/Is but for two months victualled'—that is, the voyage won't last long as there isn't enough food aboard, and therefore the marriage will be short-lived.

✕✕✕✕✕✕✕✕✕✕✕✕✕✕✕✕✕✕✕✕✕✕✕✕✕✕✕✕✕✕✕✕✕✕✕✕✕✕✕

PYGMALION

Lead-in

Bernard Shaw published *Pygmalion* in 1916, though the play was performed in 1914. The title refers to a Greek legend in which a sculptor called Galatea makes a statue called Pygmalion, falls in love with it and brings it alive. It is basically the story of a famous Professor of Phonetics (i.e., an expert in the science of speech, the sounds of language and therefore of dialects) who meets a Cockney flower-seller called Liza, and undertakes for a bet to teach her to speak standard English and pass her off as a duchess within three months. In the opening which follows, Professor Higgins is described as 'the note taker' annotating her speech—he knows so much of the fine detail of dialects that he can say exactly where people have lived 'within six miles', as he boasts: 'I can place them within two miles in London. Sometimes within two

streets.' The scene takes place in Covent Garden at night in
the pouring rain, where some wealthy people are trying to
get a taxi while 'the Gentleman' (later revealed as another
language specialist called Colonel Pickering) protects the
flower girl who has had her basket of flowers accidentally
upset. The point of the passage is mainly to focus attention
on the barriers that speech patterns can make, and the whole
play makes the point that class is (or was) largely a matter
of speech.

ACTING NOTES

Liza must be able to make a good try at cockney; Shaw gives us
quite a lot of help in pronunciation. Higgins and Pickering speak
perfect standard English. The mother, her daughter Clara and her
son Freddy (their surname, as we learn later, is Eynsford Hill)
speak a very superior 'refained' English which should make a
strong contrast with Eliza's. The bystander is a cockney and so is
'a sarcastic bystander'. A small crowd of other bystanders have a
few words to say—again mostly in London accents. Props include
a flower basket and something to serve for bunches of violets;
Higgins has a notebook and pencil and a whistle. The whole
point of the scene is to produce a kind of symphony of accents,
with Higgins as the analyst and master of them all as he writes
down other people's speeches, which he can reproduce exactly by
using phonetics.

*London at 11.15 p.m. Torrents of heavy summer rain. Cab
whistles blowing frantically in all directions. Pedestrians running for shelter into the portico of St Paul's church (not
Wren's cathedral but Inigo Jones's church in Covent Garden
vegetable market), among them a lady and her daughter in
evening dress. All are peering out gloomily at the rain, except one man with his back turned to the rest, wholly preoccupied with a notebook in which he is writing.
The church clock strikes the first quarter.*

THE DAUGHTER (*in the space between the central pillars, close
        to the one on her left*). I'm getting chilled to the bone.
    What can Freddy be doing all this time? He's been gone
    twenty minutes.
THE MOTHER (*on her* DAUGHTER'S *right*). Not so long. But

he ought to have got us a cab by this.

A BYSTANDER (*on the lady's right*). He wont get no cab not until half-past eleven, missus, when they come back after dropping their theatre fares.

THE MOTHER. But we must have a cab. We cant stand here until half-past eleven. It's too bad.

THE BYSTANDER. Well, it aint my fault, missus.

THE DAUGHTER. If Freddy had a bit of gumption, he would have got one at the theatre door.

THE MOTHER. What could he have done, poor boy?

THE DAUGHTER. Other people got cabs. Why couldnt he?
(*Freddy rushes in out of the rain from the Southampton Street side, and comes between them closing a dripping umbrella. He is a young man of twenty, in evening dress, very wet round the ankles.*)

THE DAUGHTER. Well, havnt you got a cab?

FREDDY. Theres not one to be had for love or money.

THE MOTHER. Oh, Freddy, there must be one. You cant have tried.

THE DAUGHTER. It's too tiresome. Do you expect us to go and get one ourselves?

FREDDY. I tell you theyre all engaged. The rain was so sudden: nobody was prepared; and everybody had to take a cab. Ive been to Charing Cross one way and nearly to Ludgate Circus the other; and they were all engaged.

THE MOTHER. Did you try Trafalgar Square?

FREDDY. There wasnt one at Trafalgar Square.

THE DAUGHTER. Did you try?

FREDDY. I tried as far as Charing Cross Station.. Did you expect me to walk to Hammersmith?

THE DAUGHTER. You havnt tried at all.

THE MOTHER. You really are very helpless, Freddy. Go again; and dont come back until you have found a cab.

FREDDY. I shall simply get soaked for nothing.

THE DAUGHTER. And what about us? Are we to stay here all night in this draught, with next to nothing on? You selfish pig—

FREDDY. Oh, very well: I'll go, I'll go. (*He opens his umbrella and dashes off Strandwards, but comes into collision with a flower girl who is hurrying in for shelter.*

knocking her basket out of her hands. A blinding flash of lightning, followed instantly by a rattling peal of thunder, orchestrates the incident.)

THE FLOWER GIRL. Nah than, Freddy: look wh' y' gowin, deah.

FREDDY. Sorry (*he rushes off*).

THE FLOWER GIRL (*picking up her scattered flowers and replacing them in the basket*). Theres menners f' yer! To-oo banches o voylets trod into the mad. (*She sits down on the plinth of the column, sorting her flowers, on the lady's right. She is not at all a romantic figure. She is perhaps eighteen, perhaps twenty, hardly older. She wears a little sailor hat of black straw that has long been exposed to the dust and soot of London and has seldom if ever been brushed. Her hair needs washing rather badly; its mousy colour can hardly be natural. She wears a shoddy black coat that reaches nearly to her knees and is shaped to her waist. She has a brown skirt with a coarse apron. Her boots are much the worse for wear. She is no doubt as clean as she can afford to be; but compared to the ladies she is very dirty. Her features are no worse than theirs; but their condition leaves something to be desired; and she needs the services of a dentist.*)

THE MOTHER. How do you know that my son's name is Freddy, pray?

THE FLOWER GIRL. Ow, eez yo-ooa san, is e? Wal, fewd dan y' dy-ooty bawmz a mather should, eed now bettern to spawl a pore gel's flahrzn than ran awy athaht pyin. Will ye-oo py me f'them? (*Here, with apologies, this desperate attempt to represent her dialect without a phonetic alphabet must be abandoned as unintelligible outside London.*)

THE DAUGHTER. Do nothing of the sort, mother. The idea!

THE MOTHER. Please allow me, Clara. Have you any pennies?

THE DAUGHTER. No. Ive nothing smaller than sixpence.

THE FLOWER GIRL (*hopefully*). I can give you change for a tanner, kind lady.

THE MOTHER (*to* CLARA). Give it to me. (CLARA *parts re-*

luctantly.) Now (*to the girl*) This is for your flowers.

THE FLOWER GIRL. Thank you kindly, lady.

THE DAUGHTER. Make her give you the change. These things are only a penny a bunch.

THE MOTHER. Do hold your tongue, Clara. (*To the girl*) You can keep the change.

THE FLOWER GIRL. Oh, thank you, lady.

THE MOTHER. Now tell me how you know that young gentleman's name.

THE FLOWER GIRL. I didnt.

THE MOTHER. I heard you call him by it. Dont try to deceive me.

THE FLOWER GIRL (*protesting*). Who's trying to deceive you? I called him Freddy or Charlie same as you might yourself if you was talking to a stranger and wished to be pleasant.

THE DAUGHTER. Sixpence thrown away! Really, Mamma, you might have spared Freddy that. (*She retreats in disgust behind the pillar.*)
(*An elderly gentleman of the amiable military type rushes into the shelter, and closes a dripping umbrella. He is in the same plight as* FREDDY, *very wet about the ankles. He is in evening dress, with a light overcoat. He takes the place left vacant by the daughter.*)

THE GENTLEMAN. Phew!

THE MOTHER (*to the gentleman*). Oh, sir, is there any sign of its stopping?

THE GENTLEMAN. I'm afraid not. It started worse than ever about two minutes ago. (*He goes to the plinth beside the flower girl; puts his foot on it; and stoops to turn down his trouser ends.*)

THE MOTHER. Oh dear! (*She retires sadly and joins her daughter.*)

THE FLOWER GIRL (*taking advantage of the military gentleman's proximity to establish friendly relations with him*). If it's worse, it's a sign it's nearly over. So cheer up, Captain; and buy a flower off a poor girl.

THE GENTLEMAN. I'm sorry. I havnt any change.

THE FLOWER GIRL. I can give you change, Captain.

THE GENTLEMAN. For a sovereign? Ive nothing less.

THE FLOWER GIRL. Garn! Oh do buy a flower off me, Captain. I can change half-a-crown. Take this for tuppence.

THE GENTLEMAN. Now dont be troublesome: theres a good girl. (*Trying his pockets*) I really havnt any change— Stop: heres three hapence, if thats any use to you (*he retreats to the other pillar*).

THE FLOWER GIRL (*disappointed, but thinking three half-pence better than nothing*). Thank you, sir.

THE BYSTANDER (*to the girl*). You be careful: give him a flower for it. Theres a bloke here behind taking down every blessed word youre saying. (*All turn to the man who is taking notes.*)

THE FLOWER GIRL (*springing up terrified*). I aint done nothing wrong by speaking to the gentleman. Ive a right to sell flowers if I keep off the kerb. (*Hysterically*) I'm a respectable girl: so help me, I never spoke to him except to ask him to buy a flower off me.

(*General hubbub, mostly sympathetic to* THE FLOWER GIRL, *but deprecating her excessive sensibility. Cries of* Dont start hollerin. Who's hurting you? Nobody's going to touch you. Whats the good of fussing? Steady on. Easy easy, etc., *come from the elderly staid spectators, who pat her comfortingly. Less patient ones bid her shut her head, or ask her roughly what is wrong with her. A remoter group, not knowing what the matter is, crowd in and increase the noise with question and answer:* What's the row? What-she-do? Where is she? A tec taking her down. What! him? Yes: him over there: Took money off the gentleman, etc.)

THE FLOWERGIRL (*breaking through them to* THE GENTLE-MAN, *crying wildly*). Oh, sir, dont let him charge me. You dunno what it means to me. Theyll take away my character and drive me on the streets for speaking to gentlemen. They—

THE NOTE TAKER (*coming forward on her right, the rest crowding after him*). There! there! there! there! who's hurting you, you silly girl? What do you take me for?

THE BYSTANDER. It's aw rawt: e's a genleman: look at his be-oots. (*Explaining to the note taker*) She thought you was a copper's nark, sir.

THE NOTETAKER (*with quick interest*). What's a copper's nark?

THE BYSTANDER (*inept at definition*). It's a—well, it's a copper's nark, as you might say. What else would you call it? A sort of informer.

THE FLOWER GIRL (*still hysterical*). I take my Bible oath I never said a word—

THE NOTE TAKER (*overbearing but good-humoured*). Oh, shut up, shut up. Do I look like a policeman?

THE FLOWER GIRL (*far from reassured*). Then what did you take down my words for? How do I know whether you took me down right? You just shew me what youve wrote about me. (THE NOTE TAKER *opens his book and holds it steadily under her nose, though the pressure of the mob trying to read it over his shoulders would upset a weaker man.*) Whats that? That aint proper writing. I cant read that.

THE NOTE TAKER. I can. (*Reads, reproducing her prounciation exactly*). 'Cheer ap, Keptin; n' baw ya flahr orf a pore gel.'

THE FLOWER GIRL (*much distressed*). It's because I called him Captain. I meant no harm. (*To the gentleman*) Oh, sir, dont let him lay a charge agen me for a word like that. You—

THE GENTLEMAN. Charge! I make no charge. (*To* THE NOTE TAKER) Really, sir, if you are a detective, you need not begin protecting me against molestation by young women until I ask you. Anybody could see that the girl meant no harm.

THE BYSTANDERS GENERALLY (*demonstrating against police espionage*). Course they could. What business is it of yours? You mind your own affairs. He wants promotion, he does. Taking down people's words! Girl never said a word to him. What harm if she did? Nice thing a girl cant shelter from the rain without being insulted, etc., etc., etc. (*She is conducted by the more sympathetic demonstrators back to her plinth, where she resumes her seat and struggles with her emotion.*)

THE BYSTANDER. He aint a tec. He's a blooming busybody: thats what he is. I tell you, look at his be-oots.

F

THE NOTE TAKER (*turning on him genially*). And how are all your people down at Selsey?

THE BYSTANDER (*suspiciously*). Who told you my people come from Selsey?

THE NOTE TAKER. Never you mind. They did. (*To the girl*) How did you come to be up so far east? You were born in Lisson Grove.

THE FLOWER GIRL (*appalled*). Oh, what harm is there in my leaving Lisson Grove? It wasnt fit for a pig to live in; and I had to pay four-and-six a week. (*In tears*) Oh, boo—hoo—oo—

THE NOTE TAKER. Live where you like; but stop that noise.

THE GENTLEMAN (*to the girl*). Come, come! he cant touch you : you have a right to live where you please.

A SARCASTIC BYSTANDER (*thrusting himself between* THE NOTE TAKER *and* THE GENTLEMAN). Park Lane, for instance. I'd like to go into the Housing Question with you, I would.

THE FLOWER GIRL (*subsiding into a brooding melancholy over her basket, and talking very low-spiritedly to herself*). I'm a good girl, I am.

THE SARCASTIC BYSTANDER (*not attending to her*). Do you know where I come from?

THE NOTE TAKER (*promptly*). Hoxton.
  (*Titterings. Popular interest in* THE NOTE TAKER'S *performance increases.*)

THE SARCASTIC ONE (*amazed.*) Well, who said I didnt? Bly me! you know everything, you do.

THE FLOWER GIRL (*still nursing her sense of injury*). Aint no call to meddle with me, he aint.

THE BYSTANDER (*to her*). Of course he aint. Dont you stand it from him. (*To* THE NOTE TAKER) See here : what call have you to know about people what never offered to meddle with you?

THE FLOWER GIRL. Let him say what he likes. I dont want to have no truck with him.

THE BYSTANDER. You take us for dirt under your feet, dont you? Catch you taking liberties with a gentleman!

THE SARCASTIC BYSTANDER. Yes, tell him where he come from if you want to go fortune-telling.

THE NOTE TAKER. Cheltenham, Harrow, Cambridge, and India.

THE GENTLEMAN. Quite right.

(*Great laughter. Reaction in* THE NOTE TAKER'S *favour. Exclamations of* He knows all about it. Told him proper. Hear him tell the toff where he come from? *etc.*)

THE GENTLEMAN. May I ask, sir, do you do this for your living at a music hall?

THE NOTE TAKER. I've thought of that. Perhaps I shall some day.

(*The rain has stopped; and the persons on the outside of the crowd begin to drop off.*)

THE FLOWER GIRL (*resenting the reaction*). He's no gentleman, he aint, to interfere with a poor girl.

THE DAUGHTER (*out of patience, pushing her way rudely to the front and displacing* THE GENTLEMAN, *who politely retires to the other side of the pillar*). What on earth is Freddy doing? I shall get pneumownia if I stay in this draught any longer.

THE NOTE TAKER (*to himself, hastily making a note of her pronunciation of 'monia'*). Earlscourt.

THE DAUGHTER (*violently*). Will you please keep your impertinent remarks to yourself.

THE NOTE TAKER. Did I say that out loud? I didn't mean to. I beg your pardon. Your mother's Epsom, unmistakably.

THE MOTHER (*advancing between the daughter and* THE NOTE TAKER). How very curious! I was brought up in Largelady Park, near Epsom.

THE NOTE TAKER (*uproariously amused*). Ha! ha! What a devil of a name! Excuse me. (*To* THE DAUGHTER) You want a cab, do you?

THE DAUGHTER. Dont dare to speak to me.

THE MOTHER. Oh please, please, Clara. (*Her daughter repudiates her with an angry shrug and retires haughtily.*) We should be so grateful to you, sir, if you found us a cab. (THE NOTE TAKER *produces a whistle.*) Oh, thank you. (*She joins her daughter.*)

(THE NOTE TAKER *blows a piercing blast.*)

THE SARCASTIC BYSTANDER. There! I knowed he was a plain-clothes copper.

THE BYSTANDER. That aint a police whistle: thats a sporting whistle.

THE FLOWER GIRL (*still preoccupied with her wounded feelings*). He's no right to take away my character. My character is the same to me as any lady's.

THE NOTE TAKER. I dont know whether youve noticed it; but the rain stopped about two minutes ago.

THE BYSTANDER. So it has. Why didnt you say so before? and us losing our time listening to your silliness! (*He walks off towards the Strand.*)

THE SARCASTIC BYSTANDER. I can tell where you come from. You come from Anwell. Go back there.

THE NOTE TAKER (*helpfully*). Hanwell.

THE SARCASTIC BYSTANDER (*affecting great distinction of speech*). Thenk you, teacher. Haw haw! So long (*he touches his hat with mock respect and strolls off*).

THE FLOWER GIRL. Frightening people like that! How would he like it himself?

THE MOTHER. It's quite fine now, Clara. We can walk to a motor bus. Come. (*She gathers her skirts above her ankles and hurries off towards the Strand.*)

THE DAUGHTER. But the cab— (*her mother is out of hearing*). Oh, how tiresome! (*She follows angrily.*)

(*All the rest have gone except* THE NOTE TAKER, THE GENTLEMAN, *and* THE FLOWER GIRL, *who sits arranging her basket, and still pitying herself in murmurs.*)

THE FLOWER GIRL. Poor girl! Hard enough for her to live without being worrited and chivied.

THE GENTLEMAN (*returning to his former place on* THE NOTE TAKER'S *left*). How do you do it, if I may ask?

THE NOTE TAKER. Simply phonetics. The science of speech. Thats my profession: also my hobby. Happy is the man who can make a living by his hobby! You can spot an Irishman or a Yorkshireman by his brogue. *I* can place any man within six miles. I can place him within two miles in London. Sometimes within two streets.

THE FLOWER GIRL. Ought to be ashamed of himself, unmanly coward!

THE GENTLEMAN. But is there a living in that?

THE NOTE TAKER. Oh yes. Quite a fat one. This is an age of

upstarts. Men begin in Kentish Town with £80 a year, and end in Park Lane with a hundred thousand. They want to drop Kentish Town; but they give themselves away every time they open their mouths. Now I can teach them—

THE FLOWER GIRL. Let him mind his own business and leave a poor girl—

THE NOTE TAKER (*explosively*). Woman: cease this detestable boohooing instantly; or else seek the shelter of some other place of worship.

THE FLOWER GIRL (*with feeble defiance*). Ive a right to be here if I like, same as you.

THE NOTE TAKER. A woman who utters such depressing and disgusting sounds has no right to be anywhere—no right to live. Remember that you are a human being with a soul and the divine gift of articulate speech: that your native language is the language of Shakespeare and Milton and The Bible; and dont sit there crooning like a bilious pigeon.

THE FLOWER GIRL (*quite overwhelmed, looking up at him in mingled wonder and deprecation without daring to raise her head*). Ah-ah-ah-ow-ow-oo!

THE NOTE TAKER (*whipping out his book*). Heavens! what a sound! (*He writes; then holds out the book and reads, reproducing her vowels exactly*). Ah-ah-ah-ow-ow-oo!

THE FLOWER GIRL (*tickled by the performance, and laughing in spite of herself*). Garn!

THE NOTE TAKER. You see this creature with her kerbstone English: the English that will keep her in the gutter to the end of her days. Well, sir, in three months I could pass that girl off as a duchess at an ambassador's garden party. I could even get her a place as lady's maid or shop assistant, which requires better English.

THE FLOWER GIRL. What's that you say?

THE NOTE TAKER. Yes, you squashed cabbage leaf, you disgrace to the noble architecture of these columns, you incarnate insult to the English language: I could pass you off as the Queen of Sheba. (*To* THE GENTLEMAN) Can you believe that?

THE GENTLEMAN. Of course I can. I am myself a student of Indian dialects; and—

THE NOTE TAKER (*eagerly*). Are you? Do you know Colonel Pickering, the author of Spoken Sanscrit?

THE GENTLEMAN. I am Colonel Pickering. Who are you?

THE NOTE TAKER. Henry Higgins, author of Higgins's Universal Alphabet.

PICKERING (*with enthusiasm*). I came from India to meet you.

HIGGINS. I was going to India to meet you.

PICKERING. Where do you live?

HIGGINS. 27A Wimpole Street. Come and see me tomorrow.

PICKERING. I'm at the Carlton. Come with me now and lets have a jaw over some supper.

HIGGINS. Right you are.

THE FLOWER GIRL (*to* PICKERING, *as he passes her*). Buy a flower, kind gentleman. I'm short for my lodging.

PICKERING. I really havnt any change. I'm sorry (*he goes away*).

HIGGINS (*shocked at the girl's mendacity*). Liar. You said you could change half-a-crown.

THE FLOWER GIRL (*rising in desperation*). You ought to be stuffed with nails, you ought. (*Flinging the basket at his feet.*) Take the whole blooming basket for sixpence. (*The church clock strikes the second quarter.*)

HIGGINS (*hearing in it the voice of God, rebuking him for his Pharisaic want of charity to the poor girl*). A reminder. (*He raises his hat solemnly; then throws a handful of money into the basket and follows* PICKERING.)

THE FLOWER GIRL (*picking up a half-crown*). Ah-ow-ooh! (*Picking up a couple of florins*) Aah-ow-ooh! (*Picking up several coins*) Aaaaaah-ow-ooh! (*Picking up a half-sovereign*) Aaaaaaaaaaaah-ow-ooh!!!

FREDDY (*springing out of a taxicab*). Got one at last. Hallo! (*To the girl*) Where are the two ladies that were here?

THE FLOWER GIRL. They walked to the bus when the rain stopped.

FREDDY. And left me with a cab on my hands! Damnation!

THE FLOWER GIRL (*with grandeur*). Never mind, young man. I'm going home in a taxi. (*She sails off to the cab. The driver puts his hand behind him and holds the door firmly shut against her. Quite understanding his mistrust, she shews him her handful of money.*) A taxi fare aint no object to me, Charlie. (*He grins and opens the door.*) Here. What about the basket?

THE TAXIMAN. Give it here. Tuppence extra.

LIZA. No: I dont want nobody to see it. (*She crushes it into the cab and gets in, continuing the conversation through the window.*) Goodbye, Freddy.

FREDDY (*dazedly raising his hat*). Goodbye.

TAXIMAN. Where to?

LIZA. Bucknam Pellis (Buckingham Palace).

TAXIMAN. What d'ye mean—Bucknam Pellis?

LIZA. Dont you know where it is? In the Green Park, where the King lives. Goodbye, Freddy. Dont let me keep you standing there. Goodbye.

FREDDY. Goodbye. (*He goes.*)

TAXIMAN. Here? Whats this about Bucknam Pellis? What business have you at Bucknam Pellis?

LIZA. Of course I havnt none. But I wasnt going to let him know that. You drive me home.

TAXIMAN. And wheres home?

LIZA. Angel Court, Drury Lane, next Meiklejohn's oil shop.

TAXIMAN. That sounds more like it, Judy. (*He drives off.*)

Run-out

Eliza decides she wants to be a lady in a flower shop and applies to Higgins for lessons, offering a shilling an hour, on the grounds that French teaching costs one and sixpence. She is taken into Higgins' house and looked after by his housekeeper; there is a splendid scene when her father, a dustman called Mr Doolittle, calls to take her back or get a bribe for letting her stay. Eliza finally learns standard English but continues for a while to talk on the same topics she did as a flower girl and makes a sensation at a tea party by saying 'Not bloody likely!' which was a good deal more daring then than it is now. Higgins' great triumph is at a reception where everyone takes Eliza for a duchess, or even a princess. The play ends, after some violent quarrels between Eliza and Higgins, with whom she fancies herself in love but who is really a confirmed old bachelor, when she marries the simple but affectionate Freddy and sets up a florist's shop exactly as she wanted to at the beginning.

7
War

This subject is, sadly, not a merely historical one; with two vast and appalling world wars in this century and countless more localized ones, we seem a long way from learning to live together. Drama, ahead of life in this as in other ways, offers us the sane and simple reflection that ordinary people don't benefit from wars and that both sides are the victims. The extracts from two modern plays *Sergeant Musgrave's Dance* and *The Long and the Short and the Tall* show two of the main ways in which modern dramatists handle this anti-war feeling which, in spite of current lunacies, is so widespread. The first of these is a direct attack on war by the soldiers who come to preach their doctrine in the splendidly ironic guise of a recruiting group; Musgrave *is* in a sense mad, but it is the madness of someone who is saner than the rest of us, and he wants to *demonstrate* the injustice and futility of war, even to the point of showing the actual skeleton of their dead comrade. The second shows in action what war is like by focussing on a tiny corner of it; this tender and strong relationship between Bamforth and the Japanese, Willis Hall implies, is what is natural to even the most cynical or selfish man, but war sweeps it all away: the lesson and the message are clear enough. I have prefaced these two longish passages with the famous prologue to Act IV of *Henry V*, which brings out the nobility of Henry and his troops on the night before Agincourt. We shall not expect Shakespeare to produce anti-war arguments of the kind John Arden and Willis Hall use, but it would be a mistake to believe that he takes war for granted; in many of his plays war is closely questioned, and even in this most patriotic of history plays there is a searching argument in Act IV between the disguised Henry and three rank-and-file soldiers, before the battle begins, discussing the merits and questioning the morality of war.

HENRY V

Lead-in

This may strike you as a passage of poetry rather than drama since there is only one speaker. It is the Prologue or Chorus which opens the fourth Act of Shakespeare's *Henry V*, and I have included it mainly because it seems very suitable as an introduction to a section on War, being both an introduction itself and also a fine evocation of the atmosphere before a battle begins. *Henry V* can be regarded as the third of a trilogy of plays, the first two being *Henry IV Part I* and *Henry IV Part II*. In these two plays we have a realization of the uneasy reign of Henry IV (1399–1413), beset by rebellions and the king's illness, and overshadowed by the prospect of the apparently irresponsible Prince Hal becoming king and starting the ruin of England. At the end of *Henry IV Part II* Henry dies, having been assured that Hal will reform; Hal is crowned and rejects his old friends Falstaff and his associates; *Henry V* shows him as a triumphant young king, conducting a military campaign in France, which culminates in the famous victory of Agincourt (1415). After this battle Henry marries Katherine of France, and the two kingdoms are for a short while united (though the Hundred Years War followed soon after!). This prologue describes the scene on the night before the battle of Agincourt; the French are confident, huge in numbers and splendidly equipped, while the English are exhausted by campaigning and disease, and soberly ruminating on the dangers to come. The two armies are only a short distance away from each other, and can hear the armourers and see the camp fires of each other's forces. King Henry spends the night moving among his troops, building up their morale, bringing to his humblest troops 'A little touch of Harry in the night.' The prologue ends by apologizing for the ludicrously limited stage version ('foils' are swords) of this vast battle and asks us to use our imaginations and envisage the reality beyond the 'mockery' of the theatre's presentation.

ACTING NOTES

All one needs is a really good reader who will practise this speech
a bit till it carries itself along on its own splendid rhythm, with
some regularity but no monotony. (The reader should watch out
for syllables which need sounding here but would not normally
be sounded in modern English, e.g., 'all-watched' is three syllables, not two.)

CHORUS. Now entertain conjecture of a time
  When creeping murmur and the poring dark
  Fills the wide vessel of the universe.
  From camp to camp, through the foul womb of night,
  The hum of either army stilly sounds,
  That the fix'd sentinels almost receive
  The secret whispers of each other's watch :
  Fire answers fire, and through their paly flames
  Each battle sees the other's umber'd face;
  Steed threatens steed, in high and boastful neighs
  Piercing the night's dull ear; and from the tents
  The armourers, accomplishing the knights,
  With busy hammers closing rivets up,
  Give dreadful note of preparation.
  The country cocks do crow, the clocks do toll,
  And the third hour of drowsy morning name.
  Proud of their numbers, and secure in soul,
  The confident and over-lusty French
  Do the low-rated English play at dice;
  And chide the cripple tardy-gaited night
  Who, like a foul and ugly witch, doth limp
  So tediously away. The poor condemned English,
  Like sacrifices, by their watchful fires
  Sit patiently, and inly ruminate
  The morning's danger, and their gesture sad
  Investing lank-lean cheeks and war-worn coats
  Presenteth them unto the gazing moon
  So many horrid ghosts. O now, who will behold
  The royal captain of this ruin'd band
  Walking from watch to watch, from tent to tent,
  Let him cry 'Praise and glory on his head!'
  For forth he goes and visits all his host,

Bids them good morrow with a modest smile,
And calls them brothers, friends and countrymen.
Upon his royal face there is no note
How dread an army hath enrounded him;
Nor doth he dedicate one jot of colour
Unto the weary and all-watched night;
But freshly looks and over-bears attaint
With cheerful semblance and sweet majesty;
That every wretch, pining and pale before,
Beholding him, plucks comfort from his looks:
A largess universal like the sun
His liberal eye doth give to every one,
Thawing cold fear, that mean and gentle all
Behold, as may unworthiness define,
A little touch of Harry in the night.
And so our scene must to the battle fly;
Where—O for pity!—we shall much disgrace
With four or five most vile and ragged foils,
Right ill-disposed in brawl ridiculous,
The name of Agincourt. Yet sit and see,
Minding true things by what their mockeries be.

Run-out

The battle is an overwhelming victory for the British. The
French are so certain of victory and so contemptuous of the
English that we feel they must illustrate the old proverb that
pride comes before a fall; and equally the British modesty
makes one expect that in justice they should win. The battle
is treated in a number of ways, not excluding the comic, when
the cowardly and bragging Pistol, one of the friends from
Hall's wanton youth, captures a French soldier. The play
ends with the French accepting the British peace terms and
Princess Katherine accepting a proposal of marriage from
Henry.

SERJEANT MUSGRAVE'S DANCE

Lead-in

The following extract is from John Arden's famous play *Serjeant Musgrave's Dance,* which is subtitled An Unhistorical Parable', and was first published in 1960. It is too complex a play to summarize here, and only the broad lines of the situation are needed to explain this excerpt. Serjeant Musgrave and three soldiers arrive in a strike-bound northern town during winter in the late Victorian period, apparently on a recruiting campaign; actually they are deserters from the army and opponents of the colonial war they have been engaged in, and they blame the authorities—here symbolized by the Mayor, the Parson and the Constable—for the existence of such wars. In this scene they are apparently holding a recruiting meeting in the town market-place and all the officials are present, wearing robes of office and cockades. Musgrave demonstrates rifle and bayonet and finally a Gatling gun (an early type of machine-gun) on a tripod mounting, which he loads as a demonstration, but it is pointing towards the audience. Then he reveals his real attitude to the hideous war he and his soldiers have been engaged in; they support his story and tell their own, and the climax comes when he reveals a hanging skeleton dressed as a soldier and announces that it is the remains of Billy Hicks, a citizen of the town whom everyone knew, and who was once loved by a young girl of the town called Annie. The authorities think Musgrave is mad but dare not challenge him as he has loaded weapons. But *we* understand that he sees himself as on a mission to tell the ordinary people of 'the futility and cruelty of war'.

ACTING NOTES

This passage requires careful staging; the stage audience for Musgrave's performance is of colliers on strike and the authorities and onlookers, but Musgrave is also addressing the audience in the auditorium (rather in the same way as Bri, in the first extract

in this book, is addressing both his imaginary audience of school-
boys, and the theatre audience). One of the three soldiers supporting Musgrave, called Sparky, is already dead, but the other
two, Hurst and Attercliffe, are present in this scene. Here are John
Arden's notes about them, which may help you in characteriza-
tion : 'The soldiers are regular and seasoned men. They should all
have moustaches and an ingrained sense of discipline. Musgrave
is aged between thirty and forty, tall, swart, commanding, sar-
donic but never humorous : he could well have served under Crom-
well. Attercliffe is aged about fifty, grey-haired, melancholy, a
little embittered. He is the senior O.R. ("other rank", i.e., private)
of the party and conscious of his responsibility. Hurst, in his twen-
ties, is bloody-minded, quick-tempered, handsome, cynical, tough,
but not quite as intelligent as he thinks he is. . . . The Mayor is a
bustling, shrewd, superficially jovial man with a coarse accent
and an underlying inclination to bully. The Parson is very much a
gentleman. He is conscious of the ungentlemanly nature of the
community in which he lives . . . he too has some inclination to
bully. The Constable . . . is as inefficient as he is noisy. The Bargee
is something of a grotesque, a hunchback (though this should not
be overemphasized), very rapid in his movements, with a natural
urge towards intrigue and mischief.'

The three named colliers (Walsh, the Slow Collier and the Pugnacious Collier) have little to do in this extract, and the stage
crowd have merely to respond with astonishment and fear to
Musgrave's feverish conviction.

If you have a Biology Department with a skeleton, it might be
worth trying to borrow it!

HURST *gives a roll on the drums.*
ATTERCLIFFE *swivels the gun to face out into the audience.*
MUSGRAVE *loads his rifle with a clip of cartridges.*
MUSGRAVE (*his voice very taut and hard*). The question re-
    mains as to the *use* of these weapons! (*He pushes his
    rifle-bolt home.*) You'll ask me: what is their pur-
    pose? Seeing we've beat the Russians in the Crimea,
    there's no war with France (there *may* be, but there
    isn't yet), and Germany's our friend, who do we have
    to fight? *Well*, the Reverend answered *that* for you,
    in his good short words. Me and my three lads—two

lads, I'd say rather—we belong to a regiment is a few thousand miles from here, in a little country without much importance except from the point of view that there's a Union Jack flies over it and the people of that country can write British Subject after their names. And that makes us proud!

ATTERCLIFFE. I tell you it makes us proud!

HURST. We live in tattered tents in the rain, we eat rotten food, there's knives in the dark streets and blood on the floors of the hospitals, but we stand tall and proud: because of why we are there.

ATTERCLIFFE. Because we're there to serve our duty.

MUSGRAVE. A soldier's duty is a soldier's life.

(WALSH *enters at the extreme rear of the stage and walks slowly up behind the others and listens.*)

(*A roll on the drum.*)

MUSGRAVE. A soldier's life is to lay it down, against the enemies of his Queen,

(*A roll on the drum.*)

against the invaders of his home,

(*A roll on the drum.*)

against slavery, cruelty, tyrants.

(*A roll on the drum.*)

HURST. You put on the uniform and you give your life away, and who do you give it to?

ATTERCLIFFE. You give it to your duty.

MUSGRAVE. And you give it to your people, for peace, and for honesty.

(*A roll on the drum.*)

MUSGRAVE. That's *my* book. (*He turns on the* MAYOR.) What's *yours*?

MAYOR (*very taken aback*). Eh? What? Me? I'm not a reading man, but it *sounds* all right . . . strong. Strong . . .

MUSGRAVE (*to the* PARSON). What about *yours*?

PARSON (*dubiously*). You speak with enthusiasm, yes. I hope you'll be listened to.

MUSGRAVE (*at the top of his passion*). By God, I hope I am! D'ye hear me, d'ye hear me, d'ye hear me—I'm the Queen of England's man, and I'm wearing her coat and I know her Book backwards. I'm Black Jack Musgrave, me, the hardest serjeant of the line—I work my life to bugle and drum, for eighteen years I fought for one flag only, salute it in the morning, can you haul it down at dark? The Last Post of a living life? Look— I'll show it to you all. And I'll *dance* for you beneath it—hoist up the flag, boy—up, up, *up*!

(ATTERCLIFFE *has nipped up the ladder, holding the rope. He loops the rope over the cross-bar of the lamp-bracket, drops to the plinth again, flings open the lid of the big box, and hauls on the rope.* HURST *beats frantically on his drum. The rope is attached to the contents of the box, and these are jerked up to the cross-bar and reveal themselves as an articulated skeleton dressed in a soldier's tunic and trousers, the rope noosed round the neck. The* PEOPLE *draw back in horror.* MUSGRAVE *begins to dance, waving his rifle, his face contorted with demoniac fury.*)

MUSGRAVE (*as he dances, sings, with mounting emphasis*).

Up he goes and no one knows
How to bring him downwards
Dead man's feet
Over the street
Riding the roofs
And crying down your chimneys
Up he goes and no one knows
Who it was that rose him
But white and red
He waves his head
He sits on your back
And you'll never never lose him
Up he goes and no one knows
How to bring him downwards.

(*He breaks off at the climax of the song, and stands panting. The drum stops.*)

That'll do. That'll do for *that*. (*He beckons gently to the* PEOPLE.) You can come back. Come back. Come back. We're all quiet now. But nobody move out of this market-place. You saw the gun loaded. Well, it's on a very quick swivel and the man behind it's well trained. (*He gestures with his rifle towards the platform party.*)

And *I've* won a regimental cup four year running for
small-arms marksmanship. So be good, and be gentle,
all of you.

(*That checks the* BARGEE, *who made a move. The* MAYOR
seems to be about to speak.)

Right, Mr Mayor—I'll explain the whole business.

PARSON (*in a smaller voice than usual*). Business? What
business, sir? Do you intend to imply you are *threatening* us with these weapons?

MAYOR. The man's gone barmy. Constable, do summat, grab
him, quick!

(*The* CONSTABLE *makes an indecisive move.*)

MUSGRAVE. Be *quiet*. I shan't warn agen. (*To the* MAYOR
and the PARSON) You two. Get down there! Constable,
there!

(*He gestures peremptorily and the three of them obey
him, moving downstage to stand facing the platform
and covered by the gun.*)

Now I said I'll explain. So listen. (*He points to the
skeleton.*) This, up here, was a comrade of mine—of
ours. At least, he was till a few months since. He was
killed, being there for his duty, in the country I was
telling you about, where the regiment is stationed. It's
not right a colony, you know, it's a sort of Protectorate, but British, y'know, British. This, up here, he was
walking down a street latish at night, he'd been to the
opera—*you've* got a choral society in this town, I daresay—well, he was only a soldier, but North Country,
he was full of music, so he goes to the opera. And on
his way again to camp he was shot in the back. And it's
not surprising, neither: there was patriots abroad, anti-
British, subversive; like they didn't dare to shoot him
to his face. He was daft to be out alone, wasn't he? Out
of bounds, after curfew.

ATTERCLIFFE (*with suppressed frenzy*). Get on to the words
as matter, serjeant!

MUSGRAVE (*turning on him fiercely*). *I'm* talking now; you
wait your turn! . . . So we *come* to the words as matter.
He was the third to be shot that week. He was the fif-
teenth that month. In the back and all. Add to which he

was young, he was liked, he sang songs, they say, and he joked and he laughed—he was a good soldier, too, else *I'd* not have bothered (we'll leave out his sliding off to the opera WOL, but by and large good, and I've got standards). So at twelve o'clock at night they beat up the drums and sounded the calls and called out the guard and the guard calls us *all* out, and the road is red and slippery, and every soldier in the camp no longer in the camp but in the streets of that city, rifle-butts, bayonets, every street cut off for eight blocks north and west the opera house. And that's how it began.

HURST (*the frenzy rising*). The streets is empty, but the houses is full. He says, 'no undue measures, minimum violence', he says. 'But bring in the killers.'

ATTERCLIFFE. The killers are gone, they've gone miles off in that time—*sporting* away, right up in the mountains, I told you at the time.

MUSGRAVE. That's not material, there's one man is dead, but there's *everyone's* responsible.

HURST. So bring the *lot* in! It's easy, they're all in bed, kick the front doors down, knock 'em on the head, boys, chuck 'em in the wagons.

ATTERCLIFFE. I didn't know she was only a little kid, there was scores of 'em on that staircase, pitch-dark, trampling, screaming, they're all of 'em screaming, what are we to do?

HURST. Knock 'em on the head, boy, chuck 'em in the wagons.

ATTERCLIFFE. How was I to tell she was only a little kid?

MUSGRAVE (*bringing it to an end*). THAT'S NOT MATERIAL! You were told to bring 'em in. If you killed her, you killed her! She was just one, and who cares a damn for that! Stay in your place and keep your hands on that Gatling. We've got to have order here, whatever there was *there*; and I can tell you it wasn't order . . . (*To* HURST). You, take a rifle. Leave your drum down.

(HURST *jumps on the plinth, takes a rifle and loads.*) We've *got* to have order. So I'll just tell you quietly how many there were was put down as injured—that's badly hurt, hospital, we don't count knocks and bruises, any o' that. Twenty-five men. Nine women. *No* child-

ren, whatever *he* says. She was a fully grown girl, and
she had a known record as an associate of terrorists.
That was her. Then four men, one of them elderly,
turned out to have died too. Making five. Not so very
many. Dark streets. Natural surge of rage.

HURST. We didn't find the killers.

MUSGRAVE. Of course we didn't find 'em. Not *then* we
didn't, any road. We didn't even know 'em. But *I* know
'em, now.

(*He turns on* WALSH.) So what's *your* opinion?

MAYOR. He's not balmy, he's mad, he's stark off his nut.

PARSON. Why doesn't somebody do something, Constable?
(*Noises off.*)

MUSGRAVE (*indicates* WALSH). I'm talking to *him*.

CONSTABLE (*very shakily*). I shall have to ask you to—to
come down off this platform, Sarnt Musgrave. It looks
to me like your—your meeting's got out of hand.

HURST (*covering the* CONSTABLE). Aye, it has.

MUSGRAVE (*to* WALSH). Go on, brother. Tell us.

(WALSH *climbs up at the back of the plinth.*)

WALSH (*with a certain levity*). My opinion, eh? I don't know
why you need it. You've got *him*, haven't you? (*He
waggles the skeleton's foot familiarly.*) What more
d'you want? (*He comes forward and sits on the front
of the plinth, looking at the other two* COLLIERS.) Aye,
or you too, with your natty little nosegays dandled in
your hatbands. Take 'em out, sharp! He's learnt you the
truth, hasn't he?

(*They remove their cockades, shamefacedly.*)

PUGNACIOUS COLLIER. All right, *that'll* do.

WALSH. Will it, matey, will it? If it helps you to remember
what we've been fighting for, I daresay it will. Trade
Unions aren't formed, you know, so we can all have
beer-ups on the Army.

SLOW COLLIER. He said that'll do. I'm sick and bloody tired
—I don't know *what* it's all about.

WALSH (*drops down to the forestage*). Come home and I'll
tell you. The circus is over. Come on.

MUSGRAVE. Oh no it's not. Just bide still a while. There's
more to be said yet. When I asked you your opinion

I meant about them we was talking about—them as did *this*, up here.

WALSH. Well, *what* about them—brother? Clear enough to me. You go for a soldier, you find yourself in some-one else's country, you deserve all you get. *I'd* say it stands to reason.

MUSGRAVE. And that's *all* you would say? I'd thought better of you.

WALSH (*irritated*). Now look, look here, what *are* you trying to get? You come to this place all hollering for sym-pathy, Oh you've been beating and murdering and fol-lowing your trade boo-hoo: but we're not bloody in-terested! You mend your own heartache and leave us to sort with ours—we've enough and to spare!

MUSGRAVE (*very intensely*). This *is* for your heart. Take another look at *him*. (*Points to skeleton.*) Go on, man, both eyes, and carefully. Because you all used to know him: or most of you did. Private Billy Hicks, late of this parish, welcome him back from the wars, he's bronzed and he's fit, with many a tall tale of distant campaigning to spin round the fireside—ah, *you* used to know him, *didn't* you, Mrs Hitchcock!

(MRS HITCHCOCK *has risen in great alarm.*)

SLOW COLLIER. That's never Billy Hicks, ye dirty liar.

PUGNACIOUS COLLIER. He wor my putter for two year, when I hewed coal in number five—he hewed there hisself for nigh on a year alongside o' my brother.

SLOW COLLIER. He left his clogs to me when he went to join up—that's never our Billy.

NOISES OFF. Never Billy. Never Billy.

BARGEE. 'Never Billy Hicks'—'Never Billy Hicks'—they don't dare believe it. You've knocked 'em to the root, boy. Oh the white faces!

MRS HITCHCOCK. She ought to be told. She's got a right to know.

MUSGRAVE. Go along then and tell her.

HURST (*to* MUSGRAVE). You letting her go?

MUSGRAVE. Yes.

HURST. But—

MUSGRAVE (*curtly*). Attend to your orders.

(MRS HITCHCOCK *goes out*.)

When I say it's Billy Hicks, you can believe me it's true.

WALSH. Aye, I'll believe you. And you know what I think—
it's downright indecent.

MUSGRAVE. Aye, aye? But wait. Because here is the reason.
I'm a religious man, and I see the causes of the Almighty
in every human work.

PARSON. That is absolute blasphemy!

MAYOR. This won't do you a pennorth o' good, you know.

MUSGRAVE. Not to me, no. But maybe to you Now as I
understand the workings of God, through greed and
the world, this man didn't die because he went alone
to the opera, he was killed because he had to be—it being
decided; that now the people in that city was worked
right up to killing soldiers, then more and more soldiers
should be sent for them to kill, and the soldiers in turn
should kill the people in that city, more and more, always—that's what I said to you: four men, one girl,
then the twenty-five and the nine—*and* it'll go on, there
or elsewhere, and it can't be stopped neither, except
there's someone finds out Logic and brings the wheel
round. You see, the Queen's Book, which eighteen
years I've lived, it's turned inside out for *me*. There
used to be my duty: now there's a disease—

HURST. Wild-wood mad.

MUSGRAVE. Wild-wood mad we are; and so we've fetched
it home. You've had Moses and the Prophets—that's
him— (*He points at* WALSH.)—'cos he told you. But
you were all for enlisting, it'd still have gone on. Moses
and the Prophets, what good did they do?

(*He sits down and broods. There is a pause.*)

WALSH (*awkwardly*). There's no one from this town be
over keen to join up now. You've preached your little
gospel: I daresay we can go home?

(MUSGRAVE *makes no reply. The* SOLDIERS *look at one
another doubtfully.*)

HURST. What do we do now?

ATTERCLIFFE. Wait.

HURST. Serjeant—

ATTERCLIFFE (*shushing him*). Ssh-ssh!

(*A pause. Restive noises, off.*)

HURST. Serjeant—

ATTERCLIFFE. Serjeant—they've heard your message, they'll
none of them forget it. Haven't we done what we came
for?

HURST (*astonished, to* ATTERCLIFFE). Done what we came
for?

(ATTERCLIFFE *shushes him again as* MUSGRAVE *rises.*)

MUSGRAVE (*as though to himself*). One man, and for him
five. Therefore for five of them we multiply out, *and*
we find it five-and-twenty. . . . So, as I understand
Logic and Logic to me is the mechanism of God—
that means that today there's twenty-five persons will
have to be—

(ATTERCLIFFE *jumps up in horror.* ANNIE *and* MRS
HITCHCOCK *appear at the upper window. When she sees
the skeleton* ANNIE *gasps and seems about to scream.*)

MUSGRAVE (*cutting her short*). It's true. It's him. You don't
need to cry out; you knew it when he left you.

ANNIE. Take him down. Let me have him. I'll come down
for him now.

Run-out

This powerful and mysterious play, which has been widely
performed and widely praised, reflects in 'mad Jack Musgrave' a kind of grim logic. It has been suggested that
John Arden was thinking of Cyprus where there was a na-
tionalist war against the British in the nineteen-fifties, but
it could equally apply to many other small-scale wars, then
and since. Musgrave and Hurst describe how the death of
Billy Hicks on the way back from seeing an opera is followed,
horribly and inevitably, by the death of a large number of
people, mostly innocent, in 'the Protectorate', and Musgrave,
with his passionate sense of mission and military logic got
from long acquaintance with the 'Queen's Regulations' (the
'Queen's Book') concludes that twenty-five people will have
to be killed. Hurst wants to shoot 'the ones as never get
hurt' and points to the Mayor, Parson and Constable as in-
stigators of war.

Arden has an interesting note on this: 'I think that many

of us must at some time have felt an overpowering urge to match some particularly outrageous piece of violence with an even greater and more outrageous retaliation.' But he adds that the moral of this play is pacifist even though it is 'a very hard doctrine'.

At the last moment Hurst is shot by one of a troop of dragoons who have been searching for the deserters, and Attercliffe and Musgrave are arrested. They are last seen in a prison cell awaiting hanging, and Mrs Hitchcock, the landlady of a public house, tells Musgrave he has got it all wrong in terms of tactics, but that one day the people of the town will see the point of what he has been trying to do; Attercliffe agrees with her ('You can't cure the pox by further whoring'), and finishes by singing a little ballad about an apple seed that will ultimately produce a lot of fruit—and presumably that eventually man will learn the wickedness and futility of war.

❌❌❌

THE LONG AND THE SHORT AND THE TALL

Lead-in
If you have not already read the previous extract from this play, you should do so. We won't repeat here the notes we made on the characters and general situation. The patrol is now aware that there are many Japanese soldiers in the immediate vicinity of the hut: indeed, they may be surrounded. They must try to make a break for it, and it is clear that their original plan—to take the Japanese soldier back with them—is no longer feasible. The tragedy, and the irony, lies in the fact that Bamforth has now established a real human relationship with him and is prepared to risk his own life in his defence. There follow the last pages of the play; the reference to 'the fag case' refers back to the discovery that the prisoner has an English cigarette case, which he may have acquired as a souvenir or may have looted from an English prisoner or corpse. Whitaker, himself a great collector of souvenirs, is ordered to cover the prisoner while Bamforth is overpowered, and shoots him in panic, thereby

alerting the surrounding Japanese troops who attack the patrol. At this moment contact is made by radio with the British forces, but it is too late. The final irony of all is that the only survivor is the detestable Corporal Johnstone. The indictment of war is, in fact, complete.

ACTING NOTES

Please look back to the earlier notes on this play. The most demanding part is undoubtedly that of Bamforth, who remains what used to be called a 'wide boy' in spite of the great sympathy he earns in these pages. Obviously you will need mock-ups of sten guns, bayonets, rifles, and an army water bottle, and something to represent the sound of machine guns will add a great deal to the climax. (We taped the noise made by rhythmic desk drumming and kettle drum sticks, with one of our number 'conducting' the sound to make it convincing : some experiment is probably needed.) The radio-operator's voice needs to be either taped or spoken off stage.

BAMFORTH. A handsome young private lay dying,
    At the edge of the jungle he lay.
    The Regiment gathered around him,
    To hear for the last words he'd say.
    'Take the trigger-guard out of my kidneys,
    Take the magazine out of my brain,
    Take the barrel from out of my back-bone,
    And assemble my rifle again . . .'
    (*In an attempt to restore the previous mood,* BAMFORTH *rubs the top of the* PRISONER'S *head playfully.*) Now then, Tojo, my old flowerpot, what do you think of that? That's better than you cop on from the Tokyo geisha fillies.
EVANS (*turning at window*). It'll not be long before it's dark now, Sarge.
MACLEISH (*without turning from window*). It's quiet out there. It's bloody quiet.
MITCHEM (*rising*). Time we got ready for the push then. Got packed up. Got things—sorted out.
BAMFORTH (*having taken a swig from his water bottle, he wipes the lips and offers the bottle to the* PRISONER).

Come on, Tojo son. Get a gob of this before go.
(*The* PRISONER *accepts the bottle gratefully*.)

JOHNSTONE. There's no more buckshees for the Nippo, Bamforth.
(*The* PRISONER, *sensing the meaning from* JOHN-
STONE'S *tone, returns the water bottle to Bamforth without drinking*.)

BAMFORTH (*puts down the water bottle and turns to face*
JOHNSTONE). I've warned you, Johnno. Don't over-
step them tapes. I'll not take any more of the patter. Is
it O.K. if I give the prisoner a drink, Sarge?

MITCHEM. You heard what Corporal Johnstone said, Bamforth.

BAMFORTH (*incredulous*). You what?

JOHNSTONE. There's no more water for the Nippo.

BAMFORTH. Like Hell there isn't. The bloke's got to drink.

MITCHEM. He's had a drink—earlier on this afternoon. I
gave him one myself.

BAMFORTH. He's not a camel!

MITCHEM. I'm sorry, Bamforth. We've none to spare for
him.

BAMFORTH. Sorry!

MITCHEM. We'll need every drop we've got for getting back.
It's dead certain there'll be a gang of Nips around
every water hole from here to base.

BAMFORTH. So we share out what we've got.

MITCHEM. No.

BAMFORTH. He gets half of mine.

MITCHEM. No! There's none for him.

BAMFORTH. He'll have to have a drink sometime. He can't
go the distance without—you've got to get him back
as well. (*He waits for a reply*.) We're taking him as
well!

MITCHEM. I'm sorry.

JOHNSTONE. He's stopping where he is. (*He picks up the*
PRISONER'S *bayonet from the table*.) It's cobbler's for
him.

BAMFORTH. No.

MITCHEM. I've got no choice.

BAMFORTH. You said he was going back.

MITCHEM. He was—before. The circumstances altered. The situation's changed. I can't take him along.

BAMFORTH. What's the poor get done to us?

MITCHEM. It's a war. It's something in a uniform and it's a different shade to mine.

BAMFORTH (*positioning himself between the* PRISONER *and* JOHNSTONE). You're not doing it, Johnno.

JOHNSTONE. You laying odds on that?

BAMFORTH. For Christ's sake!

JOHNSTONE. It's a bloody Nip.

BAMFORTH. He's a man!

JOHNSTONE (*crossing a few paces towards the* PRISONER). Shift yourself, Bamforth. Get out of the way.

BAMFORTH. You're not doing it.

MITCHEM. Bamforth, shift yourself.

BAMFORTH. You're a bastard, Mitchem.

MITCHEM. I wish to God I was.

BAMFORTH. You're a dirty bastard, Mitchem.

MITCHEM. As far as I'm concerned, it's all these lads or him.

BAMFORTH. It's him and me.

MITCHEM (*crossing to join* JOHNSTONE). Get to one side. That's an order.

BAMFORTH. Stick it.

MITCHEM. For the last time, Bamforth, move over.

BAMFORTH. Try moving me.

MITCHEM. I've not got time to mess about.

BAMFORTH. So come on, Whitaker! Don't sit there, lad. Who's side you on? (WHITAKER *rises slowly from the form. For a moment it would seem that he is going to stand by* BAMFORTH *but he crosses the room to stand beyond* MITCHEM *and* JOHNSTONE.) You've got no guts, Whitaker. You know that, boy? You've just got no guts.

WHITAKER. We've got to get back, Bammo.

BAMFORTH. You're a gutless slob!

WHITAKER. I've got to get back!

BAMFORTH. Evans. Taffy, Taff! (EVANS *turns from the window.*) Put the gun on these two, son.

EVANS. I reckon Mitch is right, you know. We couldn't get him back to camp, could we, boyo? The Nips must have a Div between the camp and us.

BAMFORTH. He's going to kill him, you nit!

EVANS. You never know about that fag case, do you, son?

BAMFORTH. What's the fag case got to do with it! . . .
Smudger! Smudger, now it's up to you.

SMITH. Don't ask me, Bammo. Leave me out of it.

BAMFORTH. You're in it, Smudge. You're in it up to here.

SMITH. I just take orders. I just do as I'm told. I just plod
on.

BAMFORTH. The plodding on has stopped. Right here. Right
here you stop and make a stand. He's got a wife and
kids.

SMITH. I've got a wife and kids myself. Drop it, Bammo,
it's like Mitch says—it's him or us.

BAMFORTH. Jock! . . . Jock! (MACEISH *continues to stare
out of the window.*) Macleish! . . . (MACLEISH *does
not move.*) I hope they carve your brother up. Get that?
I hope they carve your bloody brother up!

MITCHEM. All right, Bamforth, you've had your say. Now
shift.

BAMFORTH. Shift me! Come on, heroes, shift me!

MITCHEM. Whitaker! Grab a gun and cover the Nip.

BAMFORTH. Don't do it, Whitaker. Stay out of it.

MITCHEM. Whitaker!

(WHITAKER *picks up a Sten from the table and crosses
to cover the* PRISONER, *who has realized the implica-
tions and is trembling with fear.* MITCHEM *and* JOHN-
STONE *move forward to overpower* BAMFORTH. JOHN-
STONE *drops the bayonet on the floor and, together with*
MITCHEM, *grapples with* BAMFORTH. *As they fight the*
PRISONER *begins to rise to his feet.*)

WHITAKER (*already in a state of fear himself*). Get down!
. . . Sit down! . . . (*The* PRISONER *continues to rise.*)
Sit down, you stupid man, or I'll have to put a bullet
into you . . . (*The* PRISONER *is standing upright as*
WHITAKER'S *finger tightens on the trigger. A long
burst from the Sten shudders the hut and the bullets
slam home into the body of the* PRISONER *like hammer
blows. The* PRISONER *doubles up and falls to the floor.
The fight stops. There is a pause.* WHITAKER *drops the*

Sten and buries his face in his hands.) God . . . God . . . God . . . (*His voice swells.*) Oh, God!

MITCHEM. Well, that should roust out every Nip from here to Tokyo. You've made a mess of that, lad. (WHITAKER, *uncomprehending, looks at his hands.* MITCHEM *seizes him by the shoulders and shakes him savagely.*) Come on, come on! Come out of it! He's just the first.

BAMFORTH. You've got the biggest souvenir of all. You've done it this time, Whitaker. Take that and hang it on the front room wall . . .

(BAMFORTH'S *words are cut short as* MITCHEM *strikes him across the face.*)

MITCHEM. We've had enough from you.

(EVANS *and* MACLEISH *have left their posts and, together with* SMITH, *are drawn in fascination towards the body of the* PRISONER.)

JOHNSTONE. All right. Get back. It's just a corpse. You'll see a whole lot more like that before you've done.

MITCHEM. Right. All of you. We're moving out. In double time. Get your gear together. Thirty seconds and we're off. Any longer and this place will be rotten with Nips. Any man not ready stays behind. Move!

(*The members of the patrol put on their packs, ammunition pouches, etc.*)

MITCHEM. Johnno, ditch your stuff. Can you work the set? (JOHNSTONE *nods assent and crosses to radio.*) Give it one last crack. (JOHNSTONE *switches on the set and the crackle of interference grows behind.*) We haven't got a snowball's chance in Hell of getting back. So try and let them know the Japs have broken through.

JOHNSTONE (*nods and switches to 'transmit'*). Blue Patrol calling Red Leader . . . Blue Patrol calling Red Leader . . . Are you receiving me . . . Are you receiving me . . . Come in Red Leader . . . Over . . . (JOHNSTONE *switches to 'receive' and the interference swells.*) . . . Not a rotten peep.

MITCHEM. All right. Jack it in.

JOHNSTONE (*rips off headphones, leaving the set switched on. He straps on his ammunition pouches and picks up the Sten from the floor*). Let's have you then! We're pushing off!

MITCHEM (*picking up his own Sten*). Leave what you haven't got. And move!

(*The members of the patrol collect their rifles and cross to the door.* JOHNSTONE *glances out of the window.*)

JOHNSTONE. All clear.

MITCHEM (*opens the door*). I'll break the trail. Johnno, you bring up the rear. (JOHNSTONE *nods.*) All right, let's go.

(*One by one the members of the patrol follow* MITCHEM *through the door.* JOHNSTONE *is the last to leave. As the door closes behind* JOHNSTONE *the interference increases on the set and suddenly it bursts into life.*)

OPERATOR (*on distort*). . . . Red Leader calling Blue Patrol . . . Red Leader calling Blue Patrol . . . Come in Blue Patrol . . . Come in Blue Patrol . . . Over . . .

(*A machine gun chatters in the jungle and is joined by another. We hear the sound of one or two rifles and the screams of dying men. The noise of gunfire fades away, to leave only the whimper of one wounded man—it is* WHITAKER. *The door is pushed open and* JOHNSTONE *enters. He has a bullet wound in his side and the blood is seeping through his shirt. Slamming the door shut, he leans upon it to regain his breath.*)

WHITAKER (*screams out from the jungle in fear*). God! . . . God! . . . (*A final cry of terror louder than any we have heard previously.*) Mother . . . !

(*We hear the sound of a single shot and* WHITAKER *is dead.* JOHNSTONE *presses his hand to his side. The set splutters into life again.*)

OPERATOR (*on distort*). . . . Are you receiving me, Blue Patrol . . . Are you receiving me . . . Over . . .

JOHNSTONE (*crosses slowly to the set, picks up the hand-set, and switches to 'transmit'*). Get knotted! All of you! You hear! The whole damn lot of you!

(JOHNSTONE *switches off the set and crosses towards the body of the* PRISONER. *As he passes the window there is a short burst of machine-gun fire. He ducks below window level. Squatting by the side of the body, he takes the cigarette case from the* PRISONER'S *pocket and helps himself to a cigarette. Sticking the cigarette in his mouth, he returns the case to the* PRISONER'S *pocket. He tugs the white silk scarf, now spattered with blood, from the* PRISONER'S *neck and crawls across to beneath the window, where he ties the scarf round the barrel of his Sten. It has all required a great effort, and he lights a cigarette and inhales deeply before continuing. Squatting below the window, he waves the white flag and, in turn, takes long pulls at the cigarette. For a moment there is complete silence and then a bird sings out in the jungle.*)

Curtain

Run-out

We think this passage speaks for itself. The impossibility of love and sympathy—the feelings Bamforth has for the Japanese—and the empty cruel futility of the deaths are very strongly realized in dramatic terms, and above all, perhaps, the impersonality of war and its incapacity to make distinctions or save the deserving.

8
Death

We all have to face death at some time—the death of people we love, and ultimately our own death. It is right that drama should deal with this, and right that it should help us to understand it and come to terms with it. A fine novelist, E. M. Forster, wrote 'Death destroys a man; the idea of death saves him.' Coming to terms with death helps us to endure it. Lawrence's treatment brings the dead miner actually on to the stage and shows the poignant remorseful feelings of wife and mother. In contrast, Arthur Miller shows us John Proctor in his prison cell condemned to death but offered his life if he will deny himself and his own truth; he is sorely tempted but in the end goes to his death firm in his conviction. It is a shattering end to the play, and I have seen it performed so that his last exit is almost unbearable.

THE WIDOWING OF MRS HOLROYD

Lead-in
D. H. Lawrence wrote three plays as a young man, before he found his chief medium in novels and short stories. All three plays reflect his early life in Nottinghamshire, where he was born the son of a coalminer, or 'collier'. *The Widowing of Mrs Holroyd* tells the story of an unhappy marriage between a collier and his wife (Lizzie Holroyd), and clearly reflects some aspects of the life of Lawrence's own parents. Charles Holroyd drinks, partly out of despair, and the early scenes of the play show him quarrelling violently with his wife and frightening his two small children. A young bachelor, Blackmore, who works in the pit as an electrician not a collier, forms a strong attachment to Mrs Holroyd, and, after bringing her husband home drunk, he begs

her to take the children and go away with him. Holroyd falls asleep but wakes up to a confused fight with Blackmore, who lays him out. Mrs Holroyd agrees that she will leave her husband the following weekend. On the next evening Holroyd fails to appear after his day's work down the pit. His mother ('Grandmother') arrives to say that Blackmore had called at her nearby house to ask where Holroyd was, and it had been assumed that he was in one of the public houses, but he wasn't found there. In a discussion between mother and daughter-in-law, the grandmother accuses Lizzie of being stiff-necked and superior to her son, but agrees that he is difficult to live with. Then, as our extract starts, a collier, Rigley, who 'butties' and works with Charles Holroyd, arrives to say that he didn't come up from the pit with him as usual; he is obviously worried. The rest of the extract is self-explanatory; the dead man has been caught in a small fall from the tunnel roof and presumably gassed, as he is hardly marked except on his hands where he has tried to claw himself out.

The attitudes to his death shown by the three leading characters are complex and subtle, and though Lawrence is not, I think, a great dramatist, there is a fine mixture here of pity, despair and shame. Charles' mother shows a profound sadness mixed with a sense of inevitablity: this, or something like it, has happened to her before, and she knows what has to be done to make this terrible death 'seemly' in her terms. Blackmore feels a comradeship towards even the hated Holroyd, and his behaviour shows a wish to relieve Mrs Holroyd of as much pain as possible, as well as a rallying round and solidarity with a fellow-worker in the face of death. Mrs Holroyd half believes that she is responsible for her husband's death and that he wouldn't have remained behind in the pit and so been killed had it not been for their quarrel; she feels love and tenderness for him in the stillness of death—perhaps the love and tenderness that she has lost in their daily quarrels and struggles; certainly her feelings go back to the early days of their courtship. We learn in these few pages a good deal about the nature of death and the response of mother, wife and 'rival' to this immovable fact.

ACTING NOTES

The dialect is that of Nottinghamshire, and those who live in that area will have no difficulty with it; but Lawrence, like Shaw, gives us a good deal of help in showing how to pronounce it. The grandmother is old but still indomitable, and has had 'five lads in the pit'; one of her main anxieties is that Charles may have died without having had time to repent of his sins, and she is pleased to learn a little later that he survived a little while after the fall. She and Mrs Holroyd almost break down when they think of him 'making a bit of a fight', and the grandmother is anxious that he shall be properly dressed and washed for burial before he stiffens; she is proud of his fine physique, even in death. Blackmore is a straightforward and honest young man of twenty-eight who must show real devotion to Lizzie Holroyd, especially in the brief moments when the grandmother goes to get the laying-out clothes. Mrs Holroyd is described by Lawrence as a woman of thirty-two, 'tall and voluptuously built'. Hers is a difficult part to play; she needs to imply that she has come to realize too late that she has never loved her husband enough and can now do nothing for him. Her main feelings here are of remorse and guilt, but she should also show that in a sense she *has* always loved her husband. Perhaps her most important speech is just after Blackmore goes out and she talks to the dead Charles as she sponges his face : this can be very moving if well done.

Holroyd is a corpse and doesn't have to act, though 'being dead' on the stage is not the easiest of things! He is naked to the waist and has pit-dirt on his body, bloodstained hands and heavy pit-boots. Rigby and the manager are easy small parts; both are distressed and embarrassed, Rigby anxious not to be blamed and the manager trying in his own way to make the death more endurable for mother and wife. Some sound effects (the chuffing of the driving engine and so forth) can probably be improvized; some tea things on a table are needed, with a sugar bowl and something to represent lumps of sugar, and a bowl of water, with flannel, soap and towel for the washing of the corpse.

There is a knock at the door. MRS HOLROYD *opens.*
RIGLEY. They tell me, missus, as your mester's not hoom yet.
MRS HOLROYD. No—who is it?

G

GRANDMOTHER. Ask him to step inside. Don't stan' there lettin' the fog in.

(RIGLEY *steps in. He is a tall, bony, very roughly hewn collier.*)

RIGLEY. Good evenin'.

GRANDMOTHER. Oh, is it you, Mr Rigley? (*In a querulous, spiteful tone to* MRS HOLROYD.) He butties along with Charlie.

MRS HOLROYD. Oh!

RIGLEY. An' han yer seen nowt on 'im?

MRS HOLROYD. No—was he all right at work?

RIGLEY. Well, 'e wor nowt to mention. A bit short, like: 'adna much to say. I canna ma'e out what 'e's done wi' 'issen. (*He is manifestly uneasy, does not look at the two women.*)

GRANDMOTHER. An' did 'e come up i' th' same bantle wi' you?

RIGLEY. No—'e didna. As Ah was comin' out o' th' stall, Ah shouted, 'Art comin', Charlie? We're a' off.' An' 'e said, 'Ah'm comin' in a minute.' 'E wor just finishin' a stint, like, an' 'e wanted ter get it set. An' 'e'd been a bit roughish in 'is temper, like, so I thöwt 'e didna want ter walk to th' bottom wi' us....

GRANDMOTHER (*wailing*). An' what's 'e gone an' done to himself?

RIGLEY. Nay, missis, yo munna ax me that. 'E's non done owt as Ah know on. On'y I wor thinkin', 'appen summat 'ad 'appened to 'im, like, seein' as nob'dy had any knowings of 'im comin' up.

MRS HOLROYD. What is the matter, Mr Rigley? Tell us it out.

RIGLEY. I canna do that, missis. It seems as if 'e niver come up th' pit—as far as we can make out. 'Appen a bit o' stuff's fell an' pinned 'im.

GRANDMOTHER (*wailing*). An' 'ave you left 'im lying down there in the pit, poor thing?

RIGLEY (*uneasily*). I couldna say for certain where 'e is.

MRS HOLROYD (*agitated*). Oh, it's very likely not very bad, Mother! Don't let us run to meet trouble.

RIGLEY. We 'ave to 'ope for th' best, missis, all on us.

GRANDMOTHER (*wailing*). Eh, they'll bring 'im 'ome, I know

they will, smashed up an' broke! An' one of my sons they've burned down pit till the flesh dropped off 'im, an' one was shot till 'is shoulder was all of a mosh, an' they brought 'em 'ome to me. An' now there's this . . .

MRS HOLROYD (*shuddering*). Oh, don't Mother. (*Appealing to* RIGLEY.) You don't know that he's hurt?

RIGLEY (*shaking his head*). I canna tell you.

MRS HOLROYD (*in a high hysterical voice*). Then what is it?

RIGLEY (*very uneasy*). I canna tell you. But yon young electrician—Mr Blackmore—'e rung down to the night deputy, an' it seems as though there's been a fall or summat . . .

GRANDMOTHER. Eh, Lizzie, you parted from him in anger. You little knowed how you'd meet him again.

RIGLEY (*making an effort*). Well, I'd 'appen best be goin' to see what's betide. (*He goes out.*)

GRANDMOTHER. I'm sure I've had my share of bad luck, I have. I'm sure I've brought up five lads in the pit, through accidents and troubles, and now there's this. The Lord has treated me very hard, very hard. It's a blessing, Lizzie, as you've got a bit of money, else what would 'ave become of the children?

MRS HOLROYD. Well, if he's badly hurt, there'll be the Union-pay, and sick-pay—we shall manage. And perhaps it's *not* very much.

GRANDMOTHER. There's no knowin' but what they'll be carryin' him to die i' th' hospital.

MRS HOLROYD. Oh, don't say so, Mother—it won't be so bad, you'll see.

GRANDMOTHER. How much money have you, Lizzie, comin'?

MRS HOLROYD. I don't know—not much over a hundred pounds.

GRANDMOTHER (*shaking her head*). An' what's that, what's that?

MRS HOLROYD (*sharply*). Hush!

GRANDMOTHER (*crying*). Why, what?

(MRS HOLROYD *opens the door. In the silence can be heard the pulsing of the fan engine, then the driving engine chuffs rapidly: there is a skirr of brakes on the rope as it descends.*)

MRS HOLROYD. That's twice they've sent the chair down—
I wish we could see. . . . Hark!

GRANDMOTHER. What is it?

MRS HOLROYD. Yes—it's stopped at the gate. It's the doctor's.

GRANDMOTHER (*coming to the door*). What, Lizzie?

MRS HOLROYD. The doctor's motor. (*She listens acutely.*)
Dare you stop here, Mother, while I run up to the top
an' see?

GRANDMOTHER. You'd better not go, Lizzie, you'd better not.
A woman's best away.

MRS HOLROYD. It is unbearable to wait.

GRANDMOTHER. Come in an' shut the door—it's a cold that
gets in your bones.

(MRS HOLROYD *goes in.*)

MRS HOLROYD. Perhaps while he's in bed we shall have time
to change him. It's an ill wind brings no good. He'll
happen be a better man.

GRANDMOTHER. Well, you can but try. Many a woman's
thought the same.

MRS HOLROYD. Oh, dear, I wish somebody would come. He's
never been hurt since we were married.

GRANDMOTHER. No, he's never had a bad accident, all the
years he's been in the pit. He's been luckier than most.
But everybody has it, sooner or later.

MRS HOLROYD (*shivering*). It *is* a horrid night.

GRANDMOTHER (*querulous*). Yes, come your ways in.

MRS HOLROYD. Hark!

(*There is a quick sound of footsteps.* BLACKMORE *comes
into the light of the doorway.*)

BLACKMORE. They're bringing him.

MRS HOLROYD (*quickly putting her hand over her breast*).
What is it?

BLACKMORE. You can't tell anything's the matter with him
—it's not marked him at all.

MRS HOLROYD. Oh, what a blessing! And is it much?

BLACKMORE. Well—

MRS HOLROYD. What is it?

BLACKMORE. It's the worst.

GRANDMOTHER. Who is it?—What does he say?

(MRS HOLROYD *sinks on the nearest chair with a hor-*

rified expression. BLACKMORE *pulls himself together and enters the room. He is very pale.*)

BLACKMORE. I came to tell you they're bringing him home.

GRANDMOTHER. And you said it wasn't very bad, did you?

BLACKMORE. No—I said it was—as bad as it could be.

MRS HOLROYD (*rising and crossing to her Mother-in-law, flings her arms round her; in a high voice*). Oh, Mother, what shall we do? What shall we do?

GRANDMOTHER. You don't mean to say he's dead?

BLACKMORE. Yes.

GRANDMOTHER (*staring*). God help us, and how was it?

BLACKMORE. Some stuff fell.

GRANDMOTHER (*rocking herself and her daughter-in-law— both weeping*). Oh, God have mercy on us! Oh, God have mercy on us! Some stuff fell on him. An' he'd not even time to cry for mercy; oh, God spare him! Oh, what shall we do for comfort? To be taken straight out of his sins. Oh, Lizzie, to think he should be cut off in his wickedness! He's been a bad lad of late, he has, poor lamb. He's gone very wrong of late years, poor dear lamb, very wrong. Oh, Lizzie, think what's to become of him now! If only you'd have tried to be different with him.

MRS HOLROYD (*moaning*). Don't, Mother, don't. I can't bear it.

BLACKMORE (*cold and clear*). Where will you have him laid? The men will be here in a moment.

MRS HOLROYD (*starting up*). They can carry him up to bed—

BLACKMORE. It's no good taking him upstairs. You'll have to wash him and lay him out.

MRS HOLROYD (*startled*). Well—

BLACKMORE. He's in his pit-dirt.

GRANDMOTHER. He is, bless him. We'd better have him down here, Lizzie, where we can handle him.

MRS HOLROYD. Yes. (*She begins to put the tea things away, but drops the sugar out of the basin and the lumps fly broadcast.*)

BLACKMORE. Never mind, I'll pick those up. You put the children's clothes away.

(MRS HOLROYD *stares witless around. The* GRAND-

MOTHER *sits rocking herself and weeping.* BLACKMORE
*clears the table, putting the pots in the scullery. He folds
the white tablecloth and pulls back the table. The door
opens.* MRS HOLROYD *utters a cry.* RIGLEY *enters.*)

RIGLEY. They're bringing him now, missis.

MRS HOLROYD. Oh!

RIGLEY (*simply*). There must ha' been a fall directly after
we left him.

MRS HOLROYD (*frowning, horrified*). No—no!

RIGLEY (*to* BLACKMORE). It fell a' back of him, an' shut 'im
in as you might shut a loaf i' th' oven. It never touched
him.

MRS HOLROYD (*staring distractedly*). Well, then—

RIGLEY. You see, it come on 'im as close as a trap on a mouse,
an' gen him no air, an' what wi' th' gas, it smothered
him. An' it wouldna be so very long about it neither.

MRS HOLROYD (*quiet with horror*). Oh!

GRANDMOTHER. Eh, dear—dear. Eh, dear—dear.

RIGLEY (*looking hard at her*). I wasna to know what 'ud
happen.

GRANDMOTHER (*now heeding him, but weeping all the time*).
But the Lord gave him time to repent. He'd have a few
minutes to repent. Ay, I hope he did, I hope he did, else
what was to become of him. The Lord cut him off in
his sins, but He gave him time to repent.

(RIGLEY *looks away at the wall.* BLACKMORE *has made
a space in the middle of the floor.*)

BLACKMORE. If you'll take the rocking-chair off the end of
the rug, Mrs Holroyd, I can pull it back a bit from the
fire, and we can lay him on that.

GRANDMOTHER (*petulantly*). What's the good of messing
about— (*She moves.*)

MRS HOLROYD. It suffocated him?

RIGLEY (*shaking his head, briefly*). Yes. 'Appened th' after-
damp—

BLACKMORE. He'd be dead in a few minutes.

MRS HOLROYD. No—oh, think!

BLACKMORE. You mustn't think.

RIGLEY (*suddenly*). They commin'!

(MRS HOLROYD *stands at bay. The* GRANDMOTHER *half*

rises. RIGLEY *and* BLACKMORE *efface themselves as much as possible. A man backs into the room, bearing the feet of the dead man, which are shod in great pit boots. As the head bearer comes awkwardly past the table, the coat with which the body is covered slips off, revealing* HOL-ROYD *in his pit-dirt, naked to the waist.*)

MANAGER (*a little stout, white-bearded man*). Mind now, mind. Ay, missis, what a job, indeed, it is! (*Sharply*) Where mun they put him?

MRS HOLROYD (*turning her face aside from the corpse*). Lay him on the rug.

MANAGER. Steady now, do it steady.

SECOND BEARER (*rising and pressing back his shoulders*). By Guy, but 'e 'ings heavy.

MANAGER. Yi, Joe, I'll back my life o' that.

GRANDMOTHER. Eh, Mr Chambers, what's this affliction on my old age. You kept your sons out o' the pit, but all mine's in. And to think of the trouble I've had—to think o' the trouble that's come out of Brinsley pit to me.

MANAGER. It has that, it 'as that, missis. You seem to have had more'n your share; I'll admit it, you have.

MRS HOLROYD (*who has been staring at the men*). It is too much! (BLACKMORE *frowns;* RIGLEY *glowers at her.*)

MANAGER. You never knowed such a thing in your life. Here's a man, holin' a stint, just finishin', (*he puts himself as if in the holer's position, gesticulating freely*), an' a lot o' stuff falls behind him, clean as a whistle, shuts him up safe as a worm in a nut and niver touches him—niver knowed such a thing in your life.

MRS HOLROYD. Ugh!

MANAGER. It niver hurt him—niver touched him.

MRS HOLROYD. Yes, but—but how long would he be (*she makes a sweeping gesture; the* MANAGER *looks at her and will not help her out*) —how long would it take—ah—to—to kill him?

MANAGER. Nay, I canna tell ye. 'E didna seem to ha' strived much to get out—did he, Joe?

SECOND BEARER. No, not as far as Ah'n seen.

FIRST BEARER. You look at 'is 'ands, you'll see then. 'E'd non ha'e room to swing the pick.

(*The* MANAGER *goes on his knees.*)

MRS HOLROYD (*shuddering*). Oh, don't!

MANAGER. Ay, th' nails is broken a bit—

MRS HOLROYD (*clenching her fists*). Don't!

MANAGER. 'E'd be sure ter ma'e a bit of a fight. But th' gas 'ud soon get hold on 'im. Ay, it's an awful thing to think of, it is indeed.

MRS HOLROYD (*her voice breaking*). I can't bear it!

MANAGER. Eh, dear, we none on us know what's comin' next.

MRS HOLROYD (*getting hysterical*). Oh, it's too awful, it's too awful!

BLACKMORE. You'll disturb the children.

GRANDMOTHER. And you don't want *them* down here.

MANAGER. 'E'd no business to ha' been left, you know.

RIGLEY. An what man, dost think, wor goin' to sit him down on his hams an' wait for a chap as wouldna say 'thank yer' for his cump'ny? 'E'd bin ready to fall out wi' a flicker o' the candle, so who dost think wor goin' ter stop when we knowed 'e on'y kep on so's to get shut on us.

MANAGER. Tha'rt quite right, Bill, quite right. But theer you are.

RIGLEY. Ah' if we'd stopped, what good would it ha' done—

MANAGER. No, 'appen not, 'appen not.

RIGLEY. For, not known—

MANAGER. I'm sayin' nowt agen thee, neither one road nor t'other. (*There is general silence—then, to* MRS HOLROYD) I should think th' inquest'll be at th' New Inn to-morrow, missis. I'll let you know.

MRS HOLROYD. Will there have to be an inquest?

MANAGER. Yes—there'll have to be an inquest. Shall you want anybody in, to stop with you tonight?

MRS HOLROYD. No.

MANAGER. Well, then, we'd best be goin'. I'll send my missis down first thing in the morning. It's a bad job, a bad job, it is. You'll be a' right then?

MRS HOLROYD. Yes.

MANAGER. Well, good night then—good night all.

ALL. Good night. Good night.

(*The* MANAGER, *followed by the two bearers, goes out, closing the door.*)

RIGLEY. It's like this, missis. I never should ha' gone, if he hadn't wanted us to.

MRS HOLROYD. Yes, I know.

RIGLEY. 'E wanted to come up by 's sen.

MRS HOLROYD (*wearily*). I know how it was, Mr Rigley.

RIGLEY. Yes—

BLACKMORE. Nobody could foresee.

RIGLEY (*shaking his head*). No. If there's owt, missis, as you want—

MRS HOLROYD. Yes—I think there isn't anything.

RIGLEY (*after a moment*). Well—good night—we've worked i' the same stall ower four years now—

MRS HOLROYD. Yes.

RIGLEY. Well, good night, missis.

MRS HOLROYD *and* BLACKMORE. Good night.

(*The* GRANDMOTHER *all this time has been rocking herself to and fro, moaning and murmuring beside the dead man. When* RIGLEY *has gone* MRS HOLROYD *stands staring distractedly before her. She has not yet looked at her husband.*)

GRANDMOTHER. Have you got the things ready, Lizzie?

MRS HOLROYD. What things?

GRANDMOTHER. To lay the child out.

MRS HOLROYD (*she shudders*). No—what?

GRANDMOTHER. Haven't you put him by a pair o' white stockings, nor a white shirt?

MRS HOLROYD. He's got a white cricketing shirt—but not white stockings.

GRANDMOTHER. Then he'll have to have his father's. Let me look at the shirt, Lizzie. (MRS HOLROYD *takes one from the dresser drawer.*) This'll never do—a cold, canvas thing wi' a turndown collar. I s'll 'ave to fetch his father's. (*Suddenly.*) You don't want no other woman to touch him, to wash him and lay him out, do you?

MRS HOLROYD (*weeping*). No.

GRANDMOTHER. Then I'll fetch him his father's gear. We mustn't let him set, he'll be that heavy, bless him. (*She takes her shawl.*) I shan't be more than a few minutes, an' the young fellow can stop here till I come back.

BLACKMORE. Can't I go for you, Mrs Holroyd?

GRANDMOTHER. No. *You* couldn't find the things. We'll wash him as soon as I get back, Lizzie.

MRS HOLROYD. All right. (*She watches her mother-in-law go out. Then she starts, goes in the scullery for a bowl, in which she pours warm water. She takes a flannel and soap and towel. She stands, afraid to go any further.*)

BLACKMORE. Well!

MRS HOLROYD. This is a judgment on us.

BLACKMORE. Why?

MRS HOLROYD. On me, it is—

BLACKMORE. How?

MRS HOLROYD. It is.

(BLACKMORE *shakes his head.*)

MRS HOLROYD. Yesterday you talked of murdering him.

BLACKMORE. Well!

MRS HOLROYD. Now we've done it.

BLACKMORE. How?

MRS HOLROYD. He'd have come up with the others, if he hadn't felt—felt me murdering him.

BLACKMORE. But we can't help it.

MRS HOLROYD. It's my fault.

BLACKMORE. Don't be like that!

MRS HOLROYD (*looking at him—then indicating her husband*). I daren't see him.

BLACKMORE. No?

MRS HOLROYD. I've killed him, that is all.

BLACKMORE. No, you haven't.

MRS HOLROYD. Yes, I have.

BLACKMORE. We couldn't help it.

MRS HOLROYD. If he hadn't felt, if he hadn't *known*, he wouldn't have stayed, he'd have come up with the rest.

BLACKMORE. Well, and even if it was so, we can't help it now.

MRS HOLROYD. But we've killed him.

BLACKMORE. Ah, I'm tired—

MRS HOLROYD. Yes.

BLACKMORE (*after a pause*). Shall I stay?

MRS HOLROYD. I—I daren't be alone with him.

BLACKMORE (*sitting down*). No.

MRS HOLROYD. I don't love him. Now he's dead. I don't love him. He lies like he did yesterday.

BLACKMORE. I suppose, being dead—I don't know—

MRS HOLROYD. I think you'd better go.

BLACKMORE (*rising*). Tell me.

MRS HOLROYD. Yes.

BLACKMORE. You want me to go.

MRS HOLROYD. No—but *do* go. (*They look at each other.*)

BLACKMORE. I shall come tomorrow. (BLACKMORE *goes out.*)

(MRS HOLROYD *stands very stiff, as if afraid of the dead man. Then she stoops down and begins to sponge his face, talking to him.*)

MRS HOLROYD. My dear—oh, my dear! I can't bear it, my dear—you shouldn't have done it. You shouldn't have done it. Oh—I can't bear it, for you. Why couldn't I do anything for you? The children's father—my dear—I wasn't good to you. But you shouldn't have done this to me. Oh, dear, oh, dear! Did it hurt you?—oh, my dear, it hurt you—oh, I can't bear it. No, things aren't fair—we went wrong, my dear. I never loved you enough—I never did. What a shame for you! It was a shame. But you didn't—you didn't try. I *would* have loved you—I tried hard. What a shame for you! It was so cruel for you. You couldn't help it—my dear, my dear. You couldn't help it. And I can't do anything for you, and it hurt you so! (*She weeps bitterly, so her tears fall on the dead man's face; suddenly she kisses him.*) My dear, my dear, what can I do for you, what can I? (*She weeps as she wipes his face gently.*)

(*Enter* GRANDMOTHER.)

GRANDMOTHER (*putting a bundle on the table, and taking off her shawl*). You're not all by yourself?

MRS HOLROYD. Yes.

GRANDMOTHER. It's a wonder you're not frightened. You've not washed his face.

MRS HOLROYD. Why should I be afraid of him—now, Mother?

GRANDMOTHER (*weeping*). Ay, poor lamb, I can't think as ever you could have had reason to be frightened of him, Lizzie.

MRS HOLROYD. Yes—once—

GRANDMOTHER. Oh, but he went wrong. An' he was a taking lad, as iver was. (*She cries pitifully.*) And when I waked his father up and told him, he sat up in bed staring over his whiskers, and said should he come up? But when I'd managed to find the shirt and things, he was still in bed. You don't know what it is to live with a man that has no feeling. But you've washed him, Lizzie?

MRS HOLROYD. I was finishing his head.

GRANDMOTHER. Let me do it, child.

MRS HOLROYD. I'll finish that.

GRANDMOTHER. Poor lamb—poor dear lamb! Yet I wouldn't wish him back, Lizzie. He must ha' died peaceful, Lizzie. He seems to be smiling. He always had such a rare smile on him—not that he smiled much of late—

MRS HOLROYD. I loved him for that.

GRANDMOTHER. Ay, my poor child—my poor child.

MRS HOLROYD. He looks nice, Mother.

GRANDMOTHER. I hope he made his peace with the Lord.

MRS HOLROYD. Yes.

GRANDMOTHER. If he hadn't time to make his peace with the Lord, I've no hopes of him. Dear o' me, dear o' me. Is there another bit of flannel anywhere?

(MRS HOLROYD *rises and brings a piece. The* GRANDMOTHER *begins to wash the breast of the dead man.*)

GRANDMOTHER. Well, I hope you'll be true to his children at least, Lizzie.

(MRS HOLROYD *weeps—the old woman continues her washing.*)

Eh—and he's fair as a lily. Did you ever see a man with a whiter skin—and flesh as fine as the driven snow. He's beautiful, he is, the lamb. Many's the time I've looked at him, and I've felt proud of him, I have. And now he lies here. And such arms on 'im! Look at the vaccination marks, Lizzie. When I took him to be vaccinated, he had a little pink bonnet with a feather. (*Weeps.*) Don't cry, my girl, don't. Sit up an' wash him a' that side, or we s'll never have him done. Oh, Lizzie!

MRS HOLROYD (*sitting up, startled*). What—what?

GRANDMOTHER. Look at his poor hand! (*She holds up the*

right hand. The nails are bloody.)

MRS HOLROYD. Oh, no! Oh, no! No!

(*Both women weep.*)

GRANDMOTHER (*after a while*). We maun get on, Lizzie.

MRS HOLROYD (*sitting up*). I can't touch his hands.

GRANDMOTHER. But I'm his mother—there's nothing I couldn't do for him.

MRS HOLROYD. I don't care—I don't care.

GRANDMOTHER. Prithee, prithee, Lizzie, I don't want thee goin' off, Lizzie.

MRS HOLROYD (*moaning*). Oh, what shall I do!

GRANDMOTHER. Why, go thee an' get his feet washed. He's setting stiff, and how shall we get him laid out?

(MRS HOLROYD, *sobbing, goes, kneels at the miner's feet, and begins pulling off the great boots.*)

GRANDMOTHER. There's hardly a mark on him. Eh, what a man he is! I've had some fine sons, Lizzie, I've had some big men of sons.

MRS HOLROYD. He was always a lot whiter than me. And he used to chaff me.

GRANDMOTHER. But his poor hands! I used to thank God for my children, but they're rods o' trouble, Lizzie, they are. Unfasten his belt, child. We mun get his things off soon, or else we s'll have such a job.

(MRS HOLROYD, *having dragged off the boots, rises. She is weeping.*)

Curtain

Run-out

There is little to add to the comments we made earlier; this passage very much speaks for itself. Lawrence used the material of his early plays in other ways later; *A Collier's Friday Night*, for example, is very similar to some of the scenes in his novel *Sons and Lovers*. If you like this passage from *The Widowing of Mrs Holroyd* you should certainly read a beautiful short story by Lawrence on almost exactly the same theme, called *Odour of Chrysanthemums*. It is interesting to see how the effects he gets as a short-story writer compare with those he achieves on the stage. He was afraid that the limitations of the theatre would falsify his sense of reality, and all would 'end up stagily'. Raymond Williams tells us

how Lawrence revised the play in 1913, and wrote about it:
'I saw how it needed altering, refining. Particularly I hated
it in the last act, where the man and woman wrangled rather
shallowly across the dead body of the husband . . . I hope to
heaven I have come in time to have it made decent.' For Lawrence, it is the feeling that matters, and he became impatient
with the 'staginess' of the theatre, which he thought of as
artificial and restricting. Perhaps that is why he moved on to
writing novels, and there found his real genius. But the scene
of the washing of Charles Holroyd's dead body remains,
surely, a great moment. What do you think?

〰〰〰〰〰〰〰〰〰〰〰〰〰〰〰〰〰〰〰〰〰〰〰〰〰〰〰〰〰〰〰〰〰〰〰

THE CRUCIBLE

Lead-in

For the backround and the main lines of the plot of *The
Crucible* please refer to the lead-in to our previous extract
from this play (p. 88). John Proctor is duly arrested for
witchcraft on the testimony of Mary Warren, and now awaits
hanging at sunrise; his wife is carrying Proctor's child. Danforth is determined that those who will not confess shall
hang. The Reverend Hale is increasingly uneasy about the
witch-hunt and is feeling more and more guilty about his
part in it. It is decided to confront Proctor with his wife in
the hope of 'softening' him, i.e., persuading him to confess.
She is brought, chained, to a cell in Salem Jail and Hale
pleads with her to prevent her husband from 'throwing his
life away'. She makes no promise but wishes to see him.
Proctor is led in by the Marshal: he is bearded, filthy and
has been tortured to no effect (Herrick has described him
in prison thus: 'He sits like some great bird; you'd not know
he lived except he will take food from time to time'). Husband and wife have not met for three months as the extract
opens.

From his wife Proctor first hears about other victims of the
witch-hunt—how some have confessed and saved their lives,
and how Giles Corey, the fine, honest and blunt old farmer
whom Proctor loved, has been hideously 'pressed' to death.

She blames herself for Proctor's affair with Abigail, that has brought all this anguish upon them. Proctor rejects the role of martyr and determines to confess. Rebecca Nurse arrives, a saintly old woman who is to die at the same time under equally false testimony, but she refuses to confess and save herself. Danforth and Parris are delighted that Proctor will confess and try by cross-questioning to get him to inculpate Rebecca and others, and it is increasingly clear that the confession is a lie. He forces himself to sign the confession but won't give it to Danforth to be nailed on the church door. In a passion of fury and anguish he tears the paper to bits; he cannot bring himself to lie and involve others, and would rather die. Elizabeth embraces him and he kisses her for the last time. Danforth orders him to be hanged, and sweeps out. Proctor and Rebecca are led away to their deaths and the play ends with Parris and Hale desperately trying to persuade Elizabeth to intervene, and Elizabeth refusing and preferring his death in honour and truth to his survival in dishonesty.

ACTING NOTES
This extract makes great demands on acting ability, particularly for those playing John Proctor and Elizabeth. Proctor is strong, but weakened by imprisonment and torture. In our production he wore a torn shirt and trousers and was black with dirt, heavily chained from the arms and the legs. He is meeting the greatest truth of his life, and after an attempt to confess and a discovery of what this entails, not only for him but for others, he rejects it passionately and goes to his death heroically. Elizabeth has, according to the playwright, 'dirty clothes', and 'her face is pale and gaunt'. She won't press her husband either way ('I cannot judge you, John')—and of course longs for him to survive but cannot encourage him to confess to what she knows is a lie. Her two most difficult passages are when she refers to 'sins of her own'—'it were a cold house I kept', which needs to be said with tremendous effort and difficulty and yet with total conviction, and the last moments, when her love for her husband must shine nobly through her anguish at his death. Danforth is stern and unrelenting, and the two priests, Parris and Hale, anxiously try to save Proctor's life. The drum is a very dramatic note but could perhaps be imi-

tated on a desk lid if you haven't a real drum. On the stage the gradual increase of light is, of course, a very effective addition to the tension of the scene.

Alone. PROCTOR *walks to her, halts. It is as though they stood in a spinning world. It is beyond sorrow, above it. He reaches out his hand as though toward an embodiment not quite real, and as he touches her, a strange soft sound, half laughter, half amazement, comes from his throat. He pats her hand. She covers his hand with hers. And then, weak, he sits. Then she sits, facing him.*

PROCTOR. The child?

ELIZABETH. It grows.

PROCTOR. There is no word of the boys?

ELIZABETH. They're well. Rebecca's Samuel keeps them.

PROCTOR. You have not seen them?

ELIZABETH. I have not. (*She catches a weakening in herself and downs it.*)

PROCTOR. You are a —marvel, Elizabeth.

ELIZABETH. You—have been tortured?

PROCTOR. Aye.

   (*Pause. She will not let herself be drowned in the sea that threatens her.*)

They come for my life now.

ELIZABETH. I know it.

   (*Pause.*)

PROCTOR. None—have yet confessed?

ELIZABETH. There be many confessed.

PROCTOR. Who are they?

ELIZABETH. There be a hundred or more, they say. Goody Ballard is one; Isaiah Goodkind is one. There be many.

PROCTOR. Rebecca?

ELIZABETH. Not Rebecca. She is one foot in Heaven now; naught may hurt her more.

PROCTOR. And Giles?

ELIZABETH. You have not heard of it?

PROCTOR. I hear nothin', where I am kept.

ELIZABETH. Giles is dead.

   (*He looks at her incredulously.*)

PROCTOR. When were he hanged?

ELIZABETH (*quietly, factually*). He were not hanged. He would not answer aye or nay to his indictment; for if he denied the charge they'd hang him surely, and auction out his property. So he stand mute, and died Christian under the law. And so his sons will have his farm. It is the law, for he could not be condemned a wizard without he answer the indictment, aye or nay.

PROCTOR. Then how does he die?

ELIZABETH (*gently*). They press him, John.

PROCTOR. Press?

ELIZABETH. Great stones they lay upon his chest until he plead aye or nay. (*With a tender smile for the old man*) They say he give them but two words. 'More weight', he says. And died.

PROCTOR (*numbed—a thread to weave into his agony*). 'More weight.'

ELIZABETH. Aye. It were a fearsome man, Giles Corey.
(*Pause.*)

PROCTOR (*with great force of will, but not quite looking at her*). I have been thinking I would confess to them, Elizabeth. (*She shows nothing.*) What say you? If I give them that?

ELIZABETH. I cannot judge you, John.
(*Pause.*)

PROCTOR (*simply—a pure question*). What would you have me do?

ELIZABETH. As you will, I would have it. (*Slight pause.*) I want you living, John. That's sure.

PROCTOR (*pauses, then with a flailing of hope*). Giles' wife? Have she confessed?

ELIZABETH. She will not.
(*Pause.*)

PROCTOR. It is a pretence, Elizabeth.

ELIZABETH. What is?

PROCTOR. I cannot mount the gibbet like a saint. It is a fraud. I am not that man. (*She is silent.*) My honesty is broke, Elizabeth; I am no good man. Nothing's spoiled by giving them this lie that were not rotten long before.

ELIZABETH. And yet you've not confessed till now. That speak goodness in you.

PROCTOR. Spite only keeps me silent. It is hard to give a lie to dogs. (*Pause, for the first time he turns directly to her.*) I would have your forgiveness, Elizabeth.

ELIZABETH. It is not for me to give, John, I am—

PROCTOR. I'd have you see some honesty in it. Let them that never lied die now to keep their souls. It is pretence for me, a vanity that will not blind God nor keep my children out of the wind. (*Pause.*) What say you?

ELIZABETH (*upon a heaving sob that always threatens.*) John, it come to naught that I should forgive you, if you'll not forgive yourself.
(*Now he turns away a little, in great agony.*)
It is not my soul, John, it is yours.
(*He stands, as though in physical pain, slowly rising to his feet with a great immortal longing to find his answer. It is difficult to say and she is on the verge of tears.*)
Only be sure of this, for I know it now: Whatever you will do, it is a good man does it.
(*He turns his doubting, searching gaze upon her.*)
I have read my heart this three month, John. (*Pause.*) I have sins of my own to count. It needs a cold wife to prompt lechery.

PROCTOR (*in great pain*). Enough, enough—

ELIZABETH (*now pouring her heart out*). Better you should know me!

PROCTOR. I will not hear it! I know you!

ELIZABETH. You take my sins upon you, John—

PROCTOR (*in agony*). No, I take my own, my own!

ELIZABETH. John, I counted myself so plain, so poorly made, no honest love could come to me! Suspicion kissed you when I did; I never knew how I should say my love. It were a cold house I kept! (*In fright, she swerves, as* HATHORNE *enters.*)

HATHORNE. What say you, Proctor? The sun is soon up.
(PROCTOR, *his chest heaving, stares, turns to* ELIZABETH. *She comes to him as though to plead, her voice quaking.*)

ELIZABETH. Do what you will. But let none be your judge. There be no higher judge under Heaven than Proctor is! Forgive me, forgive me, John—I never knew such

goodness in the world! (*She covers her face, weeping.*)
(PROCTOR *turns from her to* HATHORNE; *he is off the
earth, his voice hollow.*)

PROCTOR. I want my life.

HATHORNE (*electrified, surprised*). You'll confess yourself?

PROCTOR. I will have my life.

HATHORNE (*with a mystical tone*). God be praised! It is a
providence! (*He rushes out the door, and his voice is
heard calling down the corridor:* He will confess! Proctor will confess!)

PROCTOR (*with a cry, as he strides to the door*). Why do you
cry it? (*In great pain he turns back to her.*) It is evil,
is it not? It is evil.

ELIZABETH (*in terror, weeping*). I cannot judge you, John,
I cannot!

PROCTOR. Then who will judge me? (*Suddenly clasping his
hands*) God in Heaven, what is John Proctor, what is
John Proctor? (*He moves as an animal, and a fury is
riding in him, a tantalized search.*) I think it is honest,
I think so; I am no saint. (*As though she had denied
this he calls angrily at her*) Let Rebecca go like a saint;
for me it is fraud!
(*Voices are heard in the hall, speaking together in
suppressed excitement.*)

ELIZABETH. I am not your judge, I cannot be. (*As though
giving him release*) Do as you will, do as you will!

PROCTOR. Would you give them such a lie? Say it. Would
you ever give them this? (*She cannot answer.*) You
would not; if tongs of fire were singeing you you would
not! It is evil. Good, then—it is evil, and I do it!
(HATHORNE *enters with* DANFORTH, *and, with them,*
CHEEVER, PARRIS, *and* HALE. *It is a businesslike, rapid
entrance, as though the ice had been broken.*)

DANFORTH (*with great relief and gratitude*). Praise to God,
man, praise to God; you shall be blessed in Heaven for
this.
(CHEEVER *has hurried to the bench with pen, ink, and
paper.* PROCTOR *watches him.*)
Now then, let us have it. Are you ready, Mr Cheever?

PROCTOR (*with a cold, cold horror at their efficiency*). Why must it be written?

DANFORTH. Why, for the good instruction of the village, Mister; this we shall post upon the church door! (*To* PARRIS, *urgently*) Where is the marshal?

PARRIS (*runs to the door and calls down the corridor*). Marshal! Hurry!

DANFORTH. Now, then, Mister, will you speak slowly, and directly to the point, for Mr Cheever's sake. (*He is on record now, and is really dictating to* CHEEVER, *who writes*.) Mr Proctor, have you seen the Devil in your life? (PROCTOR'S *jaws lock*.) Come, man, there is light in the sky; the town waits at the scaffold; I would give out this news. Did you see the Devil?

PROCTOR. I did.

PARRIS. Praise God!

DANFORTH. And when he come to you, what were his demand? (PROCTOR *is silent*. DANFORTH *helps*.) Did he bid you to do his work upon the earth?

PROCTOR. He did.

DANFORTH. And you bound yourself to his service? (DANFORTH *turns, as* REBECCA NURSE *enters, with* HERRICK *helping to support her. She is barely able to walk*.) Come in, come in, woman!

REBECCA (*brightening as she sees* PROCTOR). Ah, John! You are well, then, eh?

(PROCTOR *turns his face to the wall*.)

DANFORTH. Courage, man, courage—let her witness your good example that she may come to God herself. Now hear it, Goody Nurse! Say on, Mr Proctor. Did you bind yourself to the Devil's service?

REBECCA (*astonished*). Why, John!

PROCTOR (*through his teeth, his face turned from* REBECCA). I did.

DANFORTH. Now, woman, you surely see it profit nothin' to keep this conspiracy any further. Will you confess yourself with him?

REBECCA. Oh, John—God send his mercy on you!

DANFORTH. I say, will you confess yourself, Goody Nurse?

REBECCA. Why, it is a lie, it is a lie; how may I damn myself? I cannot, I cannot.

DANFORTH. Mr Proctor. When the Devil came to you did you see Rebecca Nurse in his company? (PROCTOR *is silent.*) Come, man, take courage—did you ever see her with the Devil?

PROCTOR (*almost inaudibly*). No.

(DANFORTH, *now sensing trouble, glances at* JOHN *and goes to the table, and picks up a sheet—the list of condemned.*)

DANFORTH. Did you ever see her sister, Mary Easty, with the Devil?

PROCTOR. No, I did not.

DANFORTH (*his eyes narrow on* PROCTOR). Did you ever see Martha Corey with the Devil?

PROCTOR. I did not.

DANFORTH (*realizing, slowly putting the sheet down*). Did you ever see anyone with the Devil?

PROCTOR. I did not.

DANFORTH. Proctor, you mistake me. I am not empowered to trade your life for a lie. You have most certainly seen some person with the Devil. (PROCTOR *is silent.*) Mr Proctor, a score of people have already testified they saw this woman with the Devil.

PROCTOR. Then it is proved. Why must I say it?

DANFORTH. Why 'must you' say it! Why, you should rejoice to say it if your soul is truly purged of any love for Hell!

PROCTOR. They think to go like saints. I like not to spoil their names.

DANFORTH (*inquiring, incredulous*). Mr Proctor, do you think they go like saints?

PROCTOR (*evading*). This woman never thought she done the Devil's work.

DANFORTH. Look you, sir. I think you mistake your duty here. It matters nothing what she thought—she is convicted of the unnatural murder of children, and you for sending your spirit out upon Mary Warren. Your soul alone is the issue here, Mister, and you will prove its whiteness or you cannot live in a Christian country. Will you tell me now what persons conspired with you in the Devil's company? (PROCTOR *is silent.*) To your knowledge was Rebecca Nurse ever—

PROCTOR. I speak my own sins; I cannot judge another. (*Crying out, with hatred*) I have no tongue for it.

HALE (*quickly to* DANFORTH). Excellency, it is enough he confess himself. Let him sign it, let him sign it.

PARRIS (*feverishly*). It is a great service, sir. It is a weighty name; it will strike the village that Proctor confess. I beg you, let him sign it. The sun is up, Excellency!

DANFORTH (*considers; then with dissatisfaction*). Come, then, sign your testimony. (*To* CHEEVER) Give it to him.

(CHEEVER *goes to* PROCTOR, *the confession and a pen in hand.* PROCTOR *does not look at it.*)

Come, man, sign it.

PROCTOR (*after glancing at the confession*). You have all witnessed it—it is enough.

DANFORTH. You will not sign it?

PROCTOR. You have all witnessed it; what more is needed?

DANFORTH. Do you sport with me? You will sign your name or it is no confession, Mister! (*His breast heaving with agonized breathing,* PROCTOR *now lays the paper down and signs his name.*)

PARRIS. Praise be to the Lord!

(PROCTOR *has just finished signing when* DANFORTH *reaches for the paper. But* PROCTOR *snatches it up, and now a wild terror is rising in him, and a boundless anger.*)

DANFORTH (*perplexed, but politely extending his hand*). If you please, sir.

PROCTOR. No.

DANFORTH (*as though* PROCTOR *did not understand*). Mr Proctor, I must have—

PROCTOR. No, no. I have signed it. You have seen me. It is done! You have no need for this.

PARRIS. Proctor, the village must have proof that—

PROCTOR. Damn the village! I confess to God, and God has seen my name on this! It is enough!

DANFORTH. No, sir, it is—

PROCTOR. You came to save my soul, did you not? Here! I have confessed myself; it is enough!

DANFORTH. You have not con—

PROCTOR. I have confessed myself! Is there no good penitence but it be public? God does not need my name nailed upon the church! God sees my name; God knows how black my sins are! It is enough!

DANFORTH. Mr Proctor—

PROCTOR. You will not use me! I am no Sarah Good or Tituba, I am John Proctor! You will not use me! It is no part of salvation that you should use me!

DANFORTH. I do not wish to—

PROCTOR. I have three children—how may I teach them to walk like men in the world, and I sold my friends?

DANFORTH. You have not sold your friends—

PROCTOR. Beguile me not! I blacken all of them when this is nailed to the church the very day they hang for silence!

DANFORTH. Mr Proctor, I must have good and legal proof that you—

PROCTOR. You are the high court, your word is good enough! Tell them I confessed myself; say Proctor broke his knees and wept like a woman; say what you will, but my name cannot—

DANFORTH (*with suspicion*). It is the same, is it not? If I report it or you sign to it?

PROCTOR (*he knows it is insane*). No, it is not the same! What others say and what I sign to is not the same!

DANFORTH. Why? Do you mean to deny this confession when you are free?

PROCTOR. I mean to deny nothing!

DANFORTH. Then explain to me, Mr Proctor, why you will not let—

PROCTOR (*with a cry of his soul*). Because it is my name! Because I cannot have another in my life! Because I lie and sign myself to lies! Because I am not worth the dust on the feet of them that hang! How may I live without my name? I have given you my soul; leave me my name!

DANFORTH (*pointing at the confession in* PROCTOR'S *hand*). Is that document a lie? If it is a lie I will not accept it! What say you? I will not deal in lies, Mister! (PROCTOR *is motionless*.) You will give me your honest confession in my hand, or I cannot keep you from the rope. (PROCTOR *does not reply*.) Which way do you go,

Mister?

(*His breast heaving, his eyes staring,* PROCTOR *tears the paper and crumples it, and he is weeping in fury, but erect.*)

DANFORTH. Marshal!

PARRIS (*hysterically, as though the tearing paper were his life*). Proctor, Proctor!

HALE. Man, you will hang! You cannot!

PROCTOR (*his eyes full of tears*). I can. And there's your first marvel, that I can. You have made your magic now, for now I do think I see some shred of goodness in John Proctor. Not enough to weave a banner with, but white enough to keep it from such dogs.

(ELIZABETH, *in a burst of terror, rushes to him and weeps against his hand.*)

Give them no tear! Tears pleasure them! Show honour now, show a stony heart and sink them with it! (*He has lifted her, and kisses her now with great passion.*)

REBECCA. Let you fear nothing! Another judgment waits us all!

DANFORTH. Hang them high over the town! Who weeps for these, weeps for corruption! (*He sweeps out past them.* HERRICK *starts to lead* REBECCA, *who almost collapses, but* PROCTOR *catches her, and she glances up at him apologetically.*)

REBECCA. I've had no breakfast.

HERRICK. Come, man.

HERRICK *escorts them out,* HATHORNE *and* CHEEVER *behind them.* ELIZABETH *stands staring at the empty doorway.*)

PARRIS (*in deadly fear, to* ELIZABETH). Go to him, Goody Proctor! There is yet time!

(*From outside a drumroll strikes the air.* PARRIS *is startled.* ELIZABETH *jerks about toward the window.*)

PARRIS. Go to him! (*He rushes out the door, as though to hold back his fate.*) Proctor! Proctor!

(*Again, a short burst of drums.*)

HALE. Woman, plead with him! (*He starts to rush out the door, and then goes back to her.*) Woman! It is pride, it is vanity.

(*She avoids his eyes, and moves to the window. He
drops to his knees.*)
Be his helper!—What profit him to bleed? Shall the
dust praise him? Shall the worms declare his truth? Go
to him, take his shame away!

ELIZABETH (*supporting herself against collapse, grips the
bars of the window, and with a cry*). He have his goodness now. God forbid I take it from him!

(*The final drumroll crashes, then heightens violently.
HALE weeps in frantic prayer, and the new sun is pouring in upon her face, and the drums rattle like bones in
the morning air.*)

Run-out

The whole play leads up to this terrible climax, which makes
one realize how witch hysteria puts its victims in impossible
positions: they must either confess to something they know
to be false or die for not doing so. Many thousands of people
died in Europe in late medieval and early modern times, and
though we still don't know what truth there was in the accu-
sations of belonging to a secret society, it is quite sure that
immense cruelty occurred and many utterly innocent people
died, in Europe and in the United States. Twenty years later
the government was 'awarding compensation to the victims
still living and to the families of the dead.' The play had
an extra interest when it was first published in 1953, because
this was in the middle of the time when a wave of anti-com-
munist fear and hysteria swept the United States, and the
infamous Senator McCarthy was conducting a series of
'hearings' accusing hundreds of people of being secret com-
munists; everyone who read or saw the play saw the parallel
between Salem in 1690 and the USA in the early nineteen-
fifties. But even now that this political meaning is less important the play has come to be seen as 'one of the profound-
est plays of the post-war world—a classic of the modern stage'
as the Penguin edition describes it. Do see the play if you
have a chance. An interesting feature of the printed text
is that Miller has included some notes about the characters
and the background, and shows that in essence these events
actually happened.

9
Alone in your skin

This solitary passage is, I think, about solitude—as well as carrying elements which belong to 'Communication' or even 'Menace'. Davies is a tramp, one who has opted (or been chosen) for solitude; his final stuttering speech is a cry of longing for identity. I find this passage, and the play from which it is taken, often funny, sometimes frightening, but mainly very sad—the despair and sadness we all share at some time, when we feel that we are 'alone in our skin'.

THE CARETAKER

Lead-in
Harold Pinter published *The Cartaker* in 1960. I have called this extract 'Alone in Your Skin' because it seems to me to be about solitude—or at least this is one aspect of the mysterious action and dialogue. The situation is easy enough to describe, in a sense, but far more difficult to explain in any straightforward way. Davies, also known as Jenkins, is a tramp who has been thrown out of a casual job in a café after a quarrel and rescued by Aston, who takes him to his room, which is a kind of junk heap. (See Acting Notes.)

Aston is kind to Davies; he gives him a pair of shoes, which Davies rejects, and Aston says he will find him a better pair. He extracts the iron bed from behind the junk and says Davies can sleep there. He confides in Davies that he plans to build a shed in his garden; he gives him some money. Davies claims that his 'papers' have been left with a man 'down at Sidcup' and that he can't get his life organized till he can get there, but the weather and his shoes prevent him from doing so. Davies is a troublesome guest, who makes noises in his sleep, but Aston is tolerant and allows him to stay. His brother, Mick, owns the flat in which he lives, and Mick's attitude to Davies is ambiguous—he tends to tease and even torture him, and yet pretends to flatter him; his general effect on Davies is to frighten the life out of him. He is a curiously menacing figure right through the play, and yet he is kind to his brother. Aston is, perhaps, the most easily explained character of the three; he describes in a very long soliloquy how he was suspected of having hallucinations, and was presumably certified as mad, and after examination in a mental hospital was treated by some kind of electrical shock therapy which obliterated his former memories but made him shy, secretive and unable really to communicate with anyone. He is unable to fix his mind on anything for more than a short time, and therefore drifts purposelessly. Davies sees his weakness and the chance of using Mick against him, so he tries to flatter Mick into working against his brother, and perhaps in the end getting rid of him; he claims that Aston wakes him up in the middle of the night, and insists on a window being open because Davies stinks. Davies is offered the job of caretaker (hence the title of the play) but is finally rejected by both brothers, and ends in a stuttering and anguished hope that he might get down to Sidcup and regain, as it were, his identity.

ACTING NOTES

Pinter describes the set as follows :

'A room. A window in the back wall, the bottom half covered by a sack. An iron bed along the left wall. Above it a small cupboard, paint buckets, boxes containing nuts, screws, etc. More boxes, vases, by the side of the bed. A door, up right. To the right of the window, a mound : a kitchen sink, a step-ladder, a coal bucket, a lawn mower, a shopping trolley, boxes, sideboard drawers. Under this mound an iron bed. In front of it a gas stove. On the gas stove a statue of Buddha. Down right, a fireplace. Around it a couple of suitcases, a rolled carpet, a blow-lamp, a wooden chair on its side, boxes, a number of ornaments, a clothes horse, a few short planks of wood, a small electric fire and a very old electric toaster. Below this a pile of old newspapers. Under Aston's bed by the left wall is an electrolux, which is not seen till used. A bucket hangs from the ceiling.' Davies 'wears a worn brown overcoat, shapeless trousers, a waistcoat, vest, no shirt, and sandals'. This extract could easily be done with no equipment at all, as its main point is in the quality of the dialogue. Harold Pinter is widely acclaimed for his subtle understanding of the speech of ordinary people—and this is not a matter of dialect, as in Wesker's *Roots* (see p. 131) but of speech rhythms and pauses. Aston needs to be very still most of the time, while Mick is lithe and vigorous : the breaking of the Buddha figurine can be mimed, though the sound of its breaking helps that moment of crisis. So long as you can imagine the acting area as a heap of complicated and discarded bits and pieces, remnants, rubbish and junk, you have enough to get the feeling of the extract.

Davies is old, bent, beaten by life—nasty when he gets the chance, against Aston for example, but in the end pathetic in his hopelessness and isolation.

Blackout.
Dim light through the window.
It is night. ASTON *and* DAVIES *are in bed,* DAVIES *groaning.* ASTON *sits up, gets out of bed, switches on the light, goes over to* DAVIES *and shakes him.*

ASTON. Hey, stop it, will you? I can't sleep.

DAVIES. What? What? What's going on?

ASTON. You're making noises.

DAVIES. I'm an old man, what do you expect me to do, stop breathing?

ASTON. You're making noises.

DAVIES. What do you expect me to do, stop breathing?

(ASTON *goes to his bed, and puts on his trousers.*)

ASTON. I'll get a bit of air.

DAVIES. What do you expect me to do? I tell you, mate, I'm not surprised they took you in. Waking an old man up in the middle of the night, you must be off your nut! Giving me bad dreams, who's responsible, then, for me having bad dreams? If you didn't keep mucking me about I wouldn't make no noises! How do you expect me to sleep peaceful when you keep poking me all the time? What do you want me to do, stop breathing?

(*He throws the cover off and gets out of bed, wearing his vest, waistcoat and trousers.*)

It's getting so freezing in here I have to keep my trousers on to go to bed. I never done that before in my life. But that's what I got to do here. Just because you won't put in any bleeding heating! I've had just about enough with you mucking me about. I've seen better days than you have, man. Nobody ever got me inside one of them places, anyway. I'm a sane man! So don't you start mucking me about. I'll be all right as long as you keep your place. Just you keep your place, that's all. Because I can tell you, your brother's got his eye on you. He knows all about you. I got a friend there, don't you worry about that. I got a true pal there. Treating me like dirt! Why'd you invite me in here in the first place if you was going to treat me like this? You think you're better than me you got another think coming. I know enough. They had you inside one of them places before, they can have you inside again. Your brother's got his eye on you! They can put the pincers on your head again, man! They can have them on again! Any time. All they got to do is to get the word. They'd carry you in there, boy. They'd come here and pick you up and carry you in! They'd keep you fixed! They'd put them pincers on your head, they'd have you fixed! They'd take one look at all this junk I got to sleep with they'd know you were a creamer. That was the greatest mistake they made, you take my tip, letting you out of that place. Nobody knows what you're at, you go out you come in, nobody knows what you're at! Well, nobody messes me about for long. You think I'm going to do your dirty work? Haaaaahhhhh! You better think again! You want me to do all the dirty work all up and down them stairs just so I can sleep in this lousy filthy hole every night? Not me, boy. Not for you, boy. You don't know what you're doing half the time. You're up the creek! You're half off! You can tell it by looking at you. Who ever saw you slip me a few bob? Treating me like a bloody animal! I never been inside a nuthouse!

(ASTON *makes a slight move towards him.* DAVIES *takes his knife from his back pocket.*)

◆

Don't come nothing with me, mate. I got this here. I
used it. I used it. Don't come it with me.
(*A pause. They stare at each other.*)
Mind what you do now.
(*Pause.*)
Don't you try anything with me.
(*Pause.*)

ASTON. I . . . I think it's about time you found somewhere
else. I don't think we're hitting it off.

DAVIES. Find somewhere else?

ASTON. Yes.

DAVIES. Me? You talking to me? Not me, man! You!

ASTON. What?

DAVIES. You! You better find somewhere else!

ASTON. I live here. You don't.

DAVIES. Don't I? Well, I live here. I been offered a job here.

ASTON. Yes . . . well, I don't think you're really suitable.

DAVIES. Not suitable? Well, I can tell you, there's someone
here thinks I am suitable. And I'll tell you. I'm staying
on here as caretaker! Get it! You brother, he's told me,
see, he's told me the job is mine. Mine! So that's where
I am. I'm going to be his caretaker.

ASTON. My brother?

DAVIES. He's staying, he's going to run this place, and I'm
staying with him.

ASTON. Look. If I give you . . . a few bob you can get down
to Sidcup.

DAVIES. You build your shed first! A few bob! When I can
earn a steady wage here! You build your stinking shed
first! That's what!
(ASTON *stares at him.*)

ASTON. That's not a stinking shed.
(*Silence.*)
(ASTON *moves to him.*)
It's clean. It's all good wood. I'll get it up. No trouble.

DAVIES. Don't come too near!

ASTON. You've no reason to call that shed stinking.
(DAVIES *points the knife.*)
You stink.

DAVIES. What!

ASTON. You've been stinking the place out.

DAVIES. Christ, you say that to me!

ASTON. For days. That's one reason I can't sleep.

DAVIES. You call me that! You call me stinking!

ASTON. You better go.

DAVIES. I'LL STINK YOU!

> (*He thrusts his arm out, the arm trembling, the knife pointing at* ASTON'S *stomach.* ASTON *does not move. Silence.* DAVIES' *arm moves no further. They stand.*)
> I'll stink you . . .
> (*Pause.*)

ASTON. Get your stuff.

> (DAVIES *draws the knife in to his chest, breathing heavily.* ASTON *goes to* DAVIES' *bed, collects his bag and puts a few of* DAVIES' *things into it.*)

DAVIES. You ain't . . . you ain't got the right . . . Leave that alone, that's mine!

> (DAVIES *takes the bag and presses the contents down.*)
> All right . . . I been offered a job here . . . you wait . . . (*He puts on his smoking-jacket*) . . . you wait . . . your brother . . . he'll sort you out . . . you call me that . . . you call me that . . . no one's ever called me that . . . (*He puts on his overcoat.*) You'll be sorry you called me that . . . you ain't heard the last of this . . . (*He picks up his bag and goes to the door.*) You'll be sorry you called me that . . . (*He opens the door,* ASTON *watching him.*)
> Now I know who I can trust.
> (DAVIES *goes out.* ASTON *stands.*)

> *Blackout.*
> *Lights up. Early evening.*
> *Voices on the stairs.*
> MICK *and* DAVIES *enter.*

DAVIES. Stink! You hear that! Me! I told you what he said, didn't I? Stink! You hear that? That's what he said to me!

MICK. Tch, tch, tch.

DAVIES. That's what he said to me.

MICK. You don't stink.

DAVIES. No, sir!

MICK. If you stank I'd be the first one to tell you.

DAVIES. I told him, I told him he . . . I said to him, you ain't heard the last of this man! I said, don't you forget your brother. I told him you'd be coming along to sort him out. He don't know what he's started, doing that. Doing that to me. I said to him, I said to him, he'll be along, your brother'll be along, he's got sense, not like you—

MICK. What do you mean?

DAVIES. Eh?

MICK. You saying my brother hasn't got any sense?

DAVIES. What? What I'm saying is, you got ideas for this place, all this . . . all this decorating, see? I mean, he's got no right to order me about. I take orders from you, I do my caretaking for you, I mean, you look upon me . . . you don't treat me like a lump of dirt . . . we can both . . . we can both see him for what he is.

(*Pause*.)

MICK. What did he say then, when you told him I'd offered you the job as caretaker?

DAVIES. He . . . he said . . . he said . . . something about . . . he lived here.

MICK. Yes, he's got a point, en he?

DAVIES. A point! This is your house, en't? You let him live here!

MICK. I could tell him to go, I suppose.

DAVIES. That's what I'm saying.

MICK. Yes. I could tell him to go. I mean, I'm the landlord. On the other hand, he's the sitting tenant. Giving him notice, you see, what it is, it's a technical matter, that's what it is. It depends how you regard this room. I mean it depends whether you regard this room as furnished or unfurnished. See what I mean?

DAVIES. No, I don't.

MICK. All this furniture, you see, in here, it's all his, except the beds, of course. So what it is, it's a fine legal point, that's what it is.

(*Pause*.)

DAVIES. I tell you he should go back where he come from!

MICK (*turning to look at him*). Come from?

DAVIES. Yes.

MICK. Where did he come from?

DAVIES. Well . . . he . . . he . . .

MICK. You get a bit out of your depth sometimes, don't you? (*Pause.*)

(*Rising, briskly.*) Well, anyway, as things stand, I don't mind having a go at doing up the place . . .

DAVIES. That's what I wanted to hear!

MICK. No, I don't mind.

(*He turns to face* DAVIES.)

But you better be as good as you say you are.

DAVIES. What do you mean?

MICK. Well, you say you're an interior decorator, you'd better be a good one.

DAVIES. A what?

MICK. What do you mean, a what? A decorator. An interior decorator.

DAVIES. Me? What do you mean? I never touched that. I never been that.

MICK. You've never what?

DAVIES. No, no, not me, man. I'm not an interior decorator. I been too busy. Too many other things to do, you see. But I . . . but I could always turn my hand to most things . . . give me . . . give me a bit of time to pick it up.

MICK. I don't want you to pick it up. I want a first-class experienced interior decorator. I thought you were one.

DAVIES. Me? Now wait a minute—wait a minute—you got the wrong man.

MICK. How could I have the wrong man? You're the only man I've spoken to. You're the only man I've told, about my dreams, about my deepest wishes, you're the only one I've told, and I only told you because I understood you were an experienced first-class professional interior and exterior decorator.

DAVIES. Now look here—

MICK. You mean you wouldn't know how to fit teal-blue, copper and parchment linoleum squares and have those colours re-echoed in the walls?

DAVIES. Now, look here, where'd you get—?

H

MICK. You wouldn't be able to decorate out a table in afro-
mosia teak veneer, an armchair in oatmeal tweed and
a beech frame settee with a woven sea-grass seat?

DAVIES. I never said that!

MICK. Christ! I must have been under a false impression!

DAVIES. I never said it!

MICK. You're a bloody impostor, mate!

DAVIES. Now you don't want to say that sort of thing to me.
You took me on here as caretaker. I was going to give
you a helping hand, that's all, for a small . . . for a small
wage, I never said nothing about that . . . you start calling
me names—

MICK. What is your name?

DAVIES. Don't start that—

MICK. No, what's your real name?

DAVIES. My real name's Davies.

MICK. What's the name you go under?

DAVIES. Jenkins.

MICK. You got two names. What about the rest? Eh? Now
come on, why did you tell me all this dirt about you
being an interior decorator?

DAVIES. I didn't tell you nothing! Won't you listen to what
I'm saying?

(*Pause.*)

It was him who told you. It was your brother who must
have told you. He's nutty! He'd tell you anything, out
of spite, he's nutty, he's half-way gone, it was him who
told you.

(MICK *walks slowly to him.*)

MICK. What did you call my brother?

DAVIES. When?

MICK. He's what?

DAVIES. I . . . now get this straight . . .

MICK. Nutty? Who's nutty?

(*Pause.*)

Did you call my brother nutty? My brother. That's a bit
of . . . that's a bit of an impertinent thing to say, isn't it?

DAVIES. But he says so himself!

(MICK *walks slowly round* DAVIES' *figure, regarding
him, once. He circles him, once.*)

MICK. What a strange man you are. Aren't you? You're really strange. Ever since you come into this house there's been nothing but trouble. Honest. I can take nothing you say at face value. Every word you speak is open to any number of interpretations. Most of what you say is lies. You're violent, you're erratic, you're just completely unpredictable. You're nothing else but a wild animal, when you come down to it. You're a barbarian. And to put the old tin lid on it, you stink from arse-hole to breakfast time. Look at it. You come here recommending yourself as an interior decorator, whereupon I take you on, and what happens? You make a long speech about all the references you've got down at Sidcup, and what happens? I haven't noticed you go down to Sidcup to obtain them. It's all most regrettable but it looks as though I'm compelled to pay you off for your caretaking work. Here's half a dollar.

(He feels in his pocket, takes out a half-crown and tosses it at DAVIES' *feet.* DAVIES *stands still.* MICK *walks to the gas stove and picks up the Buddha.)*

DAVIES *(slowly)*. All right then . . . you do that . . . you do that . . . if that's what you want . . .

MICK. THAT'S WHAT I WANT!

(He hurls the Buddha against the gas stove. It breaks.)

(Passionately.) Anyone would think this house was all I got to worry about. I got plenty of other things I can worry about. I've got other things. I've got plenty of other interests. I've got my own business to build up, haven't I? I got to think about expanding . . . in all directions. I don't stand still. I'm moving about all the time. I'm moving . . . all the time. I've got to think about the future. I'm not worried about this house. I'm not interested. My brother can worry about it. He can do it up, he can decorate it, he can do what he likes with it. I'm not bothered. I thought I was doing him a favour, letting him live here. He's got his own ideas. Let him have them. I'm going to chuck it in.

(Pause.)

DAVIES. What about me?

(Silence. MICK *does not look at him.)*

(*A door bangs.*)
(*Silence. They do not move.*)
(ASTON *comes in. He closes the door, moves into the room and faces* MICK. *They look at each other. Both are smiling, faintly.*)

MICK (*beginning to speak to* ASTON). Look . . . uh . . .
(*He stops, goes to the door, and exits.* ASTON *leaves the door open, crosses behind* DAVIES, *sees the broken Buddha, and looks at the pieces for a moment. He then goes to his bed, takes off his overcoat, sits, takes the screwdriver and plug and pokes the plug.*)

DAVIES. I just come back for my pipe.

ASTON. Oh yes.

DAVIES. I got out and . . . half-way down I . . . I suddenly . . . found out . . . you see . . . that I hadn't got my pipe. So I came back to get it .
(*Pause. He moves to* ASTON.)
That ain't the same plug, is it, you been . . . ?
(*Pause.*)
Still can't get anywhere with it, eh?
(*Pause.*)
Well, if you . . . persevere, in my opinion, you'll probably . . .
(*Pause.*)
Listen . . .
(*Pause.*)
You didn't mean that, did you, about me stinking, did you?
(*Pause.*)
Did you? You been a good friend to me. You took me in. You took me in, you didn't ask me no questions, you give me a bed, you been a mate to me. Listen. I been thinking, why I made all them noises, it was because of the draught, see, that draught was on me as I was sleeping, made me make noises without me knowing it, so I been thinking, what I mean to say, if you was to give me your bed, and you have my bed, there's not all that difference between them, they're the same sort of bed, if I was to have yourn, you sleep, wherever bed you're in, so you have mine, I have yourn, and that'll be all right,

I'll be out of the draught, see, I mean, you don't mind
a bit of wind, you need a bit of air, I can understand
that, you being in that place that time, with all them
doctors and all they done, closed up, I know them places,
too hot, you see, they're always too hot, I had a peep in
one once, nearly suffocated me, so I reckon that'd be
the best way out of it, we swap beds, and then we could
get down to what we was saying, I'd look after the place
for you, I'd keep an eye on it for you, for you, like, not
for the other . . . not for . . . for your brother, you see,
not for him, for you, I'll be your man, you say the word,
just say the word . . .

(*Pause.*)

What do you think of this I'm saying?

(*Pause.*)

ASTON. No, I like sleeping in this bed.

DAVIES. But you don't understand my meaning!

ASTON. Anyway, that one's my brother's bed.

DAVIES. Your brother?

ASTON. Any time he stays here. This is my bed. It's the only
bed I can sleep in.

DAVIES. But your brother's gone! He's gone!

(*Pause.*)

ASTON. No. I couldn't change beds.

DAVIES. But you don't understand my meaning!

ASTON. Anyway, I'm going to be busy. I've got that shed to
get up. If I don't get it up now it'll never go up. Until
it's up I can't get started.

DAVIES. I'll give you a hand to put up your shed, that's what
I'll do!

(*Pause.*)

I'll give you a hand! We'll both put up that shed together! See? Get it done in next to no time! Do you
see what I'm saying?

(*Pause.*)

ASTON. No. I can get it up myself.

DAVIES. But listen. I'm with you, I'll be here, I'll do it for
you!

(*Pause.*)

We'll do it together!

(*Pause.*)

Christ, we'll change beds!

(ASTON *moves to the window and stands with his back to* DAVIES.)

You mean you're throwing me out? You can't do that. Listen man, listen man, I don't mind, you see, I don't mind, I'll stay, I don't mind, I'll tell you what, if you don't want to change beds, we'll keep it as it is, I'll stay in the same bed, maybe if I can get a stronger piece of sacking, like, to go over the window, keep out the draught, that'll do it, what do you say, we'll keep it as it is?

(*Pause.*)

ASTON. No.

DAVIES. Why . . . not?

(ASTON *turns to look at him.*)

ASTON. You make too much noise.

DAVIES. But . . . but . . . look . . . listen . . . listen here . . . I mean . . .

(ASTON *turns back to the window.*)

What am I going to do?

(*Pause.*)

What shall I do?

(*Pause.*)

Where am I going to go?

(*Pause.*)

If you want me to go . . . I'll go. You just say the word.

(*Pause.*)

I'll tell you what though . . . them shoes . . . them shoes you give me . . . they're working out all right . . . they're all right. Maybe I could . . . get down . . .

(ASTON *remains still, his back to him, at the window.*)

Listen . . . if I . . . got down . . . if I was to . . . get my papers . . . would you . . . would you let . . . would you . . . if I got down . . . got my . . .

(*Long silence.*)

Curtain

Run-out

The lack of purpose, isolation and hopelessness of Davies' life-situation is what is left with us at the end of the play, and is beautifully rendered by the last speech with its pauses, unfinished sentences and implied questions which he knows won't and can't be answered; he is not communicating with anyone, and is indeed 'alone in his skin'. Perhaps Pinter intended him to represent the irreducible solitude that is our lot as human beings. The other two characters are perhaps more mysterious and enigmatic than the central 'Caretaker'. Mick, with his strange outbursts of fury and cruelty, is just as isolated as Davies, though he retains a protective affection for Aston. Poor Aston himself is conscious all the time of having been changed by his 'treatment' in the mental hospital. He is by far the kindest and most sympathetic of the three—and there is a deep irony in this—but he too is closed away from all other human beings and his contact with life is through things like the timber for his shed (will it *ever* be built?), picking up second-hand tools, and fiddling with electric plugs. Apart from kindness his contact even with Davies is slight, and he too is deeply alone, probably for ever. The effect of this extract—certainly of the whole play—is very disturbing and remains, I find, a haunting image in the memory. Do see the play or read it all if you can; there is a fine film version with Donald Pleasence playing the part of Davies as he did in the original stage production. Perhaps the main thought or feeling it leaves is that however much we strive to make real contact with other people, we *are* in the end alone in our skin—a chilling thought.

10
By way of conclusion

◊◊

I have said most of what I want to say in the 'lead-in' and 'run-out' about this passage from *A Day in the Death of Joe Egg*. I felt that I wanted to finish the book with a passage which I thought showed the toughness of Man's capacity to deal with problems and even insoluble disasters; especially after sections dealing with War, Death and Solitude! I felt the need of a playwright's affirmation of the splendour of human courage—how we manage to deal with 'the irreducible minimum of human misery'. I originally called this last section 'Meeting Adversity with Courage and Humour'— and this is the quality I hope it will illustrate.

A DAY IN THE DEATH OF JOE EGG

Lead-in
If you read our opening extract from this play you will remember that it starts with Bri addressing the theatre audience as though it were a classroom of naughty boys being kept in after school; and you may have thought that an audience in a theatre *is* in a sense being 'kept in'—certainly it is a captive audience like the class in a classroom, perhaps particularly in an old-fashioned school where one does little but listen or pretend to listen to a 'performance' by a teacher. Better, however, if you—the pupils, students, victims, according to your point of view—can, as it were, 'get in on the act'. This means that you take part in it, that the class is a dialogue and not merely a monologue; and when it's about drama you are acting and not merely reading aloud or listening. This seems

a good time to raise again the question of why acting is 'good
for you'. To 'enact' a situation is often to contain it, make it
more understandable, more enjoyable, and, if tragic or difficult, more endurable. People frequently come to terms with
problems or even tragedy by 'acting out' some of its features;
thus acting, though it feels mainly like fun or amusement,
may often be more than that, may be helpful, curative, thera-
peutic.

In the following longish extract we see Bri and his wife
Sheila *acting out*, by means of a series of parodies, the
revelation that their only child, their daughter Josephine
(Joe) is a helpless spastic. Their way of coming to terms
with this tragedy is, in itself, wildly funny; Sheila 'plays'
the mother worried about her baby daughter, and Bri 'plays'
in turn their family doctor, the specialist to whom they are
sent with the child, and finally the local vicar, who tries to
cheer them up. They have obviously done this before; indeed, one has the sense that they've been improving and decorating and refining this dialogue to extract every last drop
of humour from it. But—and this is true of a lot of the best
jokes—it's not *merely* funny; the more forgetful the G.P.
is, the more absurd and insensitive the specialist and the
vicar, the more real the tragedy of Joe's condition becomes,
the more difficult the question of whose fault it was (perhaps nobody's?). The humour—and I find this scene very
funny indeed—intensifies the tragedy and yet contains it,
makes it more endurable. This is one way of looking at the
function of acting in our lives.

The end of the scene is electrifying in the theatre. It is
worth going over those last few lines. Sheila has just said
ruefully, referring to Bri's insensitive and disappointed
mother Grace :

> 'And Bri's mother always says, "Wouldn't it be
> lovely if she was running about?" which makes Bri
> hoot with laughter. But I think of it too. Perhaps
> it's being a woman.'

Immediately the lights move from Sheila, and Joe appears
'running about' with a skipping rope and finishes the scene

with a skipping rhyme and an announcement to the audience about the interval. You can think of this, if you wish, as a projection of Sheila's dream; but another way of looking at it is to see that it reminds us that the whole of *A Day in the Death of Joe Egg* is a *play,* performed by actors, who are not what they seem, and that the girl who plays the hopeless spastic Joe is in fact a normal girl. This prevents us from identifying too closely with the parents or the situation or even the child, and enables us to think more about the play's meaning and message; we feel less tearful and more thoughtful. The device relates closely to Brecht's 'alienation' theories (see notes on *The Caucasian Chalk Circle,* p. 50).

ACTING NOTES

This is almost entirely a dialogue between Bri and Sheila and we have notes on them at the beginning of this volume. Bri must be a *very* good actor as he's not only got to be Bri himself, a thirtyish schoolmaster, but also three other people, the busy, bored, dense G.P., the busy, contemptuous, would-be realist middle-European specialist with a thick German accent, and the hearty, good-hearted, essentially rather stupid vicar trying hard to be 'swinging' rather than fuddy-duddy. Sheila is mainly herself—the worried parent, anxious to know even the worst—and through the little playlets acts as Bri's 'feed', i.e. the relatively straight actor by contrast with whom the funny one can make his points better (think of cross-talk comedians on radio or film or TV). Joe should be a twelve-year-old girl, hopelessly spastic and immobile for her other appearances, but here I imagine her as pretty, long-haired, free-moving, very self-contained and in control of herself. The sequence is difficult to do well and may need quite a bit of practice. The props are obvious; a cushion, a bottle of medicine, a small table, and something to serve for a telephone.

SHEILA. Soon I began to notice these funny turns. We asked
    our friends who'd had babies but they said it was most
    likely wind. So in the end we took her to our new G.P.
    (BRI *has fetched a tubular cushion from the set behind
    them, which is now in semi-darkness. The cushion is the
    size of a swaddled baby.* SHEILA *nurses it.*)
BRI. Baby. (*Points to himself.*) Doctor. Nice, bone-headed.

(In the sketches which follow, BRI *plays the funny men and* SHEILA *herself. They do it as they might repeat the dialogue from a favourite film. Sometimes they improvise, surprising or corpsing each other.)* (BRI *mimes opening a door at side of stage.* SHEILA *wanders off to opposite side and waits.)*

Bye-bye, Mrs—um—you rub that in you'll soon be as right as rain. *(Mimes closing door, returns to centre, shouts)* Next please!

(SHEILA *moves in.* BRI *bends over writing and putting away last patient's card. Has his back to* SHEILA.)

'Evening, Mister—um—feeling any better?

SHEILA. It's morning, Doctor. *(To audience.)* Not very reassuring.

BRI. 'Course it is.

SHEILA. And I've never been before.

BRI. No?

SHEILA. We're new to the district.

BRI. What seems to be the trouble?

SHEILA. I don't really know. Funny turns. Face-making.

BRI. Say 'aaah'.

SHEILA. Not me. The baby.

(BRI *looks at the cushion.)*

BRI. Nothing much wrong with this little laddie.

SHEILA. Lassie.

BRI. Lassie. Funny turns, you say. How would you describe them?

SHEILA. Frightening.

BRI. No, I meant, what form do they take?

SHEILA. Blinking with her eyes, working with her tongue, shaking her head, then going all limp.

BRI *(tickling the baby, talking to it).* Funny turns indeed at your age! Saucy beggar. We are not amused.

SHEILA. But what d'you think it is?

BRI. Wind.

SHEILA. That's what our friends said.

BRI. Always wise to get a second opinion. Have you tried Gripe Water?

SHEILA. Yes, of course.

BRI. My old mother used to swear by it. Cure anything, she

used to say. Well, let's see what we can find in here.
(*Rummages in drawer, finds medicine, reads label.*)
Ah, yes, this'll put a stop to it. Came in the post this
morning. The makers praise it very highly.

SHEILA. Doctor—I wish you could *see* one of these turns.

BRI. Oh, I've seen them, dear. Got three great monsters of
my own.

SHEILA. I am sorry.

BRI. What?

SHEILA. All your children being—um—

BRI. No, I mean great thriving brutes. Not monsters, no.
Your first, is it? First baby?

SHEILA. Yes.

BRI. Well, dear, it's like this. You're throwing an awful lot
of gubbins down the old cake-hole there. It's like running in a new car. Till all the tappets and contact breakers
get adjusted to the absolute thou, you take it easy, give
'em a chance. Same with these chaps. (*Tickles the
cushion, looks again at medicine.*) Let's see. Three times
daily after meals. How often are you feeding?

SHEILA. Every four hours.

BRI. Fours into twenty-four goes six. So six times a day—

SHEILA. Look. This may be one now.

(*They watch the cushion for ten seconds.* BRI *looks at
his watch.*)

SHEILA. No.

BRI. I've got a waiting-room full of people, dear. You try
her with this and come back if there's no improvement
in—say—a week. Make sure you wind her well. And
don't fret. (*Leading her to exit.*) They're hardy little
devils, you know. Bye-bye, Mrs—um— (*Mimes seeing
her off and shuts the door.*) Three days later. (*Mimes
opening the door and calls.*) Next please. (SHEILA
comes back at once with cushion.)
Hullo, Mrs—um—

SHEILA (*urgently*). Doctor—

BRI. Just a minute, I'll get your card.

SHEILA. But this child—

BRI. Sit down, please.

(*He seats her and looks at card.*)

Didn't I say come back in a week? Why so soon?

SHEILA. She's gone into a coma.

BRI. D'you try the medicine?

SHEILA. She won't take anything. She hasn't fed for two days.

(BRI *looks at the cushion, listens to it, claps hands by it, finally shakes it like a piggy bank.*)

BRI (*as much as to say 'so far, so good'*). Ah-ha! Mm-hum. (*Goes humming back to the table, mimes dialling.*) Get me the Children's Hospital . . . quick! No panic, dear, just a routine inquiry. Your husband with you?

SHEILA. He's in the waiting-room. Is she—?   .

BRI (*into phone*). Look—I'd like you to take a shufti at a baby—uh— (*To* SHEILA.) Girl?

SHEILA. Yes.

BRI. Baby girl . . . Off her chow and failing to respond to any stimuli whatever. (*To* SHEILA *again.*) Got a car?

SHEILA. No.

BRI. Hullo? . . . No car. Any chance of an ambulance? . . . Understood. (*Puts down phone, returns to* SHEILA.)

SHEILA. There's something seriously wrong, isn't there?

BRI. Don't start worrying, dear. Look at it this way. You know when you get a starter-motor jammed? Seems serious at the time but put it in second gear and rock the whole shoot back and forth, she's soon as right as rain.

SHEILA. We haven't got a car, I—

BRI. What I want you to do—you know the kiddies' hospital?

(*She nods.*)

You and your old man go along there—not forgetting to take the baby—you catch a bus from the end of the street. And—*nil desperandum.*

(*Sees her to door, as before, opens it, pushes her through. Is about to close it when he remembers something and shouts after her.*)

Thirty-two.

SHEILA. What?

BRI. The bus. Number thirty-two.

SHEILA. Oh.

BRI (*closing door, taking out handkerchief, wiping brow*). Strewth.

SHEILA (*turning to audience*). On the bus I said to Brian, 'I've got a feeling we shan't bring her back.' But, as you know, we did. Eventually.

BRI. Every cloud has a jet-black lining.

SHEILA. I stayed in hospital with her for a few weeks, then left her there having tests and came home to look after Brian, who'd contracted impetigo.

(BRI, *in the shadows, lights a cigarette.*)

It was painful not feeding so Brian knelt in front of me and tried to express it orally.

BRI. You should have seen that—like the Khamasutra.

SHEILA. In the end, a woman from the clinic drew it off with a sort of glass motor-horn.

(BRI *gets a coffee-table from the set, puts the cushion on it, stands behind it.*)

Few weeks later they called me to collect Joe from hospital, by which time we'd gathered that she wasn't ever going to amount to much. But I was determined to know the best we could expect. And the worst. The pediatrician was German—or Viennese, I'm not too sure.

(*For this sketch,* BRI *uses a music-hall German accent.*)

BRI. Vell, mattam, zis baby off yours has now been soroughly tested and ve need ze bets razzer battly so it's better you take her home. I sink I can promise she von't be any trouble. Keep her vell sedated you'll hartly know she's zere.

SHEILA. But, Doctor—

(*He is making for the door, turns reluctantly.*)

BRI. Ja?

SHEILA. Can't you tell me the results?

BRI. Results?

SHEILA. Of the tests.

BRI. Vitch ones? Zere vere so many—(*Slight laugh. Lists on fingers.*) Electro-encephalograph, scree-dimensional eggs-ray, blood urine and stool analyses, zis business vis needles in ze fontanelle—

SHEILA. Is that why her hair's been shaved off?

BRI. Vell of course—

SHEILA. She'd only just begun to grow it. And did the needles make that scar on her head?

BRI. Scar?

SHEILA (*pointing*). There.

BRI. Ach, nein. Zis vos a liddle biopsy to take a sample of her brain tissue.

SHEILA. That's a relief. (*She smiles quickly.*) I thought at first you'd bored a hole in her skull to let the devil out. (BRI *looks interested, confers with his assistant.*)

BRI. Sounds gut. Did you try it? . . . Ah! (*To* SHEILA) My colleague. Says ve don't do zat any more. (*Shrugs.*) Pity! Vell—if you eggscuse me.

(*Moves to go.*)

SHEILA. But—Doctor, Doctor—

BRI. Donner und blitzen!

SHEILA. What can she *do*?

BRI. Do? She can't do nozzing at all.

SHEILA. Will she ever?

BRI. Mattam, let me try and tell you vot your daughter iss like. Do you know vot I mean ven I say your daughter vos a wegetable?

(SHEILA *thinks for a moment, gets it, smiles.*)

SHEILA. Yes! You mean 'Your daughter was a vegetable'.

BRI. Ach himmel! Still is, still *is*, always will be! I have trouble vis Englisch werbs.

SHEILA. But—when people say to me what kind of cripple is your child, shall I say—she's a wegetable—a *v*egetable?

BRI. You vont a vord for her? (*Shrugs.*) You can say she iss a spastic vis a damaged cerebral cortex, multiplegic, epileptic, but vis no organic malformation of ze brain.

SHEILA. That *is* a long word.

BRI (*gaily*). Which iss vy I prefer wegetable.

SHEILA. *V*egetable.

BRI. *V*egetable.

SHEILA. But why? If her brain's physically sound, why doesn't it work?

(BRI *sighs, looks at her, thinks.*)

BRI. Imagine a svitchboard. A telephone svitchboard, ja?

SHEILA. I worked as a switchboard operator once.

BRI. Das ist wunderbar! Vell. Imagine you're sitting zere now, facing ze board. So?

SHEILA. So.

BRI. Some lines tied up, some vaiting to be used—suddenly brr-brr, brr-brr—

SHEILA. Incoming call?

BRI. Exactly! You plug in.

(SHEILA *mimes it, assuming a bright telephone voice.*)

SHEILA. Universal Shafting.

BRI (*coming out of character*). What?

SHEILA. That was the firm I worked for.

BRI. You've never put that in before.

SHEILA (*shrugs*). I thought I would this time.

BRI. Universal Shafting? Story of your life.

(*She stares coldly.* BRI *clears his throat, resumes as doctor.*)

But at zat moment anozzer incoming call—brr-brr—and you panic and plug him in to the first von and leave zem talking to each ozzer and you answer an extension and he vont the railway station but you put him on to ze cricket results and zey all start buzzing and flashing—and it's too much, you flip your lid and pull out all the lines. Kaputt! Now zere's your epileptic fit. Your Grand or Petit Mal according to ze stress, ze number of calls. All right?

(*Makes to go again.*)

SHEILA. But, Doctor, Doctor—

(*Looks at his watch.*)

BRI. Gott in himmel! I'm a wery busy man, Missis—um—

SHEILA. I know you must be—

BRI. Yours isn't ze only piecan in ze country.

SHEILA. I know—

BRI. Zere's von born every eight hours, you know.

SHEILA. No, I didn't. Is that true?

BRI. Oh, ja, ja. Not all as bad as zees case, of course—

SHEILA. Isn't there *any*thing at all we can do?

BRI. But jawohl! You must feed her, vosh her nappies, keep her varm. Just like any ozzer mozzer.

SHEILA. But for how long?

BRI. Who can tell? Anysing can happen, you know zat. Diphtheria, pneumonia . . . vooping cough . . . Colorado beetle.

(SHEILA *laughs. They come out of character.*)

SHEILA. Oh, that's terrible. Colorado beetle.

BRI. I only just thought of that.

SHEILA. It's terrible.

BRI. So—what happened then? We brought her home.

SHEILA. And the hospital passed the can back to our local G.P.

BRI. The piecan.

SHEILA. He had to supply phenobarbitone and keep us happy. He used to come once a week to explain her fits. In layman's terms.

BRI. You didn't find out much?

SHEILA. About fits, no. But I learnt a lot about what happens on a switchboard when the lines get crossed.

BRI. Or at a railway junction during fog.

SHEILA. But the time came when I asked him whose fault it was.

BRI. Which is when he suggested the vicar might call.

SHEILA. Yes. Nice vicar. Sensitive. So concerned and upset at the sight of Joe—the fits were unusually bad that day—so we left her in the cot and had our chat in another room.

(*She throws the cushion to* BRI, *who puts it on sofa.*)
(*Quite a long pause while they prepare themselves for the next scene. The mood changes slightly.* BRI *allows* SHEILA *to take the initiative and plays the Vicar quietly, even seriously, to begin with. They go upstage and she brings him down again when they are ready.*)

Here we are. Do take a pew.

(BRI, *as Vicar, laughs.*)

Oh!

(*She laughs too.*)

BRI. She's a beautiful child.

SHEILA. Yes, isn't she?

BRI. It's tragic. Tell me—when you first—knew there was nothing to be done, how did you feel?

SHEILA. Well, of course, you find out gradually, not all at

once. But there is a point when you finally accept
it. And that's—(*Shakes her head.*) Oh, very nasty.
You think 'why me?' I don't know about the other
mothers but *I* kept saying, 'Why me, why us?' all day
long. Then you get tired of that and you say, 'Why not
me?'

BRI. Indeed. You learn humility. You recognize that we are
surely in a vale of tears and you are no exception.

SHEILA. I recognized that I was worse. I'd been promiscuous,
you see. All kinds of men. It seemed to me I was responsible for Joe, being punished.

BRI. No, no.

SHEILA. No, I don't mean that either. I held the baby back.
Out of guilt.

BRI. Really, my dear, you mustn't believe this. Plenty of
women who've slept around afterwards become splendid mothers. Pre-marital intercourse is no longer considered a serious obstacle to being taken into the fold.

SHEILA. No?

BRI. Haven't you read our publications lately? You should.
The good old C. of E. is nowadays a far more swinging
scene than you seem to suppose.

SHEILA. I see.

BRI. Oh, surely. Where the action is.

SHEILA. I've never committed adultery.

BRI. There you are! That's splendid—fabulous! Crazy!
Think no more about it. Tell me, what was your husband's reaction to the child?

SHEILA. He used to say, 'Think of something worse.' And
of course that's easy. Joe could have grown older and
developed into a real person before it happened. Or she
could have been a very in*tell*igent spastic without the
use of her limbs. Which is worse, I think, than being a
kind of living parsnip.

BRI. Quote. You count your blessings.

SHEILA. Yes.

BRI. And that gives you fortitude.

SHEILA. No, but it's something to do. When you're up
against a—disaster of this kind—an Act of God—
(BRI *clears his throat.*)

—it's so *numbing* you feel you must make some sense of it—otherwise—you'd—

BRI. Give up hope?

SHEILA. Yes. My husband doesn't feel the need to make sense of anything. He lives with despair.

BRI (*coming out of character*). Did you tell him that?

SHEILA. Why not?

BRI. Bit saucy.

SHEILA. Well, don't you?

BRI. Can't argue now.

SHEILA (*resuming scene*). He says I shouldn't look for explanations.

BRI. He doesn't believe in God?

SHEILA. His own kind of God. A manic-depressive rugby footballer.

BRI. It's a start. Provides some basis for argument. (*He smiles.*)

SHEILA. He doesn't like me praying.

BRI. You have been praying?

SHEILA. What else can I do? I look at that flawless little body, those glorious eyes, and I pray for some miracle to—get her started. It seems, if we only knew the key or the combination, we could get her moving. D'you think the story of the Sleeping Beauty was about a spastic?

BRI. Who can say indeed? (*He stands, moves about.*) My dear, your child's sickness doesn't please God. In fact, it completely brings Him down.

SHEILA. Why does He allow it then?

BRI. How can we know?

SHEILA. Then how can you know it doesn't please Him?

BRI. We can't know. Only guess. It may be disease and infirmity are due to the misuse of the freedom He gave us. Perhaps they exist as a stimulus to research.

SHEILA. Research?

BRI. Against infirmity and disease.

SHEILA. But if He didn't permit disease, we shouldn't need research.

BRI. But He does so we do. (*She sighs, shakes her head.*)

My dear, the Devil is busy day and night. God does His best but we don't help Him much. Now and then some innocent bystander blunders into the cross-fire between good and evil and—

(*Makes gunfire noises, ricochet-sounds, falls elaborately clutching his chest. Stands again, dusts himself down, before proceeding.* SHEILA *watches calmly.*)

Or—if you can imagine a poisonous blight that settles on an orchard of many different varieties of tree—

SHEILA. No, please, no more parables. I've had so many from the doctor!

BRI. But how can I explain without imagery of—

SHEILA. I misled you. I don't want explanations. I've asked the people who should have been able to explain and they couldn't.

BRI. What *do* you want?

SHEILA. Magic.

BRI. I was slowly coming round to that. Once or twice, over the years, we have had in this parish children like your daughter.

SHEILA. Just as bad?

BRI. Oh, yes, I'm sure, quite as bad. Now for those poor innocents I did the Laying On Of Hands bit.

SHEILA. What is that?

BRI. A simple ceremony in your own home. A few prayers, a hymn or two, a blessing, an imposition of hands. Nothing flashy.

SHEILA. Who'd be there?

BRI. You, your husband, anyone you chose.

SHEILA. My husband?

BRI. Yes. And it sounds as though he needs instruction. His prayers would hardly help us if addressed to a manic-depressive rugby footballer.

SHEILA. No.

BRI. God might feel affronted.

SHEILA. Yes.

BRI. He's only human. No, He's not, how silly of me!

SHEILA. Perhaps you could have a word with him. Over a pint.

BRI. Ah, with your husband, yes. Not that there's anything

wrong with rugby. Scrum-half myself for years. Just
that I feel one shouldn't make a religion of it.

SHEILA. With the other children—did you have any luck?
Did God—you know—

BRI. There was one boy—no better than Joe—made such
rapid recovery after I'd done the Laying On a few times
—the medicos confessed themselves bewildered. He's
twelve now and this spring he was runner-up in the
South West Area Tap-Dancing Championships.

SHEILA. How fantastic!

(BRI *begins dancing and singing.*)

BRI. Happy Feet, I've got those Happy Feet,
Give me a low down beat—
(*Dances and sings without words. Then stops.*)

SHEILA. D'you really think you could—work a miracle?

BRI. Not me, my dear. If a miracle happens, it's only *through*
me. But remember Jairus's daughter? 'Damsel, I say unto thee, arise.' Who knows? Perhaps in a few years'
time we shall see little Joe—
(*Dances and sings again.*)
Animal crackers in my soup
Lion and tigers loop the loop.

SHEILA (*standing, breaking out of sketch*). But you
wouldn't do it! (*She moves away.* BRI *drops his Vicar
imitation.*)
He was a good man, kind and sincere.

BRI. He was, yes.

SHEILA. And that boy was cured.

BRI. Certainly improved. And, yes, he was the runner-up
in the South West Area Tap-Dancing Championships.
But. He never *had* been as bad as Joe.

SHEILA. I don't care—

BRI. I looked into it—

SHEILA. You shouldn't have.

BRI. I spoke to people—

SHEILA. Where's the harm? What else did we have?

BRI. Nothing.

SHEILA. Well!

BRI. I'd rather have nothing than a lot of lies.

SHEILA. You're unusual.

BRI. First he'd have done it for us, then he'd have got a few
of his mates in to give the prayers more Whoosh! More
Pow! And before long he'd have had us doing it in
church gloated over by all those death-watch beetles like
the victim of a disaster.

SHEILA. It could have worked. He might have magicked her.

BRI. I'm sure it was best to stop it then than later on—after
he'd raised your hopes. Sheila—
(*She looks at him, smiles.*)
Anyway, if the vicar had got her going, she'd only have
had one personality. As it is, we've given her dozens
down the years.

SHEILA (*to audience*). As soon as we were admitted to the
freemasonry of spastics parents, we saw she had even
less character than the other children. So we began to
make them for her.

BRI. Some never really suited.

SHEILA. No. Like the concert pianist dying of t.b.

BRI. Nor the girl who was tragically in love with a darkie
against her parents' wishes.

SHEILA. That was based on 'Would you let your daughter
marry one?'

BRI. I used to like the drunken bag who threw bottles at us
if we didn't fetch her gin and pipe-tobacco.

SHEILA. But they were all too active. The facial expression
wasn't right.

BRI. The one that's stuck is the coach-tour lady . . . powder-
pink felt hat, white gloves, Cuban heel shoes, swagger
coat . . .

SHEILA. And seasick pills in her handbag just in case there's
a lot of twisting and turning.

BRI. She hates foreigners—

SHEILA. And council-houses—

BRI. And shafting. She knows to her cost what that can lead to.

SHEILA. Loves the Queen—

BRI. And Jesus. She sees him as an eccentric English gentleman. Sort of Lawrence of Arabia.

SHEILA. Very disapproving of pleasure.

BRI. Not *all* pleasure. A nice Julie Andrews film with tea
after—

SHEILA. Tea in the Odeon café—

BRI. Nothing nicer. Which reminds me. I'm supposed to be giving her tea. In this play we started doing. (*Looks at his watch.*)

SHEILA. We got side-tracked.

BRI. She'll have something to say to me. She'll have me on the carpet. 'Nice thing leaving the table before you've finished eating, leaving me stuck here like Joe Egg . . .' (*Goes off.*)

(SHEILA *watches him out of sight.*)

SHEILA. I join in these jokes to please him. If it helps him live with her, I can't see the harm, can you? He hasn't any faith she's ever going to improve. Where I have, you see . . . I believe, even if she *showed* improvement, Bri wouldn't notice. He's dense about faith—faith isn't believing in fairy-tales, it's being in a receptive state of mind. I'm always on the look-out for some sign . . . (*Looks off again to wings to make sure* BRI'S *not coming.*) One day when she was—what?—about a twelve month old, I suppose, she was lying on the floor kicking her legs about and I was doing the flat. I'd made a little tower of four coloured bricks—plastic bricks— on a rug near her head. I got on with my dusting and when I looked again I saw she'd knocked it down. I put the four bricks up again and this time I watched her. First her eyes, usually moving in all directions, must have glanced in passing at this bright tower. Then the arm that side began to show real signs of intention . . . and her fist started clenching and—spreading with the effort. The other arm—held there like that— (*Raises one bent arm to shoulder level*) didn't move. At all. You see the importance—she was using for the first time one arm instead of both. She'd seen something, touched it and found that when she touched it whatever-it-was was changed. Fell down. Now her bent arm started twitching towards the bricks. Must have taken —I should think—ten minutes'—strenuous labour— to reach them with her fingers . . . then her hand jerked in a spasm and she pulled down the tower. (*Reliving the episode, she puts her hands over her face to regain composure*.) I can't tell you what that was like. But you can imagine, can't you? Several times the hand very nearly touched and got jerked away by spasm . . . and she'd try again. That was the best of it—she had a will, she had a mind of her own. Soon as Bri came home, I told him. I think he said something stupid like—you know—'That's great, put her down for piano lessons.' But when he tested her—putting piles of bricks all along the circle of her reach—both arms—and even sometimes out of reach so that she had to stretch to get there —well, of course, he saw it was true. It wasn't *much* to wait for—one arm movement completed—and even that wasn't sure. She'd fall asleep, the firelight would distract her, sometimes the effort would bring on a fit. But more often than not she'd manage . . . and a vegetable couldn't have done that. Visitors never believed it. They hadn't the patience to watch so long. And it amazed me—I remember being stunned—when I realized they thought I shouldn't deceive myself. For one thing it wasn't deception . . . and, anyway, what else could I do? We got very absorbed in the daily games. Found her coloured balls and bells and a Kelly—those clowns that won't lie down. Then she caught some bug and was very sick . . . had fit after fit—the Grand Mal, not the others—what amounted to a complete relapse. When she was over it, we tried the bricks again, but she couldn't even seem to see them. That was when Bri lost interest in her. I still try, though of course I don't bother telling him. I'll tell him when something happens. It seems to me only common sense. If she did it once, she could again. I think while there's life there's hope, don't you? (*Looks to wings again*.) I wish he'd talk more seriously about her. I wonder if he ever imagines what she'd be like if her brain worked. *I* do. And Bri's mother always says, 'Wouldn't it be lovely if she was running about?' which makes Bri hoot with laughter. But I think of it too. Perhaps it's being a woman. (*Lights off* SHEILA. *Lights on set upstage, very strong like a continuous lightning flash*.)

(JOE *skips on, using a rope*.)

JOE. Mrs D, Mrs I, Mrs FFI, Mrs C, Mrs U, Mrs LTY.
Mrs D, Mrs I, Mrs FFI, Mrs C, Mrs U, Mrs LTY.
(*Stops skipping*.)
Ladies and gentlemen, there will now be an interval.
Afterwards the ordinary play, with which we began the
performance, will continue and we shall try to show you
what happens when Sheila returns home with their
mutual friends, Freddie and Pam. Thank you.
(*She bows and resumes skipping*.)

Run-out

This has purposely been chosen for the last passage of this
collection, because it strikes two notes we specially want to
end with—one on the nature of drama, and one on the nature
of life. As to the first, *one* of the functions of the three dialogues (doctor, specialist, parson) is obviously to let us in
the audience know the early stages of Joe's life and the
parents' experience, their hope and despair. But much more
important is that the parents are acting out the three playlets,
using acting in order to come to terms with their problems.
These dialogues are impressively followed by the dramatist's
'distancing' device, which reminds us that a play *is* a play
and not a hunk of real life and that the helpless spastic is in
fact a live and lively girl. I suggested in my notes that this
helps us to be less harrowed and more thoughtful: Peter
Nichols enables us richly to imagine the situation but without
a total surrender to anguish or tears, so that understanding,
the most important constituent of sympathy, is dominant.

The second and final point we hope the extract will make
is to remind us all that even the most disastrous or appalling
situation can be tempered by two vital human resources—
humour and courage. However well society is organized and
however fortunate our individual lives, there seems to be an
irreducible minimum of human misery, of which the inevit-
ability of death—death of those we love and finally our own
death—is only the most central. Bri and Sheila in the extract
above, have found a way—and a remarkable one—of coming
to terms with this 'minimum of human misery', not by forgetting it, sweeping it under the carpet, deodorizing or dis-
infecting it out of existence, but by the opposite, facing it,

examining it, reliving it, making it endurable, human, rich —tenderly funny as well as anguishing. Humour can't obliterate anguish but it can humanize it and cure us of mere passive despair, while courage can enable us to face anxieties which might otherwise totally overwhelm us.

We have not stressed very directly the moral lessons to be derived from the many fine passages from drama which this book includes, so it is perhaps not out of place to say that in the end this is the only real purpose of reading literature, studying drama, acting play extracts; that in the process of understanding, feeling and enacting what Bamforth, or Grusha, or Bottom or Pegeen thought and felt and did, we are not only widening our own imaginative range but also building within ourselves qualities which will enable us more fully to enjoy—love, friendship, adventure; to value—loyalty, honesty; to endure—death, deprivation; to understand —prejudice, hatred, fear, war; and to come to terms with those aspects of life which we can't alter. This is well beyond the fun of acting, the interest stimulated by historical settings or new situations, and it feeds back on us and makes us to some degree better equipped to live fully and well.

Biographical Notes

ARDEN, John (1930–)
Born in Yorkshire. Educated at Cambridge and Edinburgh College of Art. Studied architecture and began to write plays. Became known when early plays were successfully produced at the Royal Court Theatre in the late 1950s. Plays include: *Live Like Pigs* (1958); *Serjeant Musgrave's Dance* (1959); *The Happy Haven* (1960); *The Workhouse Donkey* (1963); *Armstrong's Last Goodnight* (1964); *Left-Handed Liberty* (1965); *The Hero Rises Up* (1968).

BRECHT, Bertolt (1898–1956)
A German, born in Bavaria. Studied science and philosophy at university. After First World War devoted himself to writing. Exiled to the USA, he attacked Nazi Germany. Returned to East Berlin in 1947 and was provided with his own theatre and company, the Berliner Ensemble. Had full support of the Government, though the heretical opera *Lucullus* was withdrawn by Government decree after the first night. Plays include: *Baal* (1922); *Drums in the Night* (1923); *The Threepenny Opera* (1928); *The Rise and Fall of the City of Mahagonny* (1930); *St Joan of the Stockyards* (1932); *Mother Courage and Her Children* (1941); *The Life of Galileo* (1943); *The Good Person of Szechwan* (1943); *The Caucasian Chalk Circle* (1947).

HALL, Willis (1929–)
Born in Leeds, Yorkshire, and educated at Cockburn High School, Leeds. His very numerous plays include: *The Royal Astrologers* (1958); *The Long and the Short and the Tall* (1959); *A Glimpse of the Sea* (1959); *Billy Liar* (with Keith Waterhouse, 1960); *The Love Game* (1964); *Say Who You Are* (1965); *Whoops-a-Daisy* (1968); *Children's Day* (1969).

LAWRENCE, D. H. (1885–1930)
Born in Eastwood, Nottinghamshire, the son of a miner, he was

educated at Nottingham High School and trained for teaching at
Nottingham University. He taught only for a short time, in Croy-
don; the rest of his life was spent in writing and travelling. He is
most famous as a novelist (e.g., *Sons and Lovers; The Rainbow*)
and as a short-story writer, but he was also a fine essayist, travel-
writer and poet. His plays were written early in his life but were
long neglected until performed at the Royal Court Theatre in
1968. They deal with themes later reworked in fictional form.
There are three full-length plays : *A Collier's Friday Night* (1909);
The Widowing of Mrs Holroyd (1911); *The Daughter-in-Law*
(1911).

MILLER, Arthur (1915–   )
Born New York City. Educated at public schools and University
of Michigan. Journalist on *Michigan Daily*. Joined Federal Theatre Project in 1938. Most celebrated playwright in America for
two decades after the Second World War. His plays are a de-
vastating comment on the American Way of Life. Among his
most important are : *All My Sons* (1947); *Death of a Salesman*
(1949); *The Crucible* (1953); *A View from the Bridge* (1955);
The Price (1968); and the film *The Misfits* (1960).

NICHOLS, Peter (1927–   )
Educated at Bristol Grammar School. Has written several television plays and scripts for films such as *Georgie Girl*. Plays include : *The Hooded Tenor* (1965); *A Day in the Death of Joe Egg*
(1967) which won the *Evening Standard* Drama Award for the
best new play of the year; *The National Health* which won the
Evening Standard Drama Award for the best play of 1969; *For-
get-Me-Not Lane* (1971).

PINTER, Harold (1930–   )
A Londoner, educated at Hackney Downs Grammar School. He
began his career as an actor and later became a playwright. Plays
include : *The Room* and *The Dumb Waiter* (1957); *The Birthday
Party* (1958); *The Caretaker* (1960); *A Night Out* (1961); *The
Collection* (1961); *The Lover* and *The Dwarfs* (1962); *The Home-
coming* (1964). *The Caretaker* has been performed all over the
world. Pinter has written many television and radio plays.

RUDKIN, David (1936–)
Born in London of strict evangelical parents. Educated at King Edward's Grammar School, Birmingham, and St Catherine's College, Oxford. Wrote stories from early childhood and one-acters while doing National Service. Taught Latin, Greek and Music. Has written extensively for television. His first full-length play *Afore Night Come* was produced by the Royal Shakespeare Company as part of an experimental season of plays and won for him the *Evening Standard* Drama Award for the 'most promising playwright of 1962'. Has also written two opera-librettos— *Moses and Aaron* for Covent Garden and *The Grace of Todd* for Aldeburgh.

SHAKESPEARE, William (1564–1616)
Born at Stratford-upon-Avon the son of a prosperous tradesman, he was educated from seven to thirteen at Stratford Grammar School. We know surprisingly little about his life but we do know that he went to London at the age of twenty-one and became an actor. For the next twenty years he was both actor and playwright with a company called the Lord Chamberlain's Men which performed at London theatres and at Court. He achieved fame and fortune and returned to Stratford 'as a gentleman' in *c.* 1610. He wrote thirty-six plays (their exact dates are uncertain). His fame rests chiefly on the great tragedies: *Hamlet* (1601); *Othello* (1603–4); *King Lear* (1605–6); *Macbeth* (1606); *Antony and Cleopatra* (1606–7). Apart from the early *A Midsummer Night's Dream* (1594–5), there is a group of comedies including *As You Like It* (1599), *Twelfth Night* (1600) and *Much Ado About Nothing* (1598–1600). The history plays include the two parts of *Henry IV* (1597–8) and *Henry V* (1599). Of the early tragedies perhaps the finest is *Romeo and Juliet* (1594–5). There is a splendid group of late plays including *A Winter's Tale* (1611) and *The Tempest* (1612).

SHAW, George Bernard (1856–1950)
Born in Dublin of Protestant parents, he was largely self-educated. After an early attempt at novel writing he turned to journalism and became a celebrated critic of music, literature and drama, as well as a leading theorist and speaker in the Fabian Society. He started writing plays in 1892 and continued until the

mid-thirties. Among a vast list of plays some of the most famous titles are: *Arms and the Man* (1894); *Candida* (1894); *The Devil's Disciple* (1896); *Caesar and Cleopatra* (1898); *Captain Brassbound's Conversion* (1899); *Man and Superman* (1901); *Major Barbara* (1907); *The Doctor's Dilemma* (1911); *Androcles and the Lion* (1916); *Pygmalion* (1916); *Heartbreak House* (1919); *Back to Methuselah* (1921); *Saint Joan* (1924).

SYNGE, John Millington (1871–1909)
Born in Dublin into an Irish landed family. Educated at Trinity College, Dublin. Travelled for years, returning to Ireland at the suggestion of W. B. Yeats who met him in Paris in 1899. Wrote for the Abbey Theatre, Dublin, about the Aran Islanders—'a popular imagination that is fiery, magnificent and tender'. His plays include: *The Shadow of the Glen* (1903); *Riders to the Sea* (1904); *The Well of the Saints* (1905); *The Playboy of the Western World* (1907); *The Tinker's Wedding* (1908); *Deirdre of the Shadows* (1910).

WATERHOUSE, Keith (1929–   )
Was educated in Leeds, and became a journalist. Most of his plays have been written in collaboration with Willis Hall (see Hall), with whom he has also made a number of films, including *Whistle Down the Wind*, *Billy Liar*, and *A Kind of Loving*.

WESKER, Arnold (1932–   )
A Londoner, born in Stepney. He worked as a furniture-maker's apprentice, carpenter's mate, bookseller's assistant, farm labourer, kitchen porter and pastrycook, and did military service with the RAF. He developed Centre 42 to bring the Arts to a trade-union audience. Plays include: *Chicken Soup with Barley* (1958); *Roots* and *The Kitchen* (1959); *I'm Talking about Jerusalem* (1960); *Chips with Everything* (1962); *Their Very Own* and *Golden City* (1964); *The Four Seasons* (1965). He wrote a television play *Menace* in 1963.

Index to plays